Divorce: Where Next?

Issues in Law and Society
General Editor: Michael Freeman

Titles in the Series:

Children's Rights: A Comparative Perspective
Edited by Michael Freeman

Divorce: Where Next?
Edited by Michael Freeman

Exploring the Boundaries of Contract
Edited by Roger Halson

Law as Communication
Edited by David Nelken

Iraqgate: The Constitutional Implications of the Matrix-Churchill Affairs
Edited by Rodney Austin

Positivism Today
Edited by Stephen Guest

Governing Childhood
Edited by Anne McGillivray

Divorce: Where Next?

Edited by
MICHAEL FREEMAN
University College London

Dartmouth
Aldershot • Brookfield USA • Singapore • Sydney

Published by
Dartmouth Publishing Company Limited
Gower House
Croft Road
Aldershot
Hants GU11 3HR
England

Dartmouth Publishing Company
Old Post Road
Brookfield
Vermont 05036
USA

British Library Cataloguing in Publication Data
Divorce: Where Next?. – (Issues in Law & Society Series)
I. Freeman, Michael II. Series
306.890942

Library of Congress Cataloging-in-Publication Data
Divorce : where next? / [edited by] Michael Freeman.
p. cm. – (Issues in law and society)
Includes bibliographical references.
ISBN 1-85521-677-9 (hbk.). – ISBN 1-85521-682-5 (pbk.)
1. Divorce–Law and legislation–Great Britain. 2. Divorce–Great Britain. I. Freeman, Michael D. A. II. Series.
KD764.D58 1996
348.4201'66–dc20
[344.206166] 95-40760
CIP

ISBN 1 85521 677 9 HBK
ISBN 1 85521 682 5 PBK

Typeset by Manton Typesetters, 5–7 Eastfield Road, Louth, Lincolnshire LN11 7AJ, UK
Printed and bound in Great Britain by Biddles Limited, Guildford and King's Lynn

Contents

List of Tables

List of Contributors

June Carbone is an Associate Professor of Law at Santa Clara University. She writes extensively about marriage, divorce and family obligations.

Stephen M. Cretney, a Solicitor, is a Fellow of All Souls College, Oxford. He is joint author of *Principles of Family Law* (6th edn, 1996).

Ruth Deech is Principal of St Anne's College, Oxford and Chairman of the Human Fertilisation and Embryology Authority.

Michael Freeman is Professor of English Law, Faculty of Laws, University College London.

Colin Gibson is Lecturer in sociology, Department of Social Policy and Social Science, Royal Holloway College, University of London. He is joint author of *Separated Spouses* and author of *Dissolving Wedlock.*

Judith Masson is Professor of law at Warwick University. She was a member of the Joint Pensions Management Institute/Law Society Working Group which reported on Pensions and Divorce in 1993, and provided legal advice to Fairshares during passage of the Pensions bill. She is joint author of *Principles of Family Law*.

Christine Piper is Senior Lecturer in Law, Brunel University. She is the author of *The Responsible Parent*, and joint author of *How the Law Thinks about Children.*

Rhona Schuz is Lecturer in Law at Bar-Ilan University, Ramat Gan, Israel. Formerly lecturer in Law at University of Nottingham and London School of Economics; and Consultant to the Law Commission on the Ground for Divorce. She has written extensively on family law, private international law and taxation.

1 Divorce: Contemporary Problems and Future Prospects

Michael Freeman

Divorce in England today stands at a crossroads although perhaps, like roadsigns in Roman times, all routes point to the same destination. As a result of a Law Commission paper[1] and a government White Paper,[2] emanating rather surprisingly, as Stephen Cretney points out,[3] from the Lord Chancellor's Department, a divorce will be obtainable after a period of consideration and reflection (12 months was originally envisaged for this, but the period may be less or indeed greater), and mediation is going to become the norm.

We are about to witness a further retreat of law, lawyers and legal mechanisms – a further transfer of power to the citizen, but also to bureaucracy. The most recent precedent is the Child Support Act 1991, which took the assessment of child maintenance away from the courts and transferred it to the Child Support Agency. This has proved, overall, to be a monumental failure, although Ruth Deech shows in her contribution to this volume[4] that it has also had some successes. It yet may be rescued by reforms introduced in 1995, which will allow certain clean-break settlements to be taken into account[5] and amend the scheme in a number of other ways. However, criticism is likely to persist.

One of the problems with the Child Support Act, as with the Children Act 1989 before it, and now with the new divorce model, is ideological confusion.[6] The Child Support Act was based on a White Paper entitled *Children Come First*[7] but, whilst the relief of child poverty is a noble goal (albeit not one much in evidence over the last 16 years or so),[8] there was little doubt that saving the public purse was a primary motivating force.[9] Nor is this, as Ruth Deech concedes,[10] any bad thing: making men responsible for their children harmonizes well with the new emphasis on responsibility rather than rights as evidenced in the Children Act[11] and elsewhere.[12]

It is as unsurprising as it is unfortunate that the moral panic engendered around the Child Support Agency should concern its impact upon men – cases of false identity, a few suicides and punitive assessments – rather than on the plight of one-parent female-headed households or the feminization of poverty.[13] Nor is it remarkable that the whistle has for so long remained unblown[14] on the pension problem which, of course, disproportionately affects divorced women. As Judith Masson notes, until the late 1980s not only women but also their solicitors seem to have been unaware of the impact divorce would have on their retirement income.[15]

Part of the explanation for these failures is the absence of a sustained or coherent feminist response to divorce.[16] Fundamentally, the problem may be perceived to lie in the different approach that men and women have to the family, with mothers having a greater, and qualitatively different, attachment to their children. As June Carbone concedes, this may be irrelevant to the determination of public policy: nonetheless it remains the case that 'feminists are no closer to agreement on possible solutions'.[17] On one issue at least – woman battering[18] – there is agreement, and it has led to considerable concern on the impact of this phenomenon on the dynamics of mediation. Christine Piper who, with Kaganas,[19] is one of a number of commentators[20] to have written on this problem, only addresses it briefly in her contribution to this volume.[21] It is the concern of many that *Looking To The Future*, the White Paper which discusses the implementation of the proposed mediation-based divorce process, has entirely failed to grasp what is involved here.[22] With violence permeating more than one marriage in ten, and an issue in perhaps one-third of divorces, this is not a matter which can be easily swept under the carpet.

Another moral panic, addressed in this volume,[23] is the ability or otherwise of children to 'divorce' their parents. In the past, discussion on children and divorce concentrated upon the effect a parental divorce had upon dependent children. But in all this discussion children were the *objects* of concern, rather than persons in their own right. That children should be allowed to take the initiative produced consternation as well as a great deal of misinformed comment. If a feminist response to divorce has been slow in coming, then one which situates it within a child's perspective has been even more tardy.

Another problem which has rarely emerged is that of ethnic minorities' divorces, and when it has, as Rhona Schuz points out, it has provoked moral panics such as the fear of *talaqs* delivered on day-trips to Calais.[24] There remains a greater willingness to recognize the marriages of ethnic and religious minorities than their divorces. The recent case of *Berkovits* v.

Grinberg[25] is a clear illustration of this: there is a marked contrast in the attitudes of the courts to a Ghanaian marriage (in *McCabe* v. *McCabe*)[26] and to a Ghanaian divorce (in *D* v. *D*),[27] cases decided within two months of each other. A culturally pluralist perspective on divorce is yet to make its mark.

This volume addresses these issues amongst many others. Although it focuses primarily on the problems in England – appropriately, since it is in a period of transition – there is comparative material (in particular references to the US experience), and the issues raised and debated are questions common to modern states throughout the world.

Colin Gibson provides a framework for understanding divorce issues.[28] He offers a picture of the major demographic and social characteristics of divorce and sets contemporary divorce structures within our knowledge of changing family patterns and new life courses. He goes on to situate the rise in divorce within a culture and an economy which puts a premium on individual choice. Are these patterns and values which can (or should) be changed? Will waving the flag for family values[29] or injecting communitarianism with its emphasis on responsibility[30] have any impact upon these trends? And where does cohabitation fit in? The phenomenon is addressed by Gibson, as it also by Ruth Deech.[31] Is incorporation the answer[32] or would the institution merely remove to a new space?

However bad things are perceived to be, Stephen Cretney reminds us that they were once much worse. His reminiscences of Victorian values in practice (in the 1950s when Victoria 'ruled' in spirit if not in body) are a timely lesson to those – of whom the Lord Chancellor may be one – who would wish to turn the clock back. Cretney has considerable reservations about the proposed changes to the divorce process. He demonstrates how a hitherto unnoticed conflict of ideologies has been created: between 'the brusque managerialism of modern judicial administration and the social-work ideologies underlying much mediation'.[33] He is critical of the government's 'idiosyncratic notion' of mediation,[34] of the way, with no reasoned argument, it is to be extended from its 'natural' terrain of child-related issues into the unexplored territory of property and finance. He is also critical of the new ground of divorce, insofar as there is going to be one, for no amount of verbiage exhorting reflection can hide the fact that, as he puts it, the ground of divorce is to be 'the unilateral wish of one party to achieve it'.[35]

Piper is more sympathetic to the process of mediation, although she acknowledges the force of the feminist critique of it, particularly in the context of domestic violence.[36] Much discussion of the government's new proposals – possibly following the line of the White Paper itself – has perceived legal norms and mediation processes almost as polar opposites, so much so that it has failed to comprehend the extent to which lawyers are involved in the mediating of family disputes.[37] But Piper shows the important relationships that exist between legal and non-legal norms. Mediation does not necessarily provide different norms or end-products: as Piper notes, 'it may be different only in its settings and working methods'.[38] But has any thought gone into the implications of this? There is little indication in *Looking To The Future* that the issues addressed by Piper have been thought through by the Lord Chancellor's Department. Will the new proposals therefore be – as experience of the Child Support Agency has suggested – a leap in the dark?

Ruth Deech highlights the successes of the Child Support Act as well as its failures and is puzzled by the success of the campaign against the Act and the Agency. 'It would appear more logical and harmless to end maintenance to an ex-wife than to free men from responsibility for their children',[39] she pertinently notes. But, as all will have observed, it is the latter demand which has caught the public's imagination. Campaigns against 'alimony drones' in the early 1980s, which led to the Matrimonial and Family Proceedings Act 1984, attracted much attention but were subdued in comparison.[40] The problems of the Child Support Agency were, however, anticipated,[41] even if the level and scale have exceeded expectations. But could divorce reform – particularly near-compulsory mediation – apparently due, to be introduced during 1996 – prove just as unpopular?

So far as spousal maintenance is concerned, Deech shows that the three types of case she described in an important article in 1982[42] still exist. The rich, however, are a law unto themselves (consider the outrageous 'millionaire's defence').[43] As Cretney amusingly notes,[44] the thought of the new divorce processes being applied to them beggars the imagination. The concept of the Prince and Princess of Wales at an 'initial interview' before a panel belongs to the realm of television comedy! It is the middle-income group which is the most affected by recent changes. Deech anticipates a return to *Mesher* orders,[45] although the reversal of *Crozier*[46] in the Child Support Act 1995 should forestall this. Deech's survey of spousal maintenance and property issues leads her to anticipate changes but, as she concludes, no less unhappiness. Whether, as she believes, the number of divorces will also rise (or at least not fall) may ultimately depend upon whether people continue to get married.

The question of pension rights has come to public attention only recently. The issues involved are both conceptual (are they 'property' and, if so, matrimonial property?) and matters of public policy with far-reaching ramifications. These questions are addressed more fully by Masson than elsewhere, either in academic or practitioner literature. She distinguishes three models and argues for what she terms the 'third generation system',[47] Pension-splitting, which would enable courts to divide pension rights at divorce and allow the recipient to retain rights in their ex-spouse's scheme as if they were former member of it or to transfer their pension rights to another scheme. She concedes that such a change is unlikely to be popular with some men or their second families. In this case, though, surely we cannot anticipate resistance of Child Support Act proportions? Equalizing pension rights must happen because justice demands it, but finding the right solution is undoubtedly difficult and its repercussions manifold: for example, will it encourage the elderly to divorce? Masson's article guides us through the thickets of the debate.

The divorce practices of ethnic minorities are discussed by Rhona Schuz who makes a plea for mutual tolerance and for the promotion of religious and cultural pluralism.[48] These are policies more likely to be implemented in Australia,[49] Canada[50] or New Zealand[51] than in the United Kingdom. The problems she tackles, for example that of the Jewish *agunah*,[52] have not attracted the attention they deserve. Schuz examines some of the solutions, although some may consider her refusal to acknowledge that change can come from within the religious system itself unfortunate. The whole subject is ripe for re-examination and reconstruction: the current law not only contains contradictions and inconsistencies but also leaves injustice untouched, usually for women.

I approach the question of divorce from the unconventional perspective of children.[53] Much has been written on the impact of divorce upon children: I address the ways in which English law has responded to a new power in the Children Act 1989 which, although this was hardly the legislature's intention, allows children to 'divorce' parents. My article explores the limitations, examines the courts' reservations and concerns and seeks ways of improving the law. A spate of cases in 1992–93 created a moral panic[54] but this, it is concluded, is not justified.

Finally, June Carbone, in a far-ranging and comparative essay, examines a feminist perspective on divorce.[55] There is, she argues, no single feminist analysis of divorce as such. At its kernel is an examination of the failure of existing divorce policies to account for the burdens of child-rearing, which still fall largely on women despite the talk of 'symmetrical families[56] and the 'new man'.[57] As she notes, contemporary changes in women's participation in paid employment have not been met by a corresponding increase in fathers' participation in homemaking. Child-rearing duties are critical when it comes to understanding income disparities between married men and married women, and between divorced men and divorced women. There is much debate in feminist literature on the impact of no-fault divorce on women, although no feminist would return to a fault-based system. But the issue of greatest importance is, as Carbone acknowledges, whether current divorce law – and also the model proposed by the Law Commission and in

Looking To The Future – adequately provides for child-rearing in an era of divorce. That divorce is economically disastrous for many women and the children in their custody is relatively contentious. If women bear the continuing burden of child-rearing, how realistic is the goal of the clean break? And how can child support make visible caretaking efforts? Currently, undue weight is given to financial contributions.

What this volume shows is that piecemeal, rather than holistic, reform is not the answer. The future of the family and the role of the law in this need sustained attention. We will continue to get debacles like the Child Support Act until we address the problems systemically. This means looking at marriage and cohabitation, the use of lawyers and mediators, the role of the state and that of family members, the interrelationship of maintenance (spousal and child), employment and child-rearing responsibilities. It means integrating property, finance and pension questions. It means asking the 'woman question' and, we may add, 'the child question'. This cannot be done in a hurry nor can its primary motivating force be to save money. Nor can the task adequately be carried out piecemeal, with one committee examining one question, another institution a second. Nor can we allow important legislation to fail at the eleventh hour, as happened in late 1995 to the Family Homes and Domestic Violence Bill, because a small rump of bigoted MPs is blinded by prejudice.[58] We cannot look to the future unless we have a vision of what that future should look like. There is a better future than that laid out in contemporary blueprints: the essays in this collection point the way. However, further examination is required and, more than 40 years on from Morton, the answer lies in a Royal Commission with wide and flexible terms of reference. To the argument that this will delay reform I would respond that a pause (dare I say for consideration and reflection) is called for. Reform for reform's sake, or for the sake of the public purse, has little value: reform to improve the lives of citizens of this country in the next century would be worth waiting for.[59]

NOTES

1 Law Commission (1990), *Family Law: The Ground for Divorce*, Law Com. 192.
2 House of Commons (1993), *Looking to the Future: Mediation and the Ground for Divorce*, Cm 2424.
3 See Chapter 3 in this volume.
4 See Chapter 5 in this volume.
5 House of Commons, Fifth Report of the Social Security Committee (1994), *The Operation of the Child Support Act: Proposals for Change*, Session 1993–4, HC 470.
6 See L. Fox Harding (1991), 'The Children Act 1989 in context: four perspectives in child care law and policy', *Journal of Social Welfare and Family Law*, pp. 179, 285.

7 House of Commons (1991), *Children Come First*. For a good overview of the mistakes see John Eekelaar (1995), 'Child support in Britain: What went wrong?' in *Liber Amicorum Anders Agell*, Uppsala.
8 See Sue Middleton, Karl Ashworth and Robert Walker (1994), *Family Fortunes*, London: CPAG; Carey Oppenheim (1993), *Poverty: The Facts*, London: CPAG.
9 Child Poverty Action Group (1994), *Putting the Treasury First*, London: CPAG. See also John Eekelaar and Mavis Maclean (1993), 'Child support: the British solution', *International Journal of Law and the Family*, **7**, p. 205.
10 See Chapter 5 in this volume.
11 Children Act, ss. 2 and 3.
12 Even in criminal law: see Criminal Justice Act 1991 ss. 56–8.
13 See Diana Pearce (1978), 'The feminization of poverty: women, work and welfare', *Urban and Social Change Review*, February.
14 Cf. Howard Becker (1963), *Outsiders*, New York: Free Press.
15 See Chapter 6 in this volume.
16 But see Lenore Weitzman (1985), *The Divorce Revolution*, New York: Free Press.
17 See Chapter 9, p. 182.
18 See R. Emerson Dobash and Russell P. Dobash (1987), *Women, Violence and Social Change*, London: Routledge; Jalna Hanmer and Mary Maynard (1987), *Women, Violence and Social Control*, London: Macmillan.
19 See F. Kaganas and C. Piper (1994), 'Domestic violence and divorce mediation', *Journal of Social Welfare and Family Law*, p. 265.
20 See also Trina Grillo (1991), 'The mediation alternative: process dangers for women', *Yale Law Journal*, **100**, p. 1545; Penelope Bryan (1992), 'Killing us softly: divorce mediation and the politics of power', *Buffalo Law Review*, **40**, p. 441; K. Fischer, N. Vidmar and R. Ellis (1993), 'The culture of battering and the role of mediation in domestic violence cases', *Southern Methodist University Law Review*, **46**, p. 2117.
21 See Chapter 4 in this volume, pp. 78, 79, 80–82.
22 F. Kaganas and C. Piper (1994), 'The divorce consultation paper and domestic violence', *Family Law*, **24**, p. 143; H. Astor (1990), 'Domestic violence and mediation', *Australian Dispute Resolution Journal*, **1**, p. 143.
23 See Freeman, Chapter 8, in this volume.
24 See Chapter 7, p. 140
25 [1995] 1 FLR 477.
26 [1994] 1 FLR 410.
27 [1994] 1 FLR 38.
28 See Chapter 2 in this volume.
29 Three recent American articles throw light on what is involved. See Janet Dolgin (1993), 'Just a gene: judicial assumptions about parenthood', *UCLA Law Review*, **40**, p. 637; Linda Crane (1993), 'Family values and the Supreme Court', *Connecticut Law Review*, **25**, p. 427; and Barbara Bennett Woodhouse (1993), 'Hatching the egg: a child-centred perspective on parents' "rights"', *Cardozo Law Review*, **14**, p. 1747.
30 See Amitai Etzioni (1993), *The Spirit of Community*, New York: Simon and Schuster. 'New Labour' appears to have adopted this ideology.
31 See pp. 100–103.
32 See Chapter 2, pp. 39–41.
33 See Chapter 3, p. 51.
34 See p. 50.
35 See p. 52.
36 See Chapter 4.

37 See John Eekelaar (1995), 'Family justice: ideal or illusion?', *Current Legal Problems*, **48**, p. 191.
38 See p. 73.
39 See p. 93.
40 See Carol Smart (1984), 'Marriage, divorce and women's economic dependency: the politics of private maintenance' in Michael D.A. Freeman (eds), *State, Law and Family*, London: Tavistock, p. 9.
41 See Richard Collier (1994), 'The campaign against the Child Support Act', *Family Law*, **24**, p. 384.
42 R. Deech (1982), 'Financial relief: the retreat from a precedent and principle', *Law Quarterly Review*, **98**, p. 621.
43 *Van G* v. *Van G* [1995] 1 FLR 328.
44 See p. 48.
45 See p. 96. *Mesher* v. *Mesher* was decided in 1973 but reported in [1980] 1 All ER 126.
46 [1994] 1 FLR 126.
47 See p. 122.
48 See Chapter 7, p. 151.
49 Where the Law Commission has published a report on 'multi-culturalism'.
50 Where developments in Alberta and Manitoba are particularly noteworthy.
51 See Children, Young Persons and Their Families Act 1989 and also Michael Freeman (1994), 'Protecting children on both sides of the globe', *Adelaide Law Review*, **16**, p. 79. More generally see Mark Henaghan and Bill Atkin (1992), *Family Law Policy in New Zealand*, Auckland: Oxford University Press.
52 See Michael Freeman (1996), 'State, law and religion' in G. Douglas and N. Lowe (eds), *International Approaches to the Family*, Dordrecht: Nijhoff.
53 See Chapter 8.
54 On the concept see S. Cohen (1973), *Folk Devils and Moral Panics*, London: McGibbon and Kee.
55 See Chapter 9.
56 See Michael Young and Peter Willmott, *The Symmetrical Family*, London: Routledge.
57 Graphically portrayed by Patricia Hewitt (1993), 'In search of the modern father', *The Independent*, 10 May 1993. See also C. Lewis and M. O'Brien (1987), *Reassessing Fatherhood: New Observations on Fatherhood and the Modern Family*, London: Sage, and compare R. Chapman (1988), 'The great pretender: variations on the new man theme', in R. Chapman and J. Rutherford (eds), *Unwrapping Masculinity*, London: Lawrence and Wishart. On the 'old man' see Richard Collier (1995), *Masculinity, Law and the Family*, London: Routledge. For an American perspective see Mary Frances Berry (1994), *The Politics of Parenthood*, New York: Penguin.
58 They thought giving cohabitants rights to oust a violent partner would undermine the institution of marriage and deleteriously affect 'family values'. See Anna Cook, *The Independent*, 30 October 1995.
59 The government's divorce proposals are supported by 55 per cent of the population according to a recent poll (*The Guardian*, 8 November 1995).

2 Contemporary Divorce and Changing Family Patterns

*Colin Gibson**

Any analysis of the available evidence on contemporary patterns of divorce from both official data and research findings necessarily has to freeze into cold statistical aggregates the individual experiences of unhappy families. Such information does, however, provide a picture of the principal demographic and social characteristics of divorce, and these are examined in the second section of this chapter. The evidence refers to England and Wales unless otherwise noted. The same section goes on to set contemporary divorce structures within our knowledge of changing family patterns and new life courses. The relevance of remarriage and further breakdown to the field of divorce is also examined.

The third section sets down some thoughts as to some of the influences and movements behind these new patterns. It is argued that the decline of the national corporate identity, together with the joint advance of consumer freedom of choice and individualism, are the underlying structural facets behind the rising divorce rate. These changes within our post-industrial society are associated with heightened personal expectation and demand for marital happiness.

This century has witnessed the emancipation of divorce. Marriages in Victorian times were regulated by a morally and socially divisive system which sanctioned separation but harshly restricted divorce. Only a combination of statistical ignorance, historical incomprehension and legal disregard could set the 600 divorce petitions of 1900 against some 189 000 petitions of 1992 as evidence of earlier family permanency. The last 50 years especially has seen a progressive legal easing in such areas as access to divorce, the governing statutes, judicial attitudes and the regulations, procedures and administrative processing of divorce. But, as will be argued more fully later,

* Lecturer in Sociology, Royal Holloway College, University of London.

this loosening of both statute and process has been of lesser significance in explaining the increasing resort to divorce. Greater explanatory importance is attached to changing personnel expectations and practices that interact with the evolving social fabric and structure of society.

THE INCIDENCE OF DIVORCE

Divorce has now become the privately accepted and publicly approved remedy for irretrievably broken marriages. In the decade 1981–90, as Table 2.1 shows, some million and a half marriages ended in divorce. This period displayed a fairly constant picture of some 150 000 divorces annually. The early years of the 1990s have seen a slight increase on the 1980s pattern, with the 160 385 divorces of 1992 setting the highest yet recorded number. The direct witnesses of these judicial dissolutions were the 320 770 husbands and wives and their 238 134 children (of all ages).

Table 2.1 Annual number and rate of divorce, 1961–92

Year/ Period	Average*	Rate**
1961	25	2.1
1961–70	40	3.3
1971–80	122	9.8
1981–90	151	12.6
1991	159	13.5
1992	160	13.7

* Decrees absolute: dissolution and nullity, rounded to nearest thousand.
** Rate: divorces to every 1000 ongoing married population.

It is statistically prudent to show divorce totals as a rate for every 1000 married couples as divorce is a partial consequence of the married population – which has doubled between 1900 and 1990 – at risk. Since 1980 the divorce rate records some 13 in every 1000 ongoing marriages as being dissolved annually. Such a rate, if it continues at the 1987 divorce level and pattern, implies that just under four in every ten (37 per cent) newly formed marriages will ultimately end in divorce.[1] The pattern of 1987 indicates that half the newlyweds of that year will not celebrate their silver wedding anniversary; a quarter of these will be due to the death of one of the partners and three-quarters to divorce. When insuring his life the solicitous younger husband misjudges the real family threat!

Those born after 1930 have experienced an increasing divorce risk. There has been a fivefold rise in the divorce rate in the 30 years between 1961 and 1991 (see Table 2.1). This pattern is more clearly seen by studying marriage cohort trends for single women (those spinsters in a similar age group marrying in the same period of time), thereby reducing the contaminating effect of the increased divorce risk associated with those remarrying after an earlier failure. The marked trend towards divorce intensifies with more recent marriages.[2] For instance, brides aged between 20–24 years in 1961, when followed up 25 years later, had experienced twice the divorce rate (19 per cent) compared with a similar age cohort who had married in 1951 (9 per cent).

SOME DEMOGRAPHIC AND SOCIAL ASSOCIATES OF DIVORCE

Those who marry at an earlier age not only experience greater risk of divorce but are also significantly more prone to earlier breakdown. General Household Survey (GHS) evidence indicates that over a quarter (27 per cent) of young brides (under 20) marrying in Britain between 1975 and 1979 had separated within six years, compared with 15 per cent for those aged 20–24 at marriage and 9 per cent for the age group 25–29.[3] Calculations by Murphy[4] indicate that, in the younger age group, the effect of one year's reduction in age at marriage has far greater impact in raising the divorce risk than the same reduction has at an older marriage age. This means that an 18 year-old bride runs twice the risk of marital breakdown than a 21 year-old bride.

Many younger brides and grooms are low academic achievers and consequently hold low-status and poorly paid jobs or remain unemployed. The low-income dilemma of these couples are intensified by the young wife's early entry into childbearing and quicker pace of reproduction. Early childbearing is linked with increased risk of marital breakdown.[5] Low educational level, as well as being associated with earlier marriage (and now cohabitation), is also – according to US research – a significant predictor of spousal distress in early married life.[6] It is probable that early school-leaving is related to poorly developed communication skills which makes the resolution of marital problems and conflict more difficult.

However, the habit of early marriage has rapidly declined over the last 20 years. National marriage rate figures for young women (under 20) record a sixfold fall between 1970 and 1990. As a precipitating divorce factor, young bridal age at marriage is declining in terms of its numerical output. This demographic change is a feature that, by itself, should contribute towards a decline in divorce numbers.

Duration of marriage

Not only has the resort to divorce intensified since 1950, but these failed marriages are now of shorter duration than similar marriages formed 40 years ago. For example, 12 per cent of 1971 brides aged 20–24 divorced within ten years compared to 2 per cent for 1951 brides. The fact that a follow-through of the 1951 cohort's divorce pattern extends to 35 years' marriage duration before reaching a similar 12 per cent rate once more highlights how recently-formed marriages have a greater propensity, and make increasingly early resort, to divorce.

Evidence for the 1992 divorcing population records that half (50 per cent) of marriages now last under ten years. Such calculations are based upon the formal (*de jure*) length of time the union has existed as a legal entity: that is, from marriage until the decree absolute. However, awareness and experience of marital unhappiness leading on to breakdown obviously occurs at an earlier stage of the process (although each spouse will relate a unique set of meanings to their experience of breakdown). Therefore, the date of separation more realistically marks marriage breakdown. This event indicates when the withering marital fabric of affection and compatibility metamorphoses into the reality of a one-parent household, lower living standards, bruised egos and resentment. Evidence suggests that around one-third of divorcing couples have separated within five years of marrying.[7] But an even more important overall conclusion emerges from these survey findings and official figures: the majority of failed marriages do not rush from marriage to divorce.

Age at divorce

The highest risk of dissolution is found in the younger age groups. Some 3 per cent of both married men and women in the 25–29 age group experienced divorce in 1992 compared to 1 per cent for spouses aged 45–49. Those who divorce at a relatively younger age have a greater chance of remarriage and, because the manual classes tend to divorce at a younger age, they have a greater chance of establishing a second marriage than do couples in the higher-income social classes. The age at divorce pattern has remained fairly constant over the last 20 years, with wives' median age at divorce rising very slightly from 32.4 years in 1970 to 32.9 years in 1980 and 34.5 years in 1992. The more recent rise in the general population's age at marriage suggests that age upon divorce will show a slow but steady increase.

The older wife is especially vulnerable to the financially debilitating consequences of marriage breakdown and divorce. Over the ten-year period 1983–92 the courts dissolved the marriages of some quarter of a million (256 032) women aged 45 years or over: they comprised 17 per cent of all divorces in England and Wales during this period. The older woman's probability of remarriage is considerably lower than for a woman of 30.[8]

Such women have often given up earnings and work pension potential by undertaking a home-care role. With divorce they now face the loss of monetary protection and safeguard in widowhood that comes from the husband's occupational pension and life insurance schemes. The financial quagmire increases with knowledge that almost a quarter (24 per cent) of the husbands of divorcing wives of 45 years old or more in both 1991 and 1992 were experiencing their second (or more) dissolution. Proper recompense can seldom be provided by the courts to the divorced wife except in a minority of cases where the husband's earnings fall into the upper income level. In demographic terms this issue of financial support and compensation will grow because of the trend towards later marriage and the increasing number of failed further marriages. The proportion of women in the 65 years and over age group who are divorced and have not remarried is likely to increase fivefold (2.5 to 13.3 per cent) between 1985 and 2025.

Social class

Social class categorization is a powerful stratifying factor within divorce. Class is strongly associated with such significant lifestyle factors and experiences as education, employment, health, housing and income, as well as being linked with such demographic patterns as age at marriage and size of family. UK surveys report that marriages in which the husband is an unskilled worker within the Registrar General's social class groupings of employed men have the highest risk of divorce.[9] A similar pattern has been reported for the USA[10] and Finland.[11] This association between lower class and greater propensity to marriage breakdown has policy implications when discussing financial issues such as support for the mother and child.

Unemployment

The impact of poverty upon family life courses is evident in the field of unemployment. The latter has become a common, but perverse, experience within most Western countries. Within the UK in spring 1994 approximately one in six of all men under 30 were classified as unemployed. Men in all age groups record higher rates of unemployment than do women, and this gap is increasing.[12] Unsurprisingly, loss of work and status within the community creates mental distress among those made unemployed.[13] New evidence concerning the impact of unemployment on British married life emerges from a national study that interviewed some 5000 people.[14] The findings indicate that an unemployed married person is 130 per cent more likely to suffer a separation in the following year compared with those who had never been unemployed. This expectation is confirmed by GHS data for 1985.[15] The two categories 'unemployment' and 'economically inactive' when totalled together, remain significantly higher for divorcing men (16 per cent) than for married men (9 per cent) within the 'at risk' age group of 16–54 years. This once again underlines the association between low income and a high divorce risk. The structural condition of society is directly relevant to the pattern and form of family life events.

The last 50 years have witnessed reform of the divorce laws, a widening of the avenues of access to the courts and the easing of petitioning procedure. These changes have been of special benefit to the poorer members of society who had previously been largely excluded. Divorce has increasingly become accepted as the legal remedy for marital breakdown by those in the lower-income groups. Also associated with these divorcing couples are such features as younger age at marriage, earlier childbearing, larger families, rapid job changes or unemployment, poorer income and inadequate accommodation. In addition, the survey of Thornes and Collard[16] found higher neuroticism scores were registered by divorcing men and women than was found among spouses in ongoing marriages; the differences between divorcing and continuing married women were particularly marked. Those divorcing in social class 5 (unskilled manual worker) emerged as 'being relatively more at risk to marital stress resulting from environing disadvantage than did all the other groups'.[17] Material deprivations fall upon those least able to cope with the presence of tension and stress. Such social associations, together with the lowering of legal barriers, help to explain why lower socioeconomic marital households experience relatively high rates of divorce. Indeed, the highest levels are experienced by the unemployed.

Children

Behind the legal process of divorce lies the social reality of a protracted marital drama which involves children as both audience and cast within the unfolding chronology of discord, unhappiness, separation and divorce. Almost three million children under 16 years old experienced parental divorce in the 20 years between 1971 and 1990. An additional unknown minority were witnesses to parental separation. Current divorce trends suggest that one in four of all children will have first-hand knowledge of parental divorce before reaching the school-leaving age of 16. The US pattern is higher; its marital breakdown rates for the 1980s indicate that about two-fifths of all children would have experienced parental disruption by the age of 16.[18]

Over the last two decades the proportion of divorcing couples with dependent children has fallen slightly: from 62 per cent in 1970 to 57 per cent in 1992. Table 2.2 records this trend together with the linked small rise in childless divorces. These movements are a reflection of smaller family size within all marriages and a shorter marriage duration for those who will ultimately experience divorce. But over this period the annual numbers of dependent children has more than doubled to some 168 000 in 1992 as a consequence of the rising divorce numbers.

Table 2.2 Family patterns in divorce, 1970–92

Year/ Period*	Divorcing couples with children childless	All 16+ [percentages]	One or more –16	Numbers of children –16 [,000]
1970	26	12	62	71
1971–75	26	15	59	124
1976–80	29	11	60	156
1981–85	30	12	58	156
1986–90	31	14	55	150
1991	30	14	56	161
1992	29	14	57	168

Source: Calculations upon OPCS, FM2 series, table 4.4.

* Yearly average.

However, the actual numbers of dependent children experiencing parental divorce are even higher than that shown by official statistics, since government figures record children present at the time when the petition was filed. This information fails to record those who become 16 during the breakdown stage. The period of time between separation – as a delayed marker for time of breakdown – and eventual petitioning can well be a year or more.[19] A more realistic calculation showing the proportion of 1992 divorcing couples whose breakdown and separation affected one or more dependent children in their household produces 62 per cent compared with the 57 per cent recorded in Table 4.4 of the OPCS's *Marriage and Divorce Statistics* (1994) at the time of petitioning. Divorcing households have more dependent children affected by parental breakdown than official figures suggest.

Although social and legal concern focuses on the dependent child, the 1992 divorce web additionally involved some 70 000 teenage and adult offspring.[20] Continuing education, unemployment or disability causes many older children to remain dependent on their parents. Adolescent youngsters especially feel the emotional upheavals, while few older offspring escape the shock waves emanating from the disintegration of a long-lasting parental marriage. Adult–sibling relationships can be pulled apart in their reaction to a parent's decision to divorce. In some instances interfamily affection and loyalty will be permanently destroyed.

The increasing risk of children experiencing single-parent households through marital breakdown is reflected in the figures from the 1991 General Household Survey. This annually conducted survey reports that 10 per cent of all dependent children in Britain were being brought up by separated or divorced single mothers at the beginning of the 1990s.[21] When one turns to the proportion of all families with dependent children that are headed by a separated or divorced lone mother, a similar finding of 10 per cent is recorded.[22] The latter figure shows a sharp rise from 4 per cent recorded for 1971, and 6 per cent in 1981. This trend is one indicator of the move away from the traditional family pattern that predominated some 40 years ago.

For the majority of the 168 000 dependent children whose parents divorced in 1992 the family continues in a form similar to that experienced since parental separation. The decree absolute legally confirms for these children and the caring parent the reality of single parenthood. Divorce as a legal process marks one point in a particular family's life course which will continue in an amended form. For many couples, however, contact and communication is maintained because of the presence of children and family kin.

For many children the reality of being raised in a single-parent household is a short-term setting that will be replaced by a new family form of parent and step-parent. The formation of new adult relationships contained within extramarital cohabitation and remarriage are significant life events. These events impact on the consequences of divorce. For instance, a follow-up study of couples divorcing in 1973 showed that half the women had married again within four and a half years.[23] Such evidence also shows that single parenthood may represent only a fairly short period within the adult's overall life. The importance of remarriage as an increasingly occurring life event is seen in the pattern whereby women born in 1951 had three times the likelihood of experiencing remarriage by the age of 40 (16 per cent) than did women born 20 years earlier (5 per cent).[24] The reconstitution into differing new family forms has become a significant feature within the social and demographic patterning of contemporary family life.

REMARRIAGE

In the first half of this century remarriage generally concerned those who were widowed. This was a consequence of mortality's greater threat compared with the likelihood of divorce. From 1947 this was no longer the case, and the earlier divorce of one or other spouse became the increasingly common feature within a second marriage. The divorce explosion of the 1970s intensified this trend by returning increasing numbers of the unhappily married back to the single population. Linked with this transfer of status has been the desire of many divorced men and women to marry once again. This movement has had consequences for both marriage and divorce.

The remarriage patterns of the early 1990s indicate some two-thirds of all divorced people utilize their right to remarry. However, remarriage rates are affected by such factors as age, sex, social class, employment and attitude towards marriage. A demographic consequence of this propensity to remarry is that over one-third of contemporary weddings (1992: 36 per cent) involve a divorced partner. Table 2.3 records the steady rise, since 1961, in the proportion of new marriages registering a divorced person. This feature of modern marriage is a result of:

1 the high divorce rate;
2 many divorcees' desire for new marital happiness;
3 the move away from marriage by single people.

Considering their earlier marital unhappiness, it is perhaps surprising to find divorced people displaying greater willingness to re-embrace the institution of marriage than shown by single people. This pattern applies to men and women of all ages. For instance the marriage rate figures for 1992 indicate that divorced women aged 25 to 29 (119 per 1000) had a one-third

Table 2.3 Remarriage of divorced persons as a proportion of all marriages, 1961–92

Period/ Year	Annual number of marriages (,000)	Proportion involving divorced spouse (%)
1961–65	355	10
1971–75	399	23
1981–85	347	33
1986–90	345	34
1991	306	35
1992	312	36

Calculations based on OPCS (1994), *FM2*, **20**, table 3.6; and earlier numbers.

greater likelihood of marrying in that year compared with similarly aged single women. Clearly, the institution of marriage itself was not being rejected by the incompatibly married. However, the 1992 General Household Survey findings show that, since the early 1980s, premarital cohabitation has become more common for single-status divorced men (40 per cent) and women (29 per cent) aged under 50.[25] It has now become the standard precursor to marriage when one or both spouses have been previously married.[26] The increasing popularity of extramarital cohabitation, linked with the general trend to delayed marriage entry (for all marital status groups), helps to explain why remarriage rates for divorced men and women have declined from their 1972 peak. Yet even if one turns to the more typical year of 1971 as a base for comparison there is still no doubt about this increasing distaste for remarriage over the last 20 years. The 1991 marriage rate for divorced women aged 25–29 was one-third of the 1971 level; the corresponding 1991 rate for divorced women of all ages was 36 per cent of that for 1971.

In the past, marriage was the only appropriate means by which a divorced mother could shield herself and her children from the harsh realities of being a single-parent family. However, the last 30 years have seen a diminishment in prejudice against divorcees, and this has helped reduce the importance of remarriage as the set institutional process towards respectability. Changing structural patterns have especially helped divorced mothers by allowing greater freedom of choice when considering the possible benefits and disadvantages of a new marriage. The availability of improved welfare services, government financial provision, better employment opportunities and more equal pay have provided other viable alternatives for women.

Probabilities of remarriage

The time of separation indicates the *de facto* end of marriage. The couple's age at separation, with the latter's association to age at divorce, is the most important demographic factor in determining the likelihood of a further extramarital or marriage partnership. Confirmation of the greater probability of remarriage with younger age and by gender is provided by Coleman's life table calculations upon 1981 OPCS data.[27] This evidence suggests that nine out of ten of the 83 737 women *under* 35 who divorced in 1991 will marry again. Divorce is a transient state for most younger men and women. Although remarriage rates decline with age for both sexes, it is women's rates which fall most rapidly. This gender remarriage rate differential widens with each increasing year, so that, at 60, a divorced woman records only a quarter of the likelihood for similarly aged divorced men.

Discussion of remarriage trends cannot ignore the increasing importance of extramarital cohabitation (henceforth cohabitation) to family life. Cohabitation may operate as a substitute for, or as a preceding stage to, marriage, or as an state occurring before an eventual marriage. A significant minority of divorced cohabitants see and refer to their relationship as a marriage.[28] Half of the wives in Dunnell's study[29] who separated in 1970–71 had formed a new relationship, either marital (28 per cent) or cohabiting (20 per cent) within four years. The OPCS *Consequences of Divorce* study reports that a new partnership had been formed within 12 weeks of the decree absolute by 36 per cent of male informants (remarried: 11 per cent, cohabiting: 25 per cent) and 25 per cent of female informants (remarried: 7 per cent, cohabiting: 18 per cent).[30]

The existence of a child has a less negative impact on the probability of remarriage than might generally be expected.[31] In some 90 per cent of divorces the parent with responsibility for the daily care and control of the children is the mother. The majority (1991: 59 per cent) of divorcing mothers with dependent children under 16 are in the relatively high remarriage group aged under 35. The rates of remarriage and cohabitation recorded in surveys indicate that divorce is a transitional event for the majority of disunited couples and their children. Most dependent children experiencing breakdown of parental marriage are likely to find themselves in a reconstituted family unit of mother and stepfather. The formation of these new family webs create new kin associations and bonds of attachment and obligation.

The new marriage

It has been seen that contemporary marriage registers chronicle the increasing presence of previously divorced persons. The presence of children from a previous relationship means that many remarried couples begin their shared life with an existing family already around them. A resentment of the children's presence can create tension between adults attempting to mould new marital relationships in delicate and testing circumstances. A study of the consequences of divorce reports that objections to access were more likely to come from the new partner than from either the caring or the visiting parent. One father reported his experience thus: 'Her new husband [new partner of custodial mother] didn't approve of me seeing them, and didn't like me going up to the house or anything ...'.[32] These role ambiguities and uncertainties combine to increase the relationship problems contained within stepfamilies.

The reassuring presence of a new partner rekindles social links of affection and attachment within survivors of the wreckage of a collapsed marriage. Yet former marital relationship and kin networks cannot be so readily dissolved when there are dependent children. Divorced parents, particularly the mother, simply cannot make a new beginning completely severed from past familial affiliation. Remarriages containing step-parents and children have potential for far greater points of stress, conflict and ambivalence than that found within a first marriage. In Britain today, 10 per cent of all separating couples are raising children from a previous marriage.[33] The investigation of stepfamilies in Sheffield by Burgoyne and Clark[34] highlights how the economic, social and emotional inheritance from the earlier family are carried into the new marriage. The manners, habits and expectations attached to Western culture's traditional lifelong marriage have lagged behind the aftermath of the divorce explosion. All of this helps to create a web of undefined roles for the cast of the reconstituted family. Their private stage displays the personal stresses and problems associated with past ties and present ambiguity of parental behaviour.

Instability in second marriages

The complexities and problems facing those who remarry help to explain why second marriages carry a greater risk of divorce, the probability being double that of a first marriage.[35] The much higher breakdown rate of marriages involving a divorced spouse is underlined by the subsequent marital experiences of single and previously divorced men aged 20–24 who married in 1951.[36] Comparing these two cohorts some 36 years after their weddings shows that, by 1987, the bachelor grooms (16 per cent) had experienced half the divorce rate recorded by those previously divorced (32 per cent). Half the latter group will live through a further divorce. The experience of women also aged 20–24 in 1951 is very similar to that of the men; previously divorced brides (30 per cent) carried double the divorce risk of spinster brides (13 per cent). However, such variations must be qualified: the higher risk levels presented by the previously divorced is a partial demographic consequence of this group's youthful age at first marriage and subsequent early divorce, leaving them free to marry again at a still relatively young age. A strong explanatory social variable is this group's lower educational achievement, with its associated lower class and early age at marriage. Yet clear and crisp causal explanation is seldom possible in this arena of family life. The 'older' marriage age cohorts (25–29, 30–34, 35–39) still display a double marital breakdown rate among the previously divorced compared with those who were single at marriage. This finding occurred for both men and women within every one of these 1951 marriage age cohorts when recorded in 1987. The US experience – based on white women married between 1980 and 1985 – records that marriages containing a divorced spouse have a 25 per cent higher risk of divorce than do first marriages.[37] Marriages embracing a divorced person do appear to carry a greater risk of breakdown.

Those who divorce again also experience shorter durations of marriage compared with those undergoing a first divorce. The higher early breakdown propensity found within marriages involving a divorced spouse is confirmed by the subsequent marital experiences of single and previously divorced men aged 25–29 who married in 1966.[38] Comparing these two cohorts 15 years after their weddings shows the bachelor grooms (14 per cent) experienced half the divorce rate of that of those previously divorced (26 per cent). Repeating the same exercise for women also aged 25–29 produces similar findings; a quarter (24 per cent) of the previously divorced brides had experienced a further divorce compared with 15 per cent recorded by spinster brides. Supporting evidence from the USA is provided by Furstenberg and Spanier.[39] Such trends, linked with the increasing number of non-marital household relationships, affect the stability and continuity of parental socialization. One in twenty of the 1980s newborn are likely to share the confusing childhood experience of at least two more partners taking up residence with the custodial parent.

This chapter has given special attention to marriages involving the previously divorced for one principal reason: serial divorces are having an increasing influence upon the overall divorce pattern of England and Wales. A quarter of all divorces in 1992 involved a previously divorced spouse. Table 2.4, column C reports that, at the level of individual divorce experience, 17

Table 2.4 Recurring divorce as a proportion of all divorces, 1961–92

Year/ period	Annual number of divorces (A)* (,000s)	Previously divorced spouse All (B)* (,000s)	(C)** (%)	Both (D)*** (%)
1961	25	3	5	1
1966–70	48	5	5	1
1971–75	107	12	6	2
1976–80	137	24	9	3
1981–85	149	39	13	6
1986–90	152	49	16	8
1991	159	54	17	8
1992	160	56	17	9

Calculations based on OPCS (1990), *FM2*, **16**, p. 115 and OPCS (1994), *FM2*, **20**, table 4.5.

* (A) records the number of decrees absolute for dissolution and nullity, rounded to nearest thousand. (B) reports the number of previously divorced spouses within such decrees.

** (C) = B/2A times 100.

*** (D) shows the proportion of all divorces in (A) in which both spouses had previously experienced divorce.

per cent of all 1992 divorcing spouses were undergoing their second (or more) divorce. A similar calculation for 1970 produces 5 per cent.

The gender variation of 0.9 per cent (husbands: 17.4 per cent; wives: 16.5 per cent) recorded in 1991 is surprisingly small. In almost a tenth of all 1991 divorces both spouses were dissolving their marriage for the second time (see column D: 8 per cent). Of greater relevance to future breakdown trends is the rapid rise in serial divorce numbers which has helped to produce this new aspect of marital life. The 53 780 men and women experiencing a further divorce in 1991 totalled more than all the spouses divorcing in 1961 (50 788). Women under age 40 and divorcing again in 1991 formed 87 per cent of the 1961 divorcing female total (25 394).

The evidence presented concerning the previously divorced who remarry indicates that they both (a) form a growing proportion of all new marriages (1992: 36 per cent), and (b) experience twice the level of breakdown than that occurring in first marriages. These two trends help to produce (c), the increasing proportion of divorces containing one or both spouses having been previously divorced (1992: 26 per cent). For these reasons the true divorce risk for a couple both marrying for the first time will be lower than Haskey's calculated 37 per cent overall average for *all* (regardless of previous status) new marriages.[40] The interacting patterns of the early 1990s suggests that the risk of divorce for newly formed marriages uniting two previously single spouses is around one in three.

The impact of sequential divorce upon overall divorce rates is underemphasized in demographic, sociological and legal discussion. Because of the increasing numbers experiencing a further divorce it has become too simplistic to equate reconstituted families with a second marriage (or cohabitation). We now have several parallel structures of family life cycles (first, second, third or more) with their own demographic (age, fertility), social (kinship, multiple parentage) and legal (support obligations, custody) life course characteristics.

Some reasons for the previously divorced spouse's vulnerability to further breakdown emerge from studying the interaction between the structural, institutional and behavioural features which affect family life. At the structural level, the new family can experience financial hardship through the husband's ongoing maintenance liability, and this creates pressure on the second wife to earn, which in turn causes her annoyance at having to contribute to past marital obligations. The effective pressure-group activity of such couples has helped to persuade the government to propose in its 1995 White Paper, *Improving Child Support*, significant amendments to the operation of the Child Support Agency. Resentment may also be created by the divorced spouse's continuing contact with the ex-partner. These two situations are further examples of the protracted first marriage detrimentally affecting the quality and bonding of the new relationship.

Reconstituted relationships produce more opportunity for disagreement and division through the absence of effective institutional and cultural guidelines, controls and solutions found in the management of first marriages. For instance, there are no socially prescribed roles and models of behaviour for stepmothers to present to their stepchildren. Study of newly married couples shows the factor most associated with stress and unhappiness among wives was having to cope with stepchildren.[41] Earlier similar US evidence had led Cherlin in 1978 to describe remarriage as an 'incomplete institution', and to argue that it is this normative uncertainty which helps to make the preservation of family unity more difficult.[42] Though Cherlin's argument has a certain appeal, it does not entirely explain why there should be a sixfold greater propensity for further divorce found in 1992 divorce rates among younger previously divorced brides aged 25–34 (this age group avoids the special factors associated with 'older' widows) compared with similarly aged widowed brides.[43] Nevertheless, the totality of evidence does suggest that divorced persons who remarry face special family problems and strains unknown in first marriages.

A more individualistic explanation for the greater breakdown propensity found within the previously divorced contends that those who are divorce-prone display personalities and dispositions that incline them to shy away from challenges within marriage rather than resolve them. It could be that such people are less adept at choosing the right partner or more inclined to select each other. At the same time demographic reality propels the divorced together. The previously divorced or separated swell the unmarried post-30 population who potentially seek a heterosexual partnership. With increasing age the divorced have a narrower field of choice. This pattern helps to explain why six out of ten previously divorced women aged 30–49 who remarried in 1991 had similarly divorced grooms.

The experience of divorce conditions a proportion of its population who are already more temperamentally predisposed to form incompatible relationships. Those who are remarrying line up again at the institutional tape inoculated with the techniques and experiences of post-breakdown survival and knowing that there *is* life after divorce. Such an awareness ensures less hesitancy next time around if, once again, the new partner fails to provide personal happiness. Their interviews with US couples led Furstenberg and Spanier to be 'continually struck by the admissions of many of our informants that they were prepared to dissolve their second marriage if it did not work out'.[44] A more rapid conjugal assessment and pronouncement is particularly true of those remarrying at a younger age (under 35). If the arguments of personality and temperament, poor selection ability and breakdown survival knowledge can be validly related to individuals, then new partnerships bringing together two divorced persons appear especially vulnerable. This expectation of a higher risk of incompatibility leading to divorce is confirmed by both US and UK survey results.[45]

Marital and extramarital movements

National divorce patterns collate individual reactions and attitudes to marital disharmony, while, overall, they also reflect the norms and habits existing within the ongoing social structure, as well as the legal and demographic opportunity within that society. An example of the demographic input is seen in the declining married 'age at risk' population. For instance, between the years 1971 and 1991 the number of wives (including the remarried) aged 16–44 fell by 768 000 although the overall female population (single and ever-married) had increased by 17 per cent in this period. This fall in the married population is, of course, a result of the declining propensity to marry at a 'younger' age. The same pattern has also led to a decline in the proportion of newly formed marriages containing high-divorce-risk young (under 20) brides and/or grooms. The fact that marriages uniting single men and women are generally taking place at a later age has implications for future divorce patterns. The combination of 'delayed' or 'rejected' marriage will, *ceteris paribus*, lead to a drop in divorcing numbers, although such a movement could still leave the divorce rate unchanged at its historically high early 1990s level. A somewhat murky demographic crystal ball suggests that the divorce rate is likely to rise above 1992 levels for a further two or three years and then level out to a plateau of around 15 per 1000 ongoing marriages.

A study of both marital and extramarital changing patterns and habits, and their causes, is clearly necessary when trying to interpret the meaning and movement of modern-day divorce trends. The increasing popularity of marriage after the Second World War was linked to the overall trend towards marriage at a younger age that had begun in the 1930s. The year 1970 saw three out of ten brides marrying under the age of majority (then 21). The early 1970s witnessed a halt in the falling age at marriage; since then the trend has reversed to produce a clear momentum towards later entry. This is especially noticeable for women born since 1940. Table 2.5 records this changing pattern. Younger single men and women are now far less inclined to marry at the same age as their parents did. This is reflected in the proportion of women married by age 25 falling from 82 per cent for those born in 1945 to 47 per cent for those born 20 years later.

Table 2.5 The percentages of women ever married by certain ages, by birth cohort, 1940–72

Year of	Exact age			
Birth	20	25	30	45
1940	24	80	91	95
1945	29	82	92	96
1950	29	79	89	
1955	32	73	85	
1960	22	61	77	
1965	12	47		
1972	6			

Source: J. Haskey (1993) in *Population Trends*, **72**, table 1.

The above pattern can be set into a longer historical review. The average age at marriage of spinster brides in 1992 has risen to 25.9 years, and one has to turn back some 80 years to the decade 1910–19 to observe similar figures. The years between 1850 and 1894 produced an annual average of some 24 years; between 1895 and 1939 the corresponding figure was generally around 25 years. The demographic pattern remains when the mean (or average) as the statistical indicator for comparison is replaced by the median (or mid-point). The 1992 spinster bride's median age at marriage of 25.0 years is the highest recorded within the official statistics since 1850. A similar conclusion applies to the bachelor's median age at marriage (1992: 26.8 years).[46] The observable patterns of the early 1990s cannot simply be interpreted as a return to the custom and form of the early twentieth century; the demographic facts are otherwise. The trend is more dynamic, as witnessed during the 10 years between 1983 and 1992 when the spinster bride's mean age at marriage dropped by almost two and a half (2.44) years. This evidence emphasizes that these contemporary changes in marriage are a fundamental amendment to a long-established habit. The turnaround has occurred within a relatively short period, and it is increasing rapidly in momentum.

It is too early to say with confidence whether this pattern incorporates a minority's readiness to reject marriage completely or whether it is simply a delaying action by the majority. What is clear is that the postponement of marriage to a later age is a recurring feature, and it remains likely that most unmarried women in their mid-20s will eventually marry. However, it also seems probable that more younger men and women than at any time during this century will never marry. The latter belief is given credence by calculations from the OPCS which forecasts that 5 per cent of women who were 16 years old in 1974 will be unmarried at 50; a similarly aged 1991 cohort is projected at 26 per cent unmarried at 50.[47] This fivefold increase in less than two decades indicates rapidly changing social attitudes towards the appropriateness of traditional marriage.

The movement away from marriage has so far been more marked in other Northern and Western European countries. National trends (as indicated by the percentages of women born in 1960 who will remain unmarried at 50 if 1980's patterns continue) suggest that the UK (22 per cent: England and Wales) will follow a more traditional marriage approach than such countries as Austria (26 per cent), France (28 per cent), Switzerland (28 per cent), Norway (32 per cent), Denmark (39 per cent) and Sweden (45 per cent).[48] The strong cohabitation movement found within both Denmark and Sweden underlies the projection of some 40 per cent of their women remaining unmarried. Yet the British experience of the 1990s suggests that we are increasingly moving towards the Scandinavian pattern; and that 30 per cent could be a more realistic estimate of the 1960 cohort of women remaining unmarried. This movement away from marriage entry reinforces the argument that divorce numbers will fall as a direct consequence of the declining married population. This same process is also significantly reducing the numbers of young brides (aged under 20) who, through their age and associated early childbearing, are associated with a relatively high risk of divorce. Young brides formed 20 per cent of all spinster marriages in 1983; this proportion had fallen to 7 per cent in 1992.

Arm-in-arm with the evidence of delay in – or possibly abandonment of – entering marriage is the increasing popularity of extramarital cohabitation. The proportions emerging from the General Household Survey (GHS) of Great Britain annual investigation are likely to underrecord the true figure, since there is a tendency for women in long-running consensual unions to describe themselves as married. The GHS records a doubling in the proportion of all cohabiting 'non-married' (incorporating single, widowed, divorced and separated women aged 18–49) between 1981 (12 per cent) and 1991 (23 per cent). This movement is a partial reflection of the flight from marriage enrolment that is most evident among the single category. The next reported finding provides further indication of the nature of this trend. The British Household Panel Survey (henceforth BHPS) compared the experiences of British women born in the 1940s to those born in the 1960s. The Survey findings indicate that the 'partnership' rate – formed by combining both marriage and cohabitation rates – showed little variation between these two age groups.[49]

However, increasing levels of cohabitation reported by both the GHS and the BHPS is not a sufficient factor to explain away the entire decline in marriage rates. An increasing proportion of households in contemporary Britain consist of single adults (some of whom will have experienced 'partnerships') below pensionable age. This movement is particularly noticeable for men under 65 and living alone; in 1991 such men formed one in twelve of all British households compared with one in thirty in 1971.[50] This is mainly a consequence of relationship breakdown, but it also reflects the trend for an increasing minority of both men and women to remain single by choice. In other words, a significant proportion of adults who now live a single lifestyle would have been married some 20 years ago. The noticeable shift in public opinion over the last 40 years towards the moral acceptability of sexual activity by the unmarried is a further explanatory feature of this change. With changing attitudes has come the technical advances, and greater choice and freedom, in the use of contraception. Women now have a far greater control over their own fertility than was experienced by their grandmothers. Attitudinal findings upon sex before marriage underlines the general toleration felt in 1991 by both single people and those under 45 years.[51]

An acceptance of sex before marriage and the availability of willing partners means that marriage is no longer the only generally accepted setting and provider for the pleasures of such intimacy.

The overall pattern for the last 20 years is of the rapid increase in premarital cohabitation. Such a relationship in the supposedly liberal 1960s was a very uncommon practice. Only 2 per cent of women marrying before the age of 30 (both bride and groom being single) in the period 1965–69 had lived with their husbands before marriage. Twenty years later (1985–89) the proportion had risen to almost a half (47 per cent).[52] In the mid-1990s cohabitation has become both the customary route into, and also a partial replacement for, marriage, and the engagement has lost much of its traditional symbolic function. The BHPS findings confirm the extent to which consensual unions have become an accepted and practised lifestyle in contemporary Britain. Public attitudes are in accord with private habit, for less than one in ten of those under 40 regard living together outside marriage as being morally wrong. Over half of all men (55 per cent) and women (58 per cent) aged 25–29 report having lived in a consensual relationship.[53] This pattern of cohabitation displays little appreciable variation between the social classes. Parents in all strata of contemporary British society diplomatically accept and openly acknowledge their daughters' and sons' new life patterns.

This increasing tendency to live together before marriage should theoretically brush apart some couples whose unsuitability for life membership of the marriage club would have previously emerged after enrolment. In practice, however, premaritally cohabiting couples show greater vulnerability to marital breakdown. This is the conclusion reached by survey data from Canada, Sweden, the USA, as well as in the UK.[54] Evidence from 1989 GHS findings indicate that among single women marrying in 1980–84, those who had premaritally cohabited were 50 per cent more likely to have divorced within five years of marriage. The same comparison made upon earlier marrying cohorts also found a greater propensity for divorce among those who had lived together before marrying. However, the divorce risk of premarital cohabitants narrows, but does not disappear, when the partnership duration period compared with that of traditional married couples includes the premaritally cohabiting couples' total time together. For example, when a duration of 15 years' *de facto* union together becomes the comparison point, the premaritally cohabiting couples still record a 20 per cent higher divorce rate.[55] Such patterns are confirmed by the BHPS data reporting that those in the panel study who were divorced or separated were about a third more likely to have lived together before marriage than were the still married.[56] The relevance of these findings is the association between premarital cohabitation and the increased probability of divorce (although, of course, it is not being argued that the former causes the latter). Within the contemporary demographic recipe the increasing popularity of premarital cohabitation is an ingredient that, by itself, suggests an increase in the rate of divorce.

The divorced have extra reason to be cautious about re-entering marriage without first testing their suitability. Premarital cohabitation became the norm for marriages in the 1980s where one or both spouses had been previously married,[57] and these trends are set to continue during the 1990s, premarital cohabitation now being an institutionalized part of pre-marriage selection patterns among this group. In addition, postmarital cohabitation as a long-term alternative to marriage is becoming a mutual choice for the divorced:[58] OPCS figures for 1991–92 report that 26 per cent of all divorced British women under 60 were in consensual unions. Within the 35–49 age group previously divorced women were far more likely to be in such a union (29 per cent) than were widows (4 per cent).[59] This variation in lifestyles might be an indicator of the divorcees' more unorthodox attitudes and weaker commitment to the institution of marriage.

One in twenty of all dependent children are now being raised by couples living together in stable extramarital relationships.[60] It is too early to be certain that these consensual unions will eventually transform into marriage. Pregnancy does not propel couples towards matrimony, and their parents no longer coerce them towards a 'proper' wedding. This feature of contemporary family life means that marriage and parenthood are no longer inextricably linked for an increasing proportion of society.

Birth statistics for 1989 suggest that one in seven of all newborn children will have parents living in consensual unions.[61] The majority of unmarried consensual parents will eventually marry, although a significant minority will either continue to cohabit or separate. A characteristic of long-term cohabiting mothers found in McRae's 1992 survey[62] was that a quarter of the households lacked a wage-earner, and a fifth of all the fathers had been unemployed for two or more years. The low-income, poorly educated mother has less economic incentive to marry when the man cannot, or will not, offer long-term support.

Similar social changes in long-held habits are occurring in most European countries, the most noticeable movements being in Sweden and Denmark. The Swedish retreat from marriage is reflected in the finding that, among women aged 20–24 who were living in a union in 1989, some four out of five were cohabiting.[63] Over half of all Swedish children are born out of wedlock, forming the highest proportion in Europe. Figures for extramarital births (combining cohabiting and single mothers) in other European countries in 1992 show a wide variation: Denmark (46 per cent) is the next highest, the UK (31 per cent) and France (33 per cent) rank 'high' while Italy (7 per cent) and Greece (3 per cent) record the lowest proportions.

These developments are radically affecting the way we both observe family life and legislate on family matters. The existing problems of measuring marital and family stability are exacerbated when the researcher attempts to incorporate knowledge concerning the new-style partnerships. The date of marriage has become an increasingly unsatisfactory boundary mark to record such matters as length of cohabitation or child spacing patterns. Divorce remains as a legal marker within the individual's life course, but the social and demographic significance of divorce as a major indicator of broken partnerships and disrupted family life has been diminished by the force of these extra-marital patterns. The presented evidence underlines the generality of changing family custom and form within the UK and certain other European nations. With these changes comes the uncertainty as to where they may lead, and what they might produce. What is clear is that traditional familial attitudes and expectations have become less stringent over the last 25 years.

STRUCTURE, INDIVIDUAL EXPECTATION AND STATE PRESCRIPTIONS

The presented demographic and social evidence suggests that lifelong marriage will no longer be the central institutional underpin of the twenty-first-century family as it had been in 1950. The demographic momentum of the 1970s and 1980s has produced fundamental amendments to the traditional nuclear family structure model of a married couple with dependent children. The 1992 figures for both the proportion of children born out of wedlock (32 per cent: UK), and the divorce rate (13.7 per 1000 married couples: England and Wales) provide a similar twofold increase above 1970 levels. This is a pattern that is being repeated in varying degrees in most European Union states, as the divorce rates and their related increases recorded in Table 2.6 confirm. One consequence is that, in 1992, a fifth of all British families with dependent children were headed by single parents responsible for the welfare of their 2.3 million children. A further 5 per cent of families contained parents who are not married. Such trends and figures project an increasing presence of a non-traditional family form within the UK. With these diverse forms of family life comes the increased likelihood of status movement for both parents and children.

The last quarter century (1970–94) was a period in which the Conservative party, affirming its aim of personal choice juxtaposed with a belief in a well ordered traditional family life, held parliamentary power for over three-quarters of this time. Governments are generally ineffective in altering private behaviour and practice to conform with political ideals, and evidence shows that this government was no exception.

Table 2.6 Divorce trends for some European countries: 1970 and 1989

	Divorces per 1000 married population: 1989	Rate* of increase 1970 and 1989
Belgium	8.6	2.3
Denmark	13.6	0.8
Germany**	8.7	0.7
France	8.4	1.5
Ireland	–	–
Italy	2.1	0.6
Netherlands	8.1	1.4
UK	12.7	1.7

Source: Eurostat, *Demographic Statistics*

* Rates calculated upon 1970 base figures (1.0) provided by Eurostat.
** For 1988.

The condition of our divorce law has had little long-term impact on the rate of marriage breakdown. What can be seen is that those who find themselves in unhappy marriages have shown increasing readiness to turn to divorce rather than to separate or continue within unsatisfactory relationships. The demographic analysis of Schoen and Baj[64] followed the life experiences of nine successive five-year generations of men and women born between 1900 and 1944 in England and Wales. Their findings showed that each successive birth cohort's chances of divorce had increased. For instance, women born in the period 1915–19 recorded a divorce probability of 10 per cent for *all* these women (although a minority would remain single). The cohort of 1920–24 recorded 13 per cent. For the 1940–44 cohort the risk had increased to 25 per cent. Much the same pattern is provided by Haskey's similar birth cohort analysis.[65] His data shows that each succeeding generation of men and women born in the period 1925–55 registers a higher rate of divorce by the age of 40 than the preceding generation.

The next piece of relevant evidence is the 1969 Divorce Reform Act's impact upon the tendency to resort to divorce. Although its introduction did lead to an immediate surge of petitions, the 1960s had already experienced an annual rise of 9.5 per cent to a peak of 70 575 petitions in 1970. An unchanged continuation of this yearly increase would have led to over 200 000 petitions per year by 1990, compared to the actual 189 000 petitions. The 1969 legislation was partly an acknowledgement of the steadily increasing propensity to divorce, but its introduction did not lead to a long-term change in the rate of resort to divorce. All the evidence suggests that the impact of liberal divorce legislation on the divorce rate has been of a short-term nature.

Of greater significance in understanding the post-1960 divorce escalation has been the advancement of hedonistic attitudes within an increasingly pluralistic society and structure. This period has witnessed a worldwide expansion of market conditions. Whether one views social change within the context and theoretical framework of 'post-modernity' (and the death of modernity and the systems it represented), as opposed to the setting of either 'post-industrial society' or 'modernity' seems to me to be unimportant, although the concept of post-modernity does have some value by offering insights upon present social conditions and values. Traditions are being rapidly broken, and with change has come ambivalence and uncertainty. There is less willingness to make long-term public commitments within the orbit of an unpredictable world. More people choose to live single, autonomous lives. In such a privatized society the lone individual lacks binding links with the community; this has been the Swedish experience.[66] Religions increasingly display spiritual uncertainty, and their leaders no longer provide authority. Public affirmation of the existence of a God has declined to 20 per cent in the UK. A hundred years ago, nine in ten marriages were preceded by religious rites; in 1966 it was two-thirds; the proportion has now fallen to a half. With secularization has also come the loosening of the evangelical bond of rigid morality which intertwined the cultural fabric of conformist social mores and habits and the declared public conscience.

At the same time the traditional institutional displays of divorce disapproval have largely disappeared. The changing barometer of establishment social mores are indicated by the rules and practices surrounding the UK Royal Family and the Church of England. For example, the rules governing entry to Ascot's Royal Enclosure no longer debar divorcees. Such acceptability reflects both the growth of divorce within the upper and middle classes and the Royal Family's personal experience of marital breakdown. The establishment of 40 years ago would have found it inconceivable that the Queen's three married children would have revealed their marital breakdowns. A combination of political coercion and persuasion may not have healed such rifts, but divorce would have been excluded as an acceptable option. Similar pressures in the 1950s had persuaded Princess Margaret from marrying a divorced man, yet the subsequent dissolution of her marriage in 1978 caused little public comment. A combination of high technology snooping, media invasion and publication and personal indiscretion have allowed the intimate details behind the Prince and Princess of Wales' failed marriage to be exposed in every home. The Royal Family as public symbols of acceptable standards and behaviour are an institutional emblem of the rapid transition from traditional family values.

The easing of attitudes within the Church of England in 1981 allowed the Synod finally to concede that there were circumstances in which it could be proper for a divorced person to remarry in church during the lifetime of the former partner. The Church's 1980 *Alternative Service Book* declares: 'Marriage is given, that husband and wife may comfort and help each other'. Companionship has replaced the foremost justification for marriage traditionally set down in *The Book of Common Prayer*: 'for the procreation of children'. British public opinion similarly believes that successful marriages are sustained, above all, by compatibility and a friendly relationship between the spouses.[67]

Increasing enmity and incompatibility leading to irretrievable breakdown brought divorce to 920 000 husbands and wives in the three years between 1990–92. Democracy has allowed greater freedom and self-determination and, alongside these ideals, citizens have come to expect happiness and personal fulfilment. Hedonism has become a legitimate pursuit within a free-enterprise society structured on market forces and materialism. Individual expectation within a rapidly changing social structure has created the setting within which the current levels of family breakdown appear likely to increase.

Individualism and choice

Within our ambivalent enterprise culture of individualism the licence of choice dominates. The Soviet Union, the allied states of Eastern Europe and the Berlin Wall have all crumbled before the ideology of free democratic self-determination. The provision of choice allows far more citizens to examine and consider what they expect of either the government or their marriage. It is the domain of private life that offers meaning and identity within a uncertain world. Personal fulfilment has become home-centred, and individual relationships are now expected to be the primary provider of satisfaction and pleasure. Affection, companionship and togetherness have become the consummate lifestyle.

A setting of individualism and greater choice has encouraged younger couples to expect more from the emotional bonds of their relationships. If this turns into an icefield of disenchantment the victims know they can more readily judicially extricate themselves from their frozen marital wasteland. Participants know that ahead of them are others who have safely traversed the same route. The divorced are a social affirmation that the process is a transitional and survivable stage to a hopefully better life. For many men and women, divorce does create a happier future.

Women have especially benefited from the broader avenues of choice denied to their grandmothers. Improvements in the fields of education, employment, health and fertility, welfare and social security provisions, and a more equitable family law are some of the structural features which allow women greater freedom and ability to control their own lives. These changes, and the new privatized morality, have encouraged consumer emancipation. Greater freedom to judge, choose and change their minds has encouraged women to become more confident and assertive about what they expect from a marriage. An indicator of the impact of these structural and attitudinal changes upon women is reflected in the increasing proportion of petitions coming from wives: the period 1946–50 recorded 45 per cent, but by 1986–90 the rate had risen to 73 per cent. The safeguard of divorce availability provides an opportunity for women and children to escape from domestic violence and other types of antagonistic male conduct. Divorce as a reserve helps to set the standards of acceptable family behaviour.

In most Western countries divorce and remarriage have become life events which the majority of married couples will encounter either directly or through the involvement of kin. Although divorce has become more likely, some two-thirds of first-time marriages in the UK seem likely to continue. A paradoxical feature within the tapestry of forces creating both family breakdown and permanency is the continuation of conservative family attitudes. Most children are raised in two-parent households, and couples still opt to live together in conventional monogamous association rather than in the supposedly broader freedom of radical communes. Traditional family values are also reflected in the *British Values Study* which found that seven out of ten adults (of all ages) disapprove of a woman having a child outside the confines of a stable relationship.[68] The more menial child-rearing duties and household chores continue to fall upon the mother even when she is in full-time employment. Relatives are still the most likely child carers when the mother is employed. Public opinion remains strongly committed to established expectations of sexual fidelity by both spouses. But more permissive attitudes are now displayed towards premarital relationships with less than a third of the same survey informants feeling this behaviour to be always or almost always wrong.[69] Individual behaviour is no longer so formally prescribed as it was in 1950. We are witnessing transformation, but not revolution, in family attitudes and habits.

Age has become an important explanatory variable in the dissection of family life and structure. Behaviour is now increasingly prescribed by age rather than social class or gender; it is this feature that is especially noticeable in the shift in values that have been set down.

The philosophy of the 1969 divorce legislation accepted that a reformed malleable law did not itself cause breakdown. It was the reality of marital disharmony that induced movement toward divorce. The designated five 'facts' were to be seen as the symptoms and not the cause of irretrievable breakdown; but the new law compromised in readdressing as facts the three previously recognized offence grounds. Nonetheless, the expected decline and withering away of the matrimonial offence has not occurred; in 1992 three-quarters of all petitions still resorted to one or other of the fault 'facts'. Reviewing the law's efficacy in 1990, the Law Commission concluded that the working of the present system offered neither a genuine test of breakdown nor any real brake on divorce. Their original proposals for a divorce process over a one-year period, together with those of the Lord Chancellor's Department towards a far wider use of mediation, emerge as a White Paper.[70] Public discussion upon the most effective future method for handling divorce matters is clearly sensible and proper. Yet, is it seriously being proposed that the Family Proceedings Court be given a further lease of life by the incorporation of divorce business?[71] Divorce and family matters should have no part in a court designed to handle petty crime.

CONCLUSION

Divorce has become an established feature of modern life, and has been institutionalized as a legal process. It is now commonly accepted as the proper solution to irretrievable breakdown of the marital partnership. The legally directed issues and problems created by breakdown clearly must be faced by the legislators. But what can be done, if anything, to minimize the socially-oriented deprivations and disadvantages experienced by the divorced and their children? The problems experienced by the remarried are one example of the detachment experienced by divorced people in everyday family life. Goode's answer to this is to institutionalize divorce: '...accept it as we do other institutions, and build adequate safeguards as well as social understandings and pressures to make it work reasonably well'.[72] Such a prescription requires society to readjust its social norms and structures to accommodate new family patterns and habits.

Legislators cannot ignore these changes. Alternative forms of family life have become more commonplace over the last 20 years. The government recognizes that it has a duty to support families of all types. The extramarital family has grown rapidly in numbers, although of course remaining outside the divorce court's protective function. At the same time cohabiting couples are four times as likely to split up as are married couples.[73] There is already pressure to incorporate extramarital unions into quasi-married legal units. Concern over the needs and claims of children suggests that these forces towards 'incorporation' will become stronger.

Nevertheless, the fact that three out of four children in 1990 were living with their married parents confirms the most popular form of parenthood remains that which regularizes the relationship between family members, and formalizes bonds between family and society. The traditional family continues, yet today's evident and accepted non-conventional patterns will be more prevalent in the family of tomorrow.

NOTES

1 J. Haskey (1989), 'Current prospects for the proportion of marriages ending in divorce', *Population Trends*, **55**, London: HMSO, pp. 34–7.
2 See J. Haskey (1989), 'Trends in marriage and divorce, and cohort analyses of the proportions of marriages ending in divorce', *Population Trends*, **54**, London: HMSO, pp. 21–8.
3 OPCS (1989), *General Household Survey*, **16**, Table 4.9.
4 M.J. Murphy (1985), 'Demographic and socio-economic influences on recent British marital breakdown patterns', *Population Studies*, **9**, pp. 441–60 at p. 448.
5 *Ibid.*, p. 460.
6 L. Kurdek (1991), 'Predictors of increases in marital distress in newlywed couples: a 3-year prospective longitudinal study', *Developmental Psychology*, **27**, pp. 627–36 at p. 633.
7 See R. Chester (1971), 'The duration of marriage to divorce', *British Journal of Sociology*, **22**, pp. 172–82; also B. Thornes and J. Collard (1979), *Who Divorces?*, London: Routledge & Kegan Paul, p. 124; also J. Gregory and K. Foster (1990), *The Consequences of Divorce*, London: OPCS, p. 11; also C.S. Gibson (1993), *Dissolving Wedlock*, London: Routledge, p. 145.
8 D.A. Coleman (1989), 'The contemporary pattern of remarriage in England and Wales' in E. Grebenik *et al.*, (eds), *Later Phases of the Family Cycle*, Oxford: Clarendon Press, p. 99.
9 Gibson, *op. cit.*, note 7 above, p. 136.
10 W.J. Goode (1993), *World Changes in Divorce Patterns*, London: Yale University Press, p. 154.
11 K. Anntila (1977), 'Finland' in R. Chester (ed.), *Divorce in Europe*, Leiden: Nijhoff, p. 29.
12 Central Statistical Office (1995), *Social Trends*, **25**, London: HMSO, pp. 76–8.
13 British Household Panel Survey (1994), *Changing Households: The British Household Panel Survey 1990–1992*, Colchester: University of Essex, p. 178.
14 ESRC (1990), 'Unemployment and divorce', *Social Sciences*, July, p. 5.
15 OPCS (1987), *General Household Survey*, **15**, London: HMSO, p. 67.
16 Thornes and Collard, *op. cit.*, note 7 above, pp. 203–4.

17 *Ibid.*, p. 41.
18 A. Cherlin (1992), *Marriage, Divorce, Remarriage*, London: Harvard University Press, p. 26; Goode (*op. cit.*, note 10 above, p. 154) believes this rate to be almost 50 per cent.
19 Chester (*op. cit.*, note 7 above), Gibson (*op. cit.*, note 7 above, p. 142) and Gregory and Foster (*op. cit.*, note 7 above, table 2.34. The latter table, when recalculated, shows that 38 per cent of all petitions recording dependent children had such an interval of a year or more. This period must formally be so when the facts of either consensual separation or desertion (both a minimum of two years) or unilateral separation (a minimum of five years) are recorded.
20 Although in the light of the argument in note 19 above, this number should be correspondingly reduced by some 12 000 if the time focus point is separation rather than petitioning for divorce.
21 OPCS (1993), *General Household Survey*, **22**, London: HMSO, table 2.20 recalculated.
22 *Ibid.*, table 2.18.
23 R. Leete and S. Anthony (1979), 'Divorce and remarriage: a record linkage study', *Population Trends*, **16**, pp. 5–16.
24 OPCS (1994), *FM2*, **20**, London: HMSO, p. 49.
25 OPCS (1994), *General Household Survey*, **23**, London: HMSO, tables 2.6 and 2.9.
26 Gregory and Foster, *op. cit.*, note 7 above, p. 15.
27 Coleman, *op. cit.*, note 8 above, p. 89.
28 K. Dunnell (1979), *Family Formation 1976*, London: HMSO, p. 39.
29 *Ibid.*, p. 38.
30 Gregory and Foster, *op. cit.*, note 7 above, p. 13.
31 Coleman, *op. cit.*, note 8 above, p. 107; Leete and Anthony, *op. cit.*, note 23 above, p. 5; J. Ermisch (1989), 'Divorce: economic antecedents and aftermath' in H. Joshi (ed.), *The Changing Population of Britain*, Oxford: Blackwell, pp. 42–55 at p. 50.
32 Gregory and Foster, *op. cit.*, note 7 above, p. 156.
33 *Ibid.*, p. 10.
34 J. Burgoyne and D. Clark (1984), *Making a Go of It*, London: Routledge & Kegan Paul.
35 J. Haskey (1983), 'Marital status before marriage and age at marriage: their influence on the chance of divorce', *Population Trends*, **32**, London: HMSO; Coleman, *op. cit.*, note 8 above; OPCS (1993), *FM2*, **19**, London: HMSO, p. 76.
36 Haskey, *op. cit.*, note 2 above, table 5.
37 R. Martin and L. Bumpass (1989), 'Recent trends in marital disruption', *Demography*, **26**, pp. 37–51 at p. 47.
38 Haskey, *op. cit.*, note 2 above, table 5.
39 F.F. Furstenberg and G. Spanier (1984), *Recycling the Family: Remarriage after Divorce*, Beverley Hills: Sage, p. 183.
40 J. Haskey (1989), 'Current prospects for the proportion of marriages ending in divorce', *Population Trends*, **55**, pp. 34–7.
41 Kurdek *op. cit.*, note 6 above, p. 634.
42 A. Cherlin (1978), 'Remarriage as an incomplete institution', *American Journal of Sociology*, **84**, pp. 634–50.
43 OPCS (1994), *FM2*, **20**, London: HMSO, p. 76.
44 Furstenberg and Spanier, *op. cit.*, note 39 above, p. 192.
45 T. Monahan (1958), 'The changing nature and instability of remarriages', *Eugenics Quarterly*, pp. 73–85, table 5; see also Gibson, *op. cit.*, note 7 above, p. 165.
46 OPCS (1990), *FM2*, **16**, (1837–1983), London: HMSO, tables 3.4 and 3.5.

47 OPCS (1977), *FM2*, **1**, London: HMSO, p. 25; OPCS, *op. cit.*, note 35 above, p. 18.
48 J. Haskey (1992), 'Patterns of marriage, divorce and cohabitation in the different countries of Europe', *Population Trends*, **69**, pp. 27–36, table 2.
49 BHPS, *op. cit.*, note 13 above, p. 42.
50 Central Statistical Office (1995), *Social Trends*, **25**, London: HMSO, p. 30.
51 K. Wellings *et al.* (1994), *Sexual Behaviour in Britain: The National Survey of Sexual Attitudes and Lifestyles*, Harmondsworth: Penguin, pp. 246–8.
52 OPCS, *op. cit.*, note 21 above, p. 230.
53 BHPS, *op. cit.*, note 13 above, pp. 75 and 78.
54 J. Haskey (1992), 'Premarital cohabitation and the probability of subsequent divorce: analyses using new data from the General Household Survey', *Population Trends*, **68**, pp. 10–19.
55 *Ibid.*, pp. 16–17.
56 BHPS, *op. cit.*, note 13 above, p. 77.
57 OPCS, *op. cit.*, note 15 above, p. 28; BHPS, *op. cit.*, note 13 above, p. 81.
58 J. Haskey, *op. cit.*, note 48 above, p. 35.
59 CSO, *op. cit.*, note 50 above, p. 39.
60 *Ibid.*, p. 34.
61 OPCS (1990), *Population Trends*, **61**, London: HMSO, p. 58.
62 S. McRae (1993), *Cohabiting Mothers: Changing Marriage and Motherhood*, London: Policy Studies Institute.
63 Family Policy Studies Centre (1994), *Families in the European Union*, London: FPSC, p. 6.
64 R. Schoen and J. Baj (1984), 'Twentieth-century cohort marriage and divorce in England and Wales', *Population Studies*, **38**, pp. 439–49 at p. 441.
65 J. Haskey, (1993), 'First marriage, divorce, and remarriage: birth cohort analyses', *Population Trends*, **72**, London: HMSO, pp. 24–33 at p. 28.
66 D. Popenoe (1988), *Disturbing the Nest: Family Change and Decline in Modern Societies*, New York: Aldine de Gruyter.
67 S. Ashford (1987), 'Family matters', in R. Jowell *et al.* (eds), *British Social Attitudes: Special International Report*, Aldershot: Gower, at pp. 124 and 140.
68 J. Brown *et al.* (1985), 'Marriage and the family', in M. Abrams *et al.* (eds), *Values and Social Change in Britain*, London: Macmillan, p. 118.
69 R. Jowell and C. Airey (1984), *British Social Attitudes*, Aldershot: Gower, p. 137.
70 Lord Chancellor's Department (1995), *Looking to the Future: Mediation and the Ground for Divorce*, London: HMSO.
71 *Ibid.*, p. 76.
72 Goode, *op. cit.*, note 10 above, p. 345.
73 BHPS, *op. cit.*, note 13 above, p. 69.

3 Divorce Reform in England: Humbug and Hypocrisy[1] or a Smooth Transition?[2]

*Stephen M. Cretney**

INTRODUCTION: REMEMBRANCE OF THINGS PAST

The old forget, and the young have never known, the terrible things which the legal system has done, within living memory, with the professed objective of upholding the institution of marriage and promoting the welfare of children. Academic writers claim to eschew the personal and instead to rely on objective research findings, but divorce is an emotive subject and objectivity is hard to attain. I believe that it is right to make my own belief clear at the outset and that I can best do this by recounting two personal observations of the divorce process which left a deep impression and go some way to explain the values which hold weight for me in assessing current proposals for reform.

Divorce in the bad old days

In 1953 during the school holidays, I attended a three-day trial in open court of a wife's petition for the dissolution of her 30-year marriage on the ground of the adultery which (she alleged) the husband had committed with an unknown woman in one of the dark alleyways in that part of Manchester latterly romanticized in the television soap opera, *Coronation Street*. Under intensive and skilled cross-examination the husband admitted most of the allegations made against him by the private detective and other witnesses but denied that he had succeeded in having intercourse with the woman

* Fellow of All Souls College, Oxford.

concerned. The judge directed himself on the serious nature of an allegation of adultery, held that the wife had not discharged the onus of proving beyond reasonable doubt that adultery had taken place[3] and accordingly dismissed her petition.

But that was not the end of the matter. The husband had retaliated by cross-petitioning on the ground of his wife's cruelty, and the longer (and, to me, less interesting)[4] part of the hearing was devoted to a meticulous examination of his complaints. Again, most of the allegations of conjugal unkindness and other wifely failings were not denied, but the judge concluded that, as a matter of law, these incidents did not cross the dividing line, authoritatively traced by Asquith LJ,[5] between the 'ordinary wear and tear of conjugal' life on the one hand and cruelty in its legal sense on the other. Those whom the law had made one flesh were thus to remain legally yoked together, and the public interest in upholding the institution of marriage had – presumably at considerable expense to the Legal Aid Fund – been triumphantly asserted.[6]

I sometimes wonder what became of this unappealing couple – perhaps homicide achieved what the divorce court had failed to provide.[7] But whatever else might be said about the legal proceedings in which they had involved themselves, at least it was clear that the parties (unlike many of their social superiors) were wholly innocent of the crime of collusion[8] which would have created an absolute bar[9] to the dissolution of their marriage.

'Civilized' people, of course, usually managed things rather better: notwithstanding the horror voiced in the case law and elsewhere about the mere prospect of divorce by consent – 'fundamentally incompatible with the concept of marriage … to give people the right to divorce themselves would be … disastrous for the nation' as nine members of the 1956 Royal Commission were to assert[10] – in practice the marriage of a husband prepared to behave 'like a gentleman' could (so it was said) be dissolved 'as easily as [he could obtain] a motor licence and rather more easily than a passport'.[11] But even with people prepared to behave in a 'civilized' manner, professional advisers had to behave with care. There was the ever-present danger of collusion; and they had also to remember that adultery was not merely a ground for divorce but also a bar to it. An adulterous petitioner would be denied relief against her partner unless the court was prepared to exercise its discretion in the petitioner's favour. It was accordingly the duty of the petitioner's solicitor to make quite certain, so far as humanly possible, whether the client had ever committed adultery not merely by asking the question when first taking instructions, and then again when swearing the affidavit in support of the petition, but also just before the hearing[12] (although if the client were well educated and well informed the Court of

Appeal had in 1970 indicated that it would probably suffice to say 'Be sure that if you ever do between now and the time when the suit comes to be heard, let me know, because the court will have to be informed...'.[13]

The new dawn: divorce under the Divorce Reform Act 1969

To me, as to many others, the divorce process therefore seemed to be cruel, anachronistic and hypocritical. There surely had to be a better way out; and it is not surprising that progressive opinion came to favour reform along the lines achieved by the Divorce Reform Act 1969. My second observation – in the summer of 1972, 20 years after the first – seemed to confirm that, in this instance at least, progressive opinion had been right. A succession of elderly persons of eminently respectable appearance came to the witness box to give the oral testimony then required in support of divorce petitions. All had lived apart from their lawful spouse for more - usually much more - than the stipulated five years. In almost every case the story was essentially the same: the youthful wartime marriage, the long separation in service of 'King and Country', the drift apart, the formation of a new relationship, the birth of children, the woman taking the man's name, the passionate desire to legitimize those children and so on. In each case, the decree was granted; in each case the elderly couple's faces reflected happiness and quiet domestic content. Not everyone accepts that the hardship of an indissoluble marriage can be a sufficient justification for allowing divorce,[14] but one would have to be hardhearted (or highly principled) in the extreme to believe that the law had done harm rather than good in that courtroom that afternoon. And it was not difficult to see why the divorce law had been reformed. Whatever may be said about the defects of the reformed divorce law enacted in 1969, only those who would deny divorce any place[15] in the legal system are likely to disagree with the Law Commission's view that the present law is 'a considerable improvement on the previous position'.[16]

WHAT WENT WRONG?

Apart from doing away with the disgusting apparatus of the discretion statement and the enquiry agent (seeking 'proof' of adultery) and the absurd refinements of the law of cruelty and desertion the Divorce Reform Act undoubtedly did good in allowing what were called 'stable illicit unions' to be legalized and the children consequently legitimated. But the reformers' more ambitious objectives were less easily obtained. Bitterness, distress and humiliation refused to go away;[17] and within ten years[18] the Law Commission had accepted the need for a further review of the law. The main problem seemed to be that, although in theory the sole ground for divorce was the irretrievable breakdown of marriage, such a breakdown could only be established by proof of one or more of five 'facts', and that the majority of petitions were based on adultery and unreasonable behaviour. Hence, although the matrimonial offence was supposedly dead, its decaying corpse had been denied a decent burial and (it was said) threatened to become a serious hazard to the nation's emotional health.

The unsatisfactory nature of the compromise between offence-based facts and the breakdown principle was accentuated by the introduction of the so-called special procedure[19] under which undefended divorces are granted without any court hearing. A number of research studies[20] supported the criticisms of the reformed law;[21] and eventually, in 1988, the Law Commission published a powerfully argued discussion paper, *Facing the Future*[22] which concluded that the law fell 'far short' of its original objectives of buttressing the institution of marriage whilst allowing marriages which had indeed irretrievably broken down to be dissolved with the maximum fairness and the minimum bitterness, distress and humiliation.[23] The Commission's indictment of the reformed law[24] merits extended quotation:

> The present law does not, nor could it reasonably be expected to, buttress the stability of marriage by preventing determined parties from obtaining a speedy divorce. Because of the compromise nature of the 1969 Act, the benefits referred to above have been bought at the price of incoherence and increased confusion for litigants. Thus the law is neither understandable nor respected and there is evidence of not inconsiderable consumer dissatisfaction. Attaining the aims of maximum fairness and minimum bitterness has been rendered impossible by the retention of the fault element. The necessity of making allegations in the petition 'draws the battle-lines' at the outset. The ensuing hostility makes the divorce more painful, not only for the parties but also for the children, and destroys any chance of reconciliation and may be detrimental to post-divorce relationships. Underlying all these defects is the fact that whether or not the marriage can be dissolved depends principally upon what parties have done in the past. In petitions relying on fault-based facts, the petitioner is encouraged to 'dwell on the past' and to recriminate.
>
> At the same time, the present divorce process may not allow sufficient opportunity for the parties to come to terms with what is happening in their lives. A recent study of the process of 'uncoupling' points out that one party has usually gone far down that path before the other one discovers this, by which time it may be too late. Once the divorce process has been started it may have a 'juggernaut' effect, providing insufficient opportunity for the parties to re-evaluate their positions. Thus, there is little or no scope for reconciliation, conciliation or renegotiation of the relationship. It is clear that both emotionally and financially it is much less costly if ancillary matters can

be agreed between the parties. Where antagonism is created or exacerbated by the petition, or their respective bargaining power distorted, the atmosphere is not conducive to calm and sensible negotiations about the future needs of the parties and their children.

Above all, the present law fails to recognise that divorce is not a final product but part of a massive transition for the parties and their children. It is crucial in the interests of the children (as well as the parties) that the transition is as smooth as possible, since it is clear that their short and long-term adjustment depends to a large extent on their parents' adjustment and in particular on the quality of their post-divorce relationship with each parent. Although divorce law itself can do little actively to this end, it can and should ensure that the divorce process is not positively adverse to this adjustment. As Lord Hailsham has said, 'though the law could not alter the facts of life, it need not unnecessarily exaggerate the hardships inevitably involved.' There seems little doubt that the present law is guilty of just this.

DIAGNOSIS...AND CURE?

The response to the Law Commission's 1988 discussion paper made it 'absolutely plain'[25] that there was indeed a significant problem.[26] However, there was apparently 'overwhelming support' for the view that irretrievable breakdown should remain the 'fundamental basis' of the ground for divorce. The complaint, it seemed, was not of the breakdown principle itself, but of the legal rules and procedures by which breakdown is established.[27]

Smooth transitions and processes over time: the Law Commission's proposals

What, then, should supplant the existing 'facts' which provide the material from which irretrievable breakdown is inferred? The Commission rejected a number of possibilities – including the once fashionable proposal for divorce on the basis of a year's separation.[28] Instead, the Commission produced draft legislation to give effect to its proposals for 'divorce after a period for the consideration of future arrangements and for reflection'.[29]

The essence of the scheme put forward by the Law Commission[30] for determining whether the ground of irretrievable breakdown has been made out can be summarized as follows:

1 One or both parties would file a statement[31] that there was a breakdown in the marital relationship and that the person making the statement wished, as a consequence, to make arrangements for the future.[32]

2 Eleven months later,[33] either party could apply to the court for an order of divorce, and it would then be the duty of the court to make a divorce order after a further 'period of transition' of one month.[34]
3 The court would have power to make financial orders and orders relating to the upbringing of the children at any time after the filing of the statement, but property adjustment orders would only take effect before the divorce order if there were special circumstances making that course appropriate.[35]
4 The proposed legislation did not impose a requirement that the financial consequences of the breakdown (or indeed the arrangements for the children's upbringing) be settled – by agreement or court order – before the divorce order ended the marriage and gave a licence to remarry. Arguments about money and children might continue for some considerable time; but the court would have power to defer the making of the divorce order in certain circumstances – for example if the court considered it likely it would exercise its powers in relation to the children but could not yet do so, or if proper financial arrangements had not been made and postponement was desirable in order for such arrangements to be made.[36]
5 If the prescribed formalities had been completed, the court would only be able to refuse a divorce if divorce would result in grave financial or other hardship to one of the parties, and it would, in all circumstances, be wrong to dissolve the marriage.[37]
6 There would be a number of procedural measures designed to facilitate reconciliation, mediation and efficient management of the divorce process.[38]

The government acts: (i) the Consultation Paper

The Law Commission's Reports were not allowed to gather dust in the traditional Whitehall pigeonhole: in 1993 the government published its own consultation paper, *Looking to the Future. Mediation and the Ground for Divorce*.[39] The decision to do so is notable for a number of reasons, not least that for the first time in the present century government had itself contemplated[40] initiating legislation to change the ground for divorce – traditionally regarded as a matter so sensitive, divisive and controversial as to require the adoption of a neutral stance on the merits of change.[41] The consultation paper put forward proposals not only to deal with the ground on which divorce may be obtained, and with the related court procedures, but also to divert the resolution of many of the consequences of the ending of marriage away from the courts and the legal profession towards other agencies. In the circumstances, it may seem somewhat paradoxical that the minister taking the lead in this initiative is the Lord Chancellor (whose department is primarily concerned with the judiciary, the administration of the court system and with law reform) rather than by the Home Secretary or the Secretary of State for Health (who have departmental responsibility for marriage, and for the family and social service provision respectively). Finally, the emphasis of the paper was weighted very heavily towards an objective which conventional wisdom has long firmly rejected: marriage saving. 'I want saveable marriages to be saved,' said the Lord Chancellor when launching the document, 'I am aiming for a system which is better at identifying saveable marriages.'[42]

Integration of substantive law, procedural reform and mediation

Whatever views may be taken of the merits of the proposals, the government should be given credit for having the good sense and courage to seek to break down the traditional segregation between substantive law (the 'ground for divorce') on the one hand and the procedures which, in practice, so dominate the user's experience of the law in action on the other. So far as substantive law is concerned, the terms of the government's consultation paper, *Looking to the Future. Mediation and the Ground for Divorce*[43] did not in terms accept the Law Commission's proposals for a newly defined test of irretrievable breakdown as the ground for divorce, but the merits were spelt out at length.[44] So far as the process for getting a divorce is concerned, the consultation paper presented a sophisticated package:

1 *Initial interview*. There was to be a single first port of call in which those contemplating divorce would be given a personal interview, estimated to take an average of an hour,[45] 'during which essential information about the divorce process would be given and backed up with information packs and possibly a video'.[46] Information would be given about marriage guidance, mediation, the role and cost of lawyers and the availability of state funding. The government accepted that the role of the interviewer was crucial;[47] but no decision was taken about who might best fulfil it. The government did see 'practical advantages' in having the interview conducted by the person responsible at local level for allocating the public funding of mediation and legal services.[48] The interviewer would, apparently, make a preliminary assessment of the most appropriate way forward – for example, by the couple proceeding on their own, or being referred to mediation.
2 *Mediation*. This was to remain voluntary, although the government saw mediation as 'the norm rather than the exception',[49] and there were to be

'strong incentives' for the parties to 'resolve matters' and 'strong disincentives to their engaging in a protracted and expensive fight'.[50] Mediators (and others involved) were to make 'frequent reports' to ensure that issues were being handled in 'ways which are most likely to lead to resolution'[51].

3 *Agreement.* If agreement were reached in the course of mediation, the government envisaged that a solicitor might be asked to draw up the agreement, acting for both parties.[52] The courts would have only a limited role: the district judge would 'check' the agreement to ensure that it was within the court's statutory powers and would be enforceable; and the inquisitorial role of the courts to assess the fairness of the agreement between the parties was, apparently, to be removed.

4 *Legal services.* The government stated that the costs of dissolving a marriage 'like those of forming one' should be borne by the couple, but it accepted that, in certain circumstances, legal aid should be available.

5 *The courts.* The government expected the role of the courts to be greatly reduced, although they seemed to view favourably the Law Commission's proposals[53] which would require the court to hold a preliminary assessment[54] to monitor progress on the arrangements being made and to make any orders or exercise any of its powers that it considered appropriate.

The government acts: (ii) the White Paper

The government received many comments on the consultation paper, and also commissioned an attitude survey. In April 1995[55] it published its definitive proposals, in a White Paper, *Looking to the Future*.[56] This accepts that the ground for divorce should (as the Law Commission recommended) be the irretrievable breakdown of the marriage 'as demonstrated by the sole fact of a period for reflection and consideration';[57] and broadly speaking, endorses the procedural and other aspects of the earlier scheme; but there is one fundamental change, and several significant shifts of emphasis.

The fundamental change: no divorce until money and child-upbringing arrangements finalized

The original proposals[58] did not require the parties to have settled – whether by agreement or adjudication – the financial and child-upbringing consequences before the divorce order was made, although it was obviously hoped that mediation would produce a civilized outcome during the one year period of reflection. But the government has changed its mind. Under the White Paper proposals, the divorce order is not normally to be made until arrangements for children, property and finance have been settled.[59] The government has thus come to reject the Law Commission's view[60] that such a requirement would give an uncooperative spouse too powerful a bargaining chip – that someone desperately wanting a divorce would have to pay a very heavy price (perhaps in terms of the financial arrangements or even the arrangements for contact with the children) for getting the freedom to re-marry. It is true that the court is to have power to dispense with the normal requirement that all these matters be settled before the divorce order, and that this power might be used 'for example, where it would be in the best interests of the children that an order be made notwithstanding that arrangements have not been settled'. The government also intends to ensure that 'weaker or vulnerable parties and their children are sufficiently protected and that the potential for litigation is minimised'.[61] However, the White Paper is silent about how these objectives are to be achieved.

These modifications certainly weaken the force of the criticism that the Law Commission's proposals effectively constituted divorce by repudiation – after a one year waiting period – however unfair such repudiation might be. But it will only be possible to evaluate the scheme when legislation has been drafted to make clear precisely how the vulnerable are to be protected from agreeing to something inconsistent with their interests.

The initial interview – revised version

Instead of an initial, one-to-one, interview the government now proposes that the information which potential customers in the divorce market need should be dispensed at a free-of-charge group session. No one will be allowed to initiate the divorce procedure unless and until he or she has attended such a session; and the intention is that this should give a fair and unbiased view of the available services – mediation, counselling and legal services – and options, presented in the most expedient, comfortable and cost-effective way (perhaps even with the assistance of a 'well-structured video'). The government makes it clear it wants to draw a clear line between the functions of providing information and the giving of advice. The information session will be an opportunity to ask questions and seek clarification; but legal advice (in the sense of an explanation of how the law applies to the facts of a particular case, or a recommendation about the best course of action) will not be given.

The government has also dropped the plan for the person conducting the initial interview to take decisions about the customer's access to public funding. The functions of giving information and determining eligibility for legal aid or funded mediation are to be separated.[62] This decision is certainly welcome; but there are still problems about the initial interview. At one level, it is going to be difficult for some people (possibly the most vulnerable) to understand that although they 'may ask questions and seek clarification' they cannot be told anything about how the abstract statement of legal principles affects their own particular case. Take, for example, the rule[63] (which the government intends to retain[64]) that divorce can be refused if it would cause 'grave financial or other hardship'. All English family lawyers know that, if it comes to a court hearing, this bar is rarely successfully invoked;[65] but under the White Paper scheme it will be the only definitive bar to divorce and thus of great importance to many. How will the scope of this bar be explained at the information session? Many non-lawyers would assume from a mere recital of the words of the legislation that the protection is much wider than it in fact is.[66] Are their questions to be treated as inadmissible on the basis that they represent requests for 'advice' as distinct from information?

At another level – and leaving on one side the absurdity of requiring people such as the eight-times married Elizabeth Taylor or the exceedingly wealthy[67] Baron Thyssen-Bornemisza to attend a 'group session' to have the implications of marital breakdown explained – many people will find the obligation to attend what could easily seem to be a patronizing and humiliat–ing lecture about such matters as the parents' continuing parental responsibility both embarrassing and stigmatic.

Access to lawyers

The government adheres to its view that mediation should be the normal method of dealing with the consequences of divorce.[68] Couples whose marriage is in difficulties should no longer habitually use a solicitor's office as 'the automatic first port of call'.[69] The new scheme will discourage uncontrolled access to lawyer representation (as opposed to specific advice on specific issues) during the mediation process and the use of solicitors employed at the expense of the taxpayer 'to go over the ground already covered ...'.[70] The White Paper does accept that 'most couples...contemplating divorce will need to obtain...some specific legal advice about their own legal rights and obligations', that they 'may also need some assistance with the preparation of the necessary divorce papers',[71] and that 'there may be a need for them to seek legal assistance' – perhaps from a lawyer advising both husband and wife – in translating the agreement they have reached in mediation 'into either an enforceable agreement or a draft consent order...correctly phrased and...within the powers of the court'.[72] But the White Paper makes it quite clear that there is to be a dramatic reduction in public funding for legal services. The general objective is that the total costs borne by the taxpayer in providing information sessions, mediation and any attendant legal advice and negotiation or litigation 'should not exceed those which would have been borne by the Legal Aid Fund under the present system'.[73] To put the matter rather crudely, the cake which is at present consumed entirely by lawyers will now have to be shared with the mediators and the information givers.

The White Paper did not spell out how this dramatic reduction in state expenditure on legal services is to be achieved; but this omission was subsequently remedied by publication of the government's consultation paper on the future of the legal aid system:[74] a client will have to show 'acceptable reasons' – for instance, the need for protection from violence – for requiring legal representation rather than mediation.[75] This reduction in provision for advice designed to protect the vulnerable from exploitation comes rather oddly at a time when the courts[76] are emphasizing the need for independent professional advice to minimize the dangers that emotional involvement and pressure will result in a spouse assuming unwise *financial* obligations. What justification is there for the government to think that the pressures are likely to be less when a marriage is collapsing, and the future of all the family's assets is in issue?

The main element in the government's thinking is confidence in mediation as the process for dealing with the consequences of divorce; and it is time to consider whether such confidence is well founded.

Some reservations

Mediation a panacea?

In 1983 the Inter-Departmental Committee on Conciliation concluded that out-of-court mediation schemes did not save money overall and seemed to be less cost-effective than in-court schemes; 12 years later the government intends to make mediation the bedrock of the divorce process. Few conversions have been so dramatic; and no doubt the new-found enthusiasm reflects increased experience both of the reality of mediation – National Family Mediation provides out of court mediation to some 6500 families[77] a year, while the Family Mediators Association provides mediation for some 1500 families[78] and also of research findings. Perhaps the vast amount of writing which has been devoted to the subject – not to mention the persistent, wide-scale and well-organized lobbying – have also been influential.

The White Paper is vague about many important issues of machinery and procedure. How, precisely, are people to be steered to mediation – other than by being told that mediation is the only procedure for which public funding is to be available? What is to happen in a situation in which one party has the means to pay lawyers to fight (and wishes to do so) whereas the other has no means? What is to be done to deter people from initiating actions under the domestic violence legislation – perhaps because lawyers[79] advise them to do so – so as to exercise pressure on the other spouse, rather than following the government's preferred route into mediation?

It is clear that mediation is to remain in the private sector[80] and that the government does not intend to tell mediators how to do their job. But the government does seem to have a somewhat idiosyncratic notion of the objectives of mediation. The White Paper claims[81] that mediation 'enables spouses to accept responsibility for the breakdown, to acknowledge responsibility for the ending of the marriage, to address face to face the questions of fault and blame' and that, where conduct is in issue, mediation 'offers an opportunity to address what went wrong with the marriage'. Some people might regard these matters as being more appropriate for the confessional or indeed for the re-education programmes associated with totalitarian regimes. Possibly they might form a part of the mediation process; but claims of this kind have not in the past often been made by those involved in conciliation. Indeed the most recent study[82] states that 'not addressing the past is much appreciated by clients who are feeling guilt. For them it came as a relief to discover that the mediators were not judgmental and that fault was not an issue'.

Again, not everyone will share the enthusiasm displayed in the White Paper for the extension of mediation from child-related issues to financial matters. Routine low- to medium-net worth divorce financial negotiations could often be well handled by the specialist profession made up of people with no formal legal qualification – after all, there is some[83] evidence that settlements under the present system are often arrived at in a rather unsophisticated 'back of the envelope' way, and para-legals play an important part in conducting solicitors' matrimonial work. But a weakness of the White Paper is that it does not go into any detail about the relationship between the courts and the parties in this area; and in particular it fails to give any real guidance about the extent to which the court is to be involved in investigating the fairness of agreements which have been reached in mediation.[84] This is perhaps part of a more general weakness of the White Paper proposals – that the role of the court is left disturbingly unclear.

What is the court's role?

The Law Commission thought the court should play a central part in the divorce process. In particular, the court was to hold a preliminary assessment 'no later than twelve weeks from the date when the statement of marital breakdown is made'[85] in order to 'review progress' in the making of arrangements for the future.[86] The inspiration for these procedures would seem to be the robust summons for directions now familiar in some Children Act proceedings: the court is not to stand for any nonsense, but is to make the parties aware of the realities, and above all to make progress for the efficient disposal of the case.

This is all very well. But what has become of the concern, expressed elsewhere by the Law Commission, that the parties should have sufficient opportunity to come to terms with what is happening in their lives? What about the so-called 'juggernaut' effect of divorce?[87] Perhaps the court will wish to 'encourage' – not, of course, to 'direct', because such procedures are, at least up to a point, voluntary – the parties to 'participate in ...conciliation or mediation procedures';[88] and yet – it seemed – the pressure would be on all the time for (under the original Law Commission scheme) each spouse would know that:- 'at the end of twelve months you will be divorced, like it or not', 'stick it out for twelve months, be charming and courteous to the mediator, and at the end of the twelve months you will almost certainly[89] get your divorce without really having had to give anything away'.

It is true that under the revised proposals the pressure of having to do everything within twelve months has gone; but the White Paper[90] continues, eminently reasonably, to urge 'efficient and effective' conduct of ancillary relief applications. Yet one person's effective efficiency may be another's ruthless disregard of feelings and of the need for time for adjustment; one person's sensible 'clarification of the issues to be resolved' may be another's insistence on excluding the matters – such as responsibility for the breakdown – of real importance and a determination to force important human problems into meaningless lawyers' categories. There seems to be something of an unresolved conflict here between the brusque managerialism of modern judicial administration and the social work ideologies underlying much mediation practice, between the demands of an increasingly managerial court system, heavily dependent on the assessment of 'outcomes' and other performance indicators on the one hand, and the need for the parties to be allowed to 'plan for the future at a pace which suits them both and within a time-scale which does not push them into making hasty and ill-considered decisions'[91] on the other. It is almost as if the 'mediation' parts of the White Paper and the Court Administration sections of the earlier consultation paper had been written by different people, and that they never got together to discuss just how things were to work. The question whether the government still intend the courts to have the leading role in determining how the process of 'transition' is to be negotiated – and indeed the underlying question of what the courts and the legal system have to contribute to the settlement of issues arising from marital breakdown – remains unanswered.

Consideration and reflection – wishful thinking?

As already mentioned, the Law Commission's draft Bill[92] would require a person seeking divorce to file a statement of marital breakdown with the court; and there would follow a period 'for consideration to be given to what (if any) arrangements should be made for the future and for the parties to the marriage to reflect on whether the breakdown is irreparable',[93] and the White Paper[94] claims that couples 'will be required to spend time reflecting on whether their marriage can be saved, and, if not to face up to the consequences of their actions and make arrangements to meet their responsibilities'.

This is a very laudable aspiration. But how is this 'requirement' to be enforced? May not some of those concerned prefer to spend their time in the far more pleasurable activity of conceiving – necessarily illegitimate – babies? May not some spend the time seeking means of exploiting their emotional or financial advantage, or brooding on grievances and perhaps using the available legal procedures as a way of seeking satisfaction for the wrongs they have suffered? The way in which the Law Commission's proposals were presented seemed almost reminiscent of those earnest Victorian reformers who invented the so-called 'separate system' – prisoners deprived of all corrupting influences would be driven to reflect in their solitude on the evil of their ways and thereby be well prepared to receive the sympathy, advice and religious consolation provided for those truly humbled by their experience'.[95] It was, of course, all very well-intentioned; and yet succeeded in inflicting scarcely imaginable cruelty on hundreds of helpless human beings. We would all hope that the parties will indeed give anxious consideration to whether their marriage has broken down irretrievably and to the consequential arrangements. We must all hope that mediation and counselling will be successful in this respect. But the evidence for believing that these expectations will be fulfilled is not overwhelmingly convincing.[96]

It is in concealing the reality - that divorce is to be available at the unilateral wish of either party – behind a comforting facade of consideration, reflection, reconciliation and counselling – that the government's proposals are most vulnerable to the charge of perpetuating the tradition of hypocrisy and humbug.[97] It is true that the government's proposals will end the sometimes damaging ritual of filing a petition alleging – perhaps unjustly – that the other spouse has committed adultery or been guilty of behaviour such as to make it unreasonable for the spouses to go on living together. But a man who has behaved cruelly and unreasonably will still be able to insist on divorce against the wishes of his wife; and the wife's anger, grief and bitterness may reasonably not be assuaged by assurances that the new law promotes consideration and reflection – and that since her case is a simple one she is not to receive any public help to pay a lawyer who will defend her interests. There seems to be a serious risk that countless people will find themselves uncomprehendingly ensnared in a monstrous and costly legal/social work/counselling nightmare. The Law Commission, as we have seen,[98] identifies the 'incoherence' of the law and the confusion thereby caused to people caught up in the divorce process as one of the law's most significant weaknesses; and the Commission rightly attributes these defects to the compromise nature of the 1969 divorce reforms.[99] But there is a serious risk that the incoherence and confusion will be perpetuated and even increased. We shall still have to pretend that the ground for divorce is the breakdown of the marriage; whereas the reality is that it is the wish of one party to divorce the other. The information and mediation sessions merely conceal that simple truth[100] and, in so doing, they make matters worse.

Rash gamble – or bold experiment

These reservations seem to me to justify considerable scepticism about the likelihood of the proposals achieving the objectives which their promoters seek. But opinion – largely, it seems, in reliance on the view that the proposed system will mark the end of the 'quicky' divorce and of 'adversarial' court process, and convinced by the eminently plausible and attractively presented claims made on behalf of mediation – seems to favour the proposals. At the time of going to press, legislation seems probable; and only experience will tell how far the reservations expressed in this paper are well founded. Many of them are based on the fact that the White Paper leaves so many things vague and unclear; and those reservations may be overcome by judicious modifications of the details of the scheme. For that reason, I welcome the government's acceptance of the view[101] that a comprehensive pilot project is an 'essential step' in preparing for implementation. It may be thought that careful piloting is sufficient to transform a rash and irresponsible gamble into a bold experiment; but the difficulty is that once primary legislation effectively making unilateral repudiation on one year's notice the ground for divorce is on the statute book it will be possible for all the safeguards to be removed by ministerial order with the minimum of fuss. Historical precedents are, in this context, not encouraging. Does anyone imagine that the Divorce Reform Act would ever have got onto the statute book if Parliament had known that within a few years the requirement of 'careful judicial scrutiny' would be scrapped by delegated legislation in favour of the so-called special procedure? It still seems very questionable whether reform along the lines of the White Paper proposals will achieve significant improvements in the working of the divorce process. On the contrary, there is a very real risk that the divorce process will, at best, not be improved and that, at worst, it will become even more damaging for the parties and their families. For all its faults, the 1969 Act made a real improvement to the divorce process;[102] it is far from clear that the 1995 proposals will do so.

NOTES

1 The apt description by L. Stone of much of the debate on the Matrimonial Causes Act 1923 (which allowed wives the privilege, previously confined to husbands, of founding a divorce petition solely on the spouse's adultery): L. Stone (1990), *Road to Divorce, England 1530–1987*, Oxford: Oxford University Press, p. 396.

2 The reference is to the terminology at one time used by the Law Commission in its Report, *Facing the Future: A Discussion Paper on the Ground for Divorce* (Law Com. no. 170, 1988, para. 6.3) to describe its favoured reform of the divorce law.

3 *Ginesi* v. *Ginesi* [1948] P 179, CA; *Preston-Jones* v. *Preston-Jones* [1951] AC 391, HL.

4 An earlier encounter with divorce law had been the prominent and extensive coverage in the national press of a divorce suit brought by the wife of a local dentist on the ground of his alleged adultery with a woman teacher. The evidence established that the teacher was *virgo intacta* and the suit was dismissed. These events did a lot to increase my admiration for the teacher's dignified behaviour in the classroom, but little to increase my respect for either the legal system or the press (which was permitted to report the material which aroused such prurient interest in myself and my contemporaries because the judge had dealt with the relevant matters in his judgment: Judicial Proceedings (Regulation of Reports) Act 1926, s.1 (1)(b)(iv).

5 In *Buchler* v. *Buchler* [1947] P. 25, CA. The son of Prime Minister H.H. Asquith and stepson of the legendary Lady Margot (said to have been a woman of unrestrained candour who could never believe that truth could wound: see L.P. Hartley, *Dictionary of National Biography* 1941–50, Oxford: Oxford University Press), was likely to have had ample opportunity of witnessing the strains of married life.

6 Proof of adultery could sometimes lead to financial compensation, since statute [Matrimonial Causes Act 1965, s.41 (1)] preserved the husband's right to seek damages in respect of his wife's adultery; and as recently as 1962 Scarman J in a hotly contested case, awarded a civil servant £1500 – somewhat in excess of £15 000 in 1994 values – against a 'prosperous and attractive barrister' who had wooed the wife (evidently successfully) over a period of years.

7 In 1925 Home Office officials produced charts showing the significant correlation between domestic homicides (in those days usually resulting in the death of the perpetrator by judicial execution) in an (unsuccessful) attempt to secure the removal from the Summary Jurisdiction (Separation and Maintenance) Act 1925 of a provision which empowered a wife to initiate maintenance proceedings before leaving the matrimonial home.

8 Which might have been committed by a couple who agreed not to defend: see, for

example *Churchward* v. *Churchward and Holliday (The Queen's Proctor Showing Cause)* [1895] P. 7 (adulterous wife's agreement not to defend and to settle all her capital on child of marriage and pay costs of proceedings if husband would petition and not claim damages for adultery: held, agreement, albeit disclosed to court, collusive, divorce refused, divorce suit ought not to be the price of any pecuniary consideration, per Sir F.H. Jeune P). Cf. under the modern law, *N* v. *N (Divorce: Agreement not to Defend)* [1992] 1 FLR 266, Ewbank J (although allowing that false case to be put forward remains improper, agreement on terms not to defend divorce petition enforceable).

9 Supreme Court of Judicature (Consolidation) Act 1925, s.178(2).

10 *Royal Commission on Marriage and Divorce* (Cmd. 6678, 1956) para. 69(vii) and (viii).

11 A.P. Herbert (1934), *Holy Deadlock*; and note the description of a 'civilized' upper-middle-class divorce in E. Waugh (1934), *A Handful of Dust*, London: Chapman and Hall, Ch.4.

12 *Shiers* v. *Shiers (King's Proctor Showing Cause)* [1942] 2 All ER 417. This guidance was authoritatively reiterated in 1969: *Pearson* v. *Pearson* [1971] P. 16.

13 *Ibid.* Any confession of adultery by a petitioner had to be recorded in a discretion statement filed with the court; and the Queen's Proctor was charged with the duty of intervening in cases in which the rules about disclosure of a petitioner's adultery appeared to have been breached. The possibility that a member of the public would successfully intervene in the divorce suit which was to free Mrs Ernest Simpson to marry King Edward VIII led the Cabinet to discuss (albeit ultimately to reject) a suggestion that provision be included in His Majesty's Declaration of Abdication Act 1936 making absolute her decree forthwith: see P. Ziegler (1990), *King Edward VIII*, London: Collins, pp. 318, 320. The King's Proctor did, after the abdication, and in the light of representations from members of the public, carry out investigations and eventually decided that there were no grounds upon which Mrs Simpson could be denied the decree absolute.

14 The words of Lord Hugh Cecil – 'The path of virtue may often lead to unspeakable misery. It was hard in the War to stay in the front line places, it was hard to be wounded, mutilated and maimed for life, it was hard to be scourged and crucified. Is any unhappy marriage worse? If not the Christian must endure as his Lord endured' – have been quoted in successive editions of S.M. Cretney's *Principles of Family Law*, London: Sweet and Maxwell.

15 It is important to remember the legal background against which the reforms were effected: notwithstanding considerable improvements brought about by the Family Law Reform Act 1969 the children of parents who were not able to marry suffered serious legal discrimination. Had the reforms in the legal position of children born to parents who are not married to one another been in place in 1969, and had cohabitation outside marriage then been as common (and indeed in some circles fashionable) as it has subsequently become, it might have been possible to argue that the hardship caused by denying to those whose marriage had failed the opportunity to remarry so long as the other partner survived would be outweighed by the general public benefit of a firm and unwavering assertion of the principle that marriage is indeed, for better or worse, a lifelong commitment.

16 Law Commission (1988), *Facing the Future. A Discussion Paper on the Ground for Divorce*, Law Com. no. 170, para. 3.47.

17 It appears that a discussion paper prepared by The Law Society's Family Law Subcommittee (*A Better Way Out*, 1979) was influential in supporting this view: see Law

Commission (1980), *Law Commission Fourteenth Annual Report 1978–9*, Law Com. no. 97, para. 2.24, note 34.

18 *Ibid.*, para. 2.24.

19 For an authoritative summary, see *Pounds* v. *Pounds* [1994] 1 FLR 776, CA, per Waite LJ:

> Following presentation of the petition, the petitioner's solicitor lodges an application for 'directions for trial' together with a standard affidavit in the form required to verify the particular ground alleged in the petition. In routine cases...the [district judge] gives 'directions for trial' by entering the cause in the special procedure list and thereafter considers the evidence filed by the petitioner. If he is satisfied that the petitioner has sufficiently proved the contents of the petition and is entitled to the decree sought and any costs prayed for, he will make and file a certificate to that effect. The court then sends notification to the parties of the date, time and place fixed for the pronouncement of the decree nisi, The parties are also told that their attendance at the pronouncement of decree is not necessary. The actual process of pronouncement of the decree has become reduced to a very brief ceremony of a purely formal character in which decrees are listed together in batches for a collective mention in open court before a judge who speaks (or nods) his assent. The right to a decree absolute 6 weeks thereafter is automatic...[T]he sole truly judicial function in the entire process is that of the [District Judge] when granting his certificate. Everything that follows is automatic and administrative, and the open court pronouncement of the decree is pure formality, to which the pronouncing judge...has no option but to consent....

20 G. Davis and M. Murch (1988), *Grounds for Divorce*, Oxford: OUP was particularly influential, not least in casting doubt on whether many marriages had indeed irretrievably broken down at the time when divorce proceedings were initiated.

21 Firmly adopted in the *Report of the Matrimonial Causes Procedure Committee* (Chairman, the Hon. Mrs Justice Booth DBE) (1985), para. 2.10: '...the bitterness and unhappiness of divorcing couples is frequently exacerbated and prolonged by the fault element in divorce, and ...this is particularly so where the fact relied on is behaviour...'.

22 Law Commission, *op. cit.*, note 16 above.

23 The objectives of a good divorce law as prescribed by the Law Commission in 1966: see Law Commission (1966), *Reform of the Grounds of Divorce: The Field of Choice*, Cmnd. 3123, Law Com. no 6, para. 15.

24 Law Commission, *op .cit.*, note 16 above, paras 3.48–50.

25 Law Commission (1990), *The Ground for Divorce*, Law Com. no 192, para. 1.5.

26 The response 'overwhelmingly endorsed the criticisms of the current law and practice which it contained': *ibid.*

27 *Ibid.*, para. 1.7.

28 In *Facing the Future* (*op. cit.*, note 16 above) para. 5.16, the Law Commission said that a separation-based divorce law might not work fairly between the spouses and would discriminate against particular categories of spouse; it would not necessarily ensure that dead marriages would be buried where it was not possible to effect a separation; it would not be as simple and easily understandable as would appear; there would be too much scope for abuse and perjury; there would be a considerable risk that issues of fault, with their attendant risks of unfairness, bitterness and humiliation, would reappear but at the point of separation rather than divorce; it could prejudice rather than encourage reconciliation; and above all it could prejudice rather

than promote the interests of the children. In *The Ground for Divorce* (*op. cit.*, note 25 above) the Commission concluded that a separation-based divorce law would be unlikely to provide much of an obstacle to those determined and agreed upon a speedy divorce, but that it would undoubtedly make divorce very much more difficult for some, including the victims of prolonged marital violence and persistent infidelity and parents who wish to protect their children from serious abuse.

29 This is the language used in the draft bill annexed to the Law Commission's report, (*op. cit.*, note 25 above) *The Ground for Divorce*; somewhat different terminology is used elsewhere to describe the same concept (for example, 'divorce by a process over time' and 'divorce after a period of transition') in the Law Commission's earlier report, (*op. cit.*, note 16 above), *Facing the Future* para 6.3.

30 For comments, see A. Bainham (1994), 'Divorce and the Lord Chancellor: looking to the future or getting back to basics', *Cambridge Law Journal*, **53**, p. 253; R. Deech (1990), 'Divorce law and empirical studies', *Law Quarterly Review*, **106**, p. 229; R. Schuz (1993), 'Divorce Reform', *Family Law*, **23**, pp. 580, 630.

31 This must be accompanied by a *declaration* that the maker or makers of the declaration believes that the breakdown is irreparable.

32 Clause 2(1) of the Draft bill annexed to the Law Commission report, *The Ground for Divorce* (*op. cit.*, note 25 above). Future references are abbreviated to 'draft bill'.

33 The Commission propose to retain the existing bar on divorce petitions within the first year of marriage, and it is accordingly provided that, where the statement of marital breakdown is made within the first year of marriage, the period of 11 months shall be extended by 'a further period equal to the time between the day on which the statement was made' and the first anniversary: clause 5(3).

34 Draft bill, clauses 2(1), 2(2) and 5.

35 Draft bill, clauses 11, 12, and 13.

36 Draft bill, clause 6. In considering whether to exercise its power to enable financial arrangements to be made, the court is directed to consider certain matters, including the conduct of the parties in relation to the making of those arrangements: draft bill, clause 6(3). It is not difficult to envisage such applications being frequent and acrimonious.

37 Draft bill, clause 4(1) (which, in substance, is identical to the largely ineffective provision of the Matrimonial Causes Act 1973, s. 5; see p. 48 and note 1 above).

38 These were subsequently amplified in the government's consultation paper (1993), *Looking to the Future. Mediation and the Ground for Divorce*, Cm. 2424, and in its White Paper, discussed below.

39 *Ibid.* Members of the public and interested organizations were invited to give their comments on the proposals; and the Lord Chancellor commissioned a survey to ascertain the current attitudes of people to divorce and mediation 'whether single, married or divorced': Lord Mackay of Clashfern's speech at the launch of the consultation paper on 6 December 1993.

40 *Looking to the Future* (*op. cit.*, note 38 above) states, at para. 12.1, that: 'No decisions have yet been taken. Divorce is an important and sensitive subject on which many people have strong views and the Government wishes to consult widely about the options for reform... The Government will then decide whether to introduce legislation.'

41 As distinct from making legislative time available for measures introduced by backbench MPs and providing the services of parliamentary counsel with the objective of ensuring that the expressed will of the legislature should not be defeated: see B.H. Lee (1974), *Divorce Reform in England,* London: Peter Owen (on the passage of the Divorce Reform Act 1969) and S. Redmayne (1993), 'The Matrimonial Causes Act 1937: a lesson in the art of compromise', *Oxford Journal of Legal Studies*, p. 183.

42 And note that *Looking to the Future* (*op. cit.*, note 38 above), para. 6.46 sees the period which has to elapse between the filing of the initial statement of breakdown and divorce as 'very importantly' providing the couple with the opportunity to seek help through guidance/counselling with a view to saving their marriage.

43 *Op. cit.*, note 38 above.

44 The consultation paper (*ibid.*) states at para. 6.46 that the Commission's recommendations would 'seem to have a number of advantages' including (a) many of the advantages of divorce after a fixed period of separation but without discriminating against those who cannot find or afford alternative accommodation; (b) allowing for divorce by agreement, without putting a heavy premium on consent, and so promote sharing of responsibility for bringing the marriage to an end; (c) avoiding the injustices and other problems such as humiliation bitterness and resentment associated with allegations of fault made by one party against the other with no real opportunity for that party to respond. Moreover (d) the passage of time would act as a brake on hasty or rash applications for divorce and an opportunity to reflect on the past without recriminating; (e) there would be no need for collusion in respect of evidence to establish breakdown; (f) there would be no risk of perjury or cheating on time periods of separation; (g) the parties would not be required to separate unless they wished to do so, thus giving them time to make alternative arrangements and explore possibilities for saving the marriage; (h) the parties could attempt reconciliation without worrying about whether they might be prejudiced if the attempt failed; (g) parents could cooperate as much as they liked concerning children without prejudicing their own position; and (as already mentioned) (j) the couple could during the 'period of consideration and reflection...seek help through guidance/counselling with a view to saving their marriage. If this were not possible then it would be open to the couple to make arrangements for the future with the help of mediation services and without litigating.' A number of possible criticisms are briefly mentioned and cursorily despatched, but these do not include the confusion and complexity to which I have drawn attention in (1992) *Family Law*, p. 630.

45 *Looking to the Future* (*op. cit.*, note 38 above), para. 8.12.

46 *Ibid.*, para. 8.1.

47 *Ibid.*, para. 8.9.

48 *Ibid.*, para. 8.11.

49 *Ibid.*, para. 7.11.

50 *Ibid.*, para. 9.20. It appears to be contemplated that the interviewer's report might be made available to the court so that it could take failure to agree to enter into mediation into account when considering an application for a costs order (para. 9.22).

51 *Ibid.*, para. 9.25.

52 *Ibid.*, para. 9.19.

53 *The Ground for Divorce*, *op. cit.*, note 25 above, para. 7.32.

54 The government thinks that this should *not* necessarily involve a hearing: *Looking to the Future*, *op. cit.*, note 38 above, para. 11.7.

55 After the resignation of Mrs Margaret Thatcher. She has recorded that she 'did not accept that we should follow the Law Commission's recommendation...that this should just become a process in which fault was not at issue. In some cases – for example where there is violence – I considered that divorce was not just permissible but unavoidable. Yet I also felt strongly that if all the remaining culpability was removed from marital desertion, divorce would be that much more common...': see M. Thatcher (1995), *The Downing Street Years*, London: p. 630.

56 1995, Cmd. 2799. This is hereafter referred to as *White Paper*.

57 *Ibid.*, para. 4.7.
58 See p. 43 above.
59 *White Paper, op. cit.*, see note 56, paras 4.26–4.30.
60 See p. 44 above.
61 *White Paper, op. cit.*, see note 56, para. 4.30.
62 *Ibid.*, paras 6.15, 7.13–7.28
63 Matrimonial Causes Act 1973, s. 5.
64 See *White Paper, op. cit.*, note 56, paras 4.46–4.47.
65 There is no reported case in which a divorce decree has been withheld on the ground that divorce would cause hardship other than financial hardship; and there are precious few cases in which divorce – as distinct from separation – is found to have caused financial hardship: see e.g. most recently *Jackson* v. *Jackson* [1993] 2 FLR 848, CA.
66 The *White Paper* itself suggests that this is the case. It appears that 'many consultees' considered that the bar in its present form 'does provide significant protection from hardship which could arise as a result of divorce, even where that hardship is not financial'; but this belief is hardly consistent with the reported case-law.
67 His assets were thought to be worth in excess of a hundred million pounds: *Thyssen-Bornemisza* v. *Thyssen-Bornemisza* [1986] Fam 1.
68 See p. 49 for comments on whether the government's confidence is well-founded.
69 *White Paper, op. cit.*, note 56, para. 7.3.
70 *Ibid.*, para 6.21.
71 *Ibid.*, para 6.17.
72 *Ibid.*, para 6.20.
73 *Ibid.*, para 6.27.
74 *Legal Aid - Targeting Need* (1995) Cm. 2854.
75 *Ibid.*, paras 9.7–9.16.
76 See *Barclays Bank plc* v. *O'Brien* [1994] 1 AC 180, HL.
77 But these figures need to be kept in context: in 1964 the National Marriage Guidance Council gave 57 040 interviews and had at that period some 120 counselling centres staffed by nearly 100 volunteers: see J. Dominian (1968), *Marital Breakdown* (Harmondsworth: Penguin), Ch. 16; and generally on the (illuminating) history of The National Marriage Guidance Council (which, in 1988, changed its name to Relate) see J. Lewis, D. Clark and D. Morgan (1992), *Whom God Hath Joined Together: The Work of Marriage Guidance* (London: Routledge). The most recent official publication on the scope of marriage guidance is *Marriage Matters* (a consultative paper by the Working Party on Marriage Guidance issued by the Home Office and DHSS; London: HMSO, 1979).
78 These figures are taken from *Facing the Future, op. cit.*, note 38 above, para 7.14. Relationships between the two organizations have not always been harmonious: see for example the description of the FMA scheme by M. Roberts (Training Coordinator of NFM) as 'a private sector initiative catering for a small, well-off clientele': [1992] *Journal of Social Welfare and Family Law*, pp. 372, 373.
79 Who will be able to handle such claims under the legal aid scheme: see p. 49 above.
80 However, eligibility for public funding is to depend on those concerned meeting quality assurance criteria: see *White Paper*, para 6.24. The government considers there to be a role for a 'national professional body or bodies for mediators that lay(s) down and enforce(s)' rules about selection, training and accreditation, client care, complaints, and disciplinary procedures: paras 6.25-26. It may seem rather odd that a government which has perhaps not shown itself particularly well disposed to the

existing professions should in this way be contemplating the creation of a wholly new one.

81 *Looking to the Future* , *op. cit.*, note 38 above, para. 7.5.

82 J. Walker, P. McCarthy and N. Timms (1994), *Mediation: the Making and Remaking of Co-operative relationships*, p. 62.

83 See Davis *et. al.* (1994), *Simple Quarrels* (Oxford: OUP).

84 The present law is unsatisfactory – note the comments in *Pounds* v. *Pounds* [1994] 1 FLR 775, and particularly the view of Hoffmann LJ that the doctrine derived from the decisions in *Hyman* v. *Hyman* [1929] AC 601, HL, and *Edgar* v. *Edgar* [1980] 1 WLR 1410, CA, secures the worst of both worlds. But paras 7.37–7.38 of the White Paper seem unnecessarily obscure.

85 *The Ground for Divorce, op. cit* ., note 25 above, para 7.32; also draft bill, clause 8.

86 The court was also to have a number of specific duties, including considering whether the parties are agreed on financial matters: draft bill, clause 8(2)(e).

87 See the quotation from *Facing the Future*, *op. cit.*, note 38 above, at p. 42 above.

88 Draft bill, Clause 8(2)(a).

89 A qualification necessary because of the provision whereby the court could, in certain circumstances, defer the making of the decree – a proposal which I regard as potentially disastrous unless the court discouraged applications.

90 *White Paper*, *op. cit.*, note 56, para 9.7.

91 *Ibid.*, para. 5.5

92 *Op. cit.*, note 29 above.

93 Draft bill, clauses 2 and 5.

94 Para 4.16.

95 See the views of J. Kingsmill, Chaplain of Pentonville Prison, quoted by U.R.Q. Henriques (1972) 'The rise and decline of the separate system of prison discipline', *Past and Present*, **54**, pp. 61, 79.

96 The same could be said about the commitment to marriage saving (which pervades the White Paper) and the belief that the period of reflection will enable saveable marriages to be saved: see e.g. *White Paper,* para. 4.32. It is nearly fifty years since the (Denning) *Committee on Procedure in Matrimonial Causes, Final Report* (1947, Cmd. 7024, para. 3) asserted 'the principle that the preservation of the marriage tie is of the highest importance in the interests of society' and that accordingly 'reconciliation should be attempted in every case where there is a prospect of success'; but notwithstanding consideration by various other bodies the goal still appears elusive: see note 77 above. Again, it is not easy to evaluate success of measures such as those which require schools to provide sex education {Education Act 1993, s. 241] that is to be given in such a manner as to encourage pupils to have 'due regard to moral considerations and the value of family life': Education (No. 2) Act 1986, s. 46.

97 See L. Stone, *op. cit.*, note 1 above.

98 P. 42 above.

99 In 1969 it was necessary to convince the Church of England and others that the Divorce Reform Act was based on the principle (favoured by the Church) of irretrievable breakdown as the sole ground for divorce. But the reality was that the Act did little more than add two and five years living apart as grounds for divorce to the existing grounds for divorce: see S.M. Cretney and J.M. Masson (1996), *Principles of Family Law* (6th ed., London: Sweet and Maxwell).

100 The writer's preference amongst the options for reform of the divorce law remains that it should be based on an open acceptance of the principle that marriage can – subject to measures to protect children and the vulnerable – be dissolved by the

agreement of the parties: see S.M. Cretney (1992) *Family Law*, **22**, 472 'Divorce, A Smooth Transition?' There would of course have to be provision for those cases in which the parties do not agree: the Scottish Law Commission's proposals [Scottish Law Com. No 116 (1989)] for retaining the substance of the existing law but minimizing unnecessary reliance on 'behaviour' by reducing the required period of separation seem attractive to those who favour an evolutionary approach to law reform.

101 *White Paper, op. cit.*, note 57, para. 7.39.

102 See above p. 41. It does not follow from this that the writer believes (consistently with the view expressed at the time by the Law Commission and others but contrary to the view of R. Deech (1990) 'Divorce Law and Empirical Studies' *Law Quarterly Review*, 106) that the 1969 Act had no impact on the incidence of marital breakdown, a matter on which he remains agnostic.

4 Norms and Negotiation in Mediation and Divorce

*Christine Piper**

> First, let's talk a little bit about what mediation is. Many of you have perhaps had this explained to you by your lawyer or by someone else, but some of you have not. Mediation is what we call an alternative dispute resolution programme. It's another way of trying to find a solution to a problem other than in the court room. Mediation focuses on you finding your own solution to the problem that brings you here.[1]

> If it's a case where I think it's important that the other party needs to be grabbed by the collar and shook a bit, then I'll opt for mediation as soon as possible.[2]

These two comments about mediation (or conciliation)[3] were made by legal professionals involved in the use of mediation in the USA,[4] where mediation has had a longer and more varied development than in the UK. They convey quite different attitudes to, and assumptions about, the role of mediation. The first statement is part of a talk to couples prior to attendance at mediation on court premises; it assumes that mediation is an alternative to judicial adjudication and is a form of alternative dispute resolution that provides the benefit of parent (that is, party) control. The second comment, made by an attorney specializing in divorce cases, was elicited as part of research into the divorce process: he or she sees mediation primarily as part of, and only partly as an alternative to, a process of lawyer-controlled negotiation in which mediation is a 'tool' to avoid court adjudication or prolonged lawyer negotiation.

Both comments are made on the basis of experience in states where mediation is mandatory if an application is made to the court for adjudication of contested issues concerning children. Yet similar comments can be

* Senior Lecturer in Law, Brunel University.

found in regard to voluntary out-of-court mediation in the UK. For instance, the consultation paper on divorce reform issued by the Lord Chancellor's Department[5] highlights 'parent control' in its summary of the benefits of mediation:

> The overall objectives are to help separating couples reach their own agreements about the future, to improve communications between them, to help them cooperate in bringing up their children .... It empowers them to plan the future for themselves at a pace which suits both of them.[6]
> [Mediation] offers a credible and professional method of helping families to resolve their problems with reduced involvement from lawyers and the courts....[7]

On the other hand, a comment made by a wife about her referral to an English mediation service has echoes of the attitude of the attorney quoted above:

> She [the client's solicitor] obviously thought it would be a good idea for us to try that [mediation] because we hadn't got anywhere with these letters in over a year, going back and forth between solicitors.[8]

All comments, whether they focus on control by parents or lawyers, perceive mediation as an alternative to part of the traditional legal process of divorce but they reveal ambivalent attitudes to the relationship between that process and mediation. The law-centred perspective of the comments is hardly surprising, given that they are made by, or refer to, lawyers, but what is of interest is why lawyers should wish to 'abdicate' part or all of their traditional role in the current legal process. To rephrase the issue, lawyers are promoting mediation as, at least in some circumstances, a 'better' way. If mediation is therefore a 'solution' to procedures perceived as less good, what is the problem?

THE CASE FOR MEDIATION

Answers can be found in the complex history of mediation, developed in various jurisdictions out of the needs and problems of very diverse groups of people and institutions. One need, predominant in pro-mediation pressure in the UK in the early 1980s[9] but not influential until the early 1990s when the soaring costs of the legal aid bill have given it fresh impetus, has been the search for a cheaper alternative to lawyers and courts. This has led to economic criteria for effectiveness and a research focus on settlement rates and the cost of a mediation 'package'. Yet, so far in the UK, the choice of mediation by the client has been little influenced by cost savings, in that state funding has often been more readily available for lawyer than mediator assistance. The promotion, by the mediation lobby, of the economic benefits of mediation has been aimed rather at the government whose eventual funding of mediation services has been seen as crucial for the survival of mediation as more than a fringe activity in the UK. The consultation paper,[10] reveals the success of such lobbying: para. 7.22, referring to the advantages of the new method of dispute resolution, points out that the reduced involvement of lawyers and courts will have 'subsequent savings in court and other costs'.

However, not all those promoting mediation have done so for financial benefits and nor do such benefits adequately fulfil the political imperatives of 'selling' a major change. For most of the 1980s those committed to mediation as a 'better way' put forward other criteria for judging its success.[11] The most compelling argument has been in relation to the benefits for children of their parents using mediation. Pressure to address the problem of children distressed and disturbed by marital discord, separation or conflict after separation had arisen from the concerns of mental health professionals in previous decades. It led to research on parental 'harmony' and disturbance levels in children with a resulting emphasis on mediation as a process to encourage *future* parental agreement as well as current settlement of disputes. The consultation paper refers to the 'considerable amount of research' and concludes:

> What is important about this research is not that it confirms what we must all know already – namely the awful trauma children suffer when their parents split up – it is that this trauma can be reduced in certain circumstances. A major factor is the reduction of conflict between their parents.[12]

The subsequent White Paper on divorce reform reiterated this message, adding that

> Further research carried out at Exeter University... has confirmed that marital conflict is harmful to children. These findings are significant... the Government is of the view that the reduction of conflict should be high on the list of objectives for a good divorce process.[13]

The research is perhaps not as clear as this would suggest,[14] but Kelly's research in California[15] on middle-class samples collected during 1983–86 and also the California Statewide Snapshot Study data collected in 1991 shows at least that mediation has short-term effects in 'diffusing and reducing' parental conflict during the divorce process and up to one year afterwards.[16]

The 'problem' of the children has also been highlighted by the difficulty of a judiciary, under pressure of time, to investigate adequately whether the arrangements for children on divorce are satisfactory.[17] This has encouraged the translation of the adage that 'parents know best' into a controlling principle in relation to court intervention. By this principle the law can legitimately retire from active consideration of the welfare of the individual child affected by divorce and, instead, promote mediation as an arena in which parents can use their superior knowledge of their children within a process under their control. Such a stance has led to research on consumer satisfaction with mediation and debate about the amount of control which parents 'actually' have.[18]

Finally, the tensions within particular professions have led to pressure for mediation as a method of working with clients, which is both more effective in terms of client outcome and also more productive of 'worker' satisfaction. This particularly applies to the Probation Service in the UK. Ambivalence about the role of the divorce court welfare officer in the late 1970s and early 1980s, and the increasing influence of family systems theory within social work knowledge, led to the development of a method of compiling welfare reports for the courts, using sessions of mediation, or something akin to mediation, in the course of such reporting. In addition, court welfare officers staff court-based mediation: nationally the Family Court Welfare Service completed 19 280 'conciliations' and 31 160 reports under the Children Act (1989) in 1992–93.[19]

Coming together, these diverse professional dilemmas have fuelled a demand for mediation but, in terms of a market for mediation, this demand has been largely 'supply-led' with few actual 'clients' demanding mediation. In statistical terms it is still a minority pursuit: the consultation paper[20] gives National Family Mediation's 58 affiliated services as providing mediation for 6500 families per year and the Family Mediators' Association as providing 1500. However, over 150 000 couples divorce each year in England and Wales and about 60 per cent of such couples have children under 16. Either through ignorance of its existence or through an unwillingness to negotiate directly, divorcing couples are not using out-of-court mediation in large numbers. Some judges would argue that non-attendance is the result of misguided motives on the part of those divorcing: 'The problem of bitterness and the emotional fall-out of marriage breakdown can include a blind refusal to be reasonable.'[21]

Those couples who do use mediation do so for a variety of reasons,[22] only some of which match up with the reasons used to promote mediation. As Simpson *et al.* found, mediators were referred to as 'Social Welfare Officer, Social Worker, Probation Officer, Welfare Man, Reconciliation Officer and Welfare Rights Lady',[23] indicating a variety of functions being attributed to mediators. In my small sample of parents who had attended mediation, about a third felt they had been 'sent' to mediation and had no clear idea of what it might entail whilst, of the remainder, slightly more had viewed it as 'a place to talk' than had believed it to be an advice agency.[24]

The views of lawyers at the beginning of this chapter therefore reflect the fact that not only is divorce today 'controlled' by substantive law and legal procedures, but the cost implications of that fact are a major element in the pressure for greater use of mediation. The focus on financial savings has been encouraged: research on outcomes and consumer satisfaction has frequently been based on the assumption that mediation is simply a better, cheaper way to a negotiated settlement – that is, to the same outcomes. Yet the existence of other pressures for mediation and much that has been written on mediation would belie this assumption. Statements such as the following, written by UK researchers, suggest that mediation can be very different in kind:

> [Mediation] is seen by proponents and practitioners alike as more than a sensible strategy for the settling of disputed issues. It is said to be a civilised and civilising procedure, a process which returns to, or keeps control in, the couple, and a way of ensuring reliable arrangements for the future. As such it cannot be fully appreciated without consideration of such concepts as civility, friendship, trust and the pursuit of mutual interests.[25]

This somewhat purple prose needs to be put alongside the fact that it is now taken for granted that divorce is part of a complicated process of separation over a period of time.[26] As Gwynn Davis wrote in the first sentence of his book, *Partisans and Mediators*:

> The term 'divorce' may be understood in a number of different ways - most obviously as an event which entails massive disruption and reorganisation for individuals and families. But 'divorce' may also be conceived as an area of substantive law destroying the status of marriage, or as a legal process (involving visits to solicitors, court appearances and so on).[27]

Given that divorce is a process of emotional and situational change as well as a process of legal change, it is evident that knowledges and processes other than those of law are relevant to the process of ending a relationship. Such knowledges are evident in the pressures for mediation stemming from, *inter alia*, divorce court welfare officers and child psychologists. The questions which run throughout the whole of this book are therefore those concerning the choice of professionals, institutions and rules associated with different types of knowledge to influence and structure that process and the extent to which professionals, rather than the separating partners, should control that process.

However, the issue of the role of law and the role of 'the other' in the divorce and the mediation processes is more complex than a struggle for influence (with resulting employment and funding) by two or more professional groups. Rather, it entails a discussion of the role of law and the role of the 'other' in the way lawyers and mediators currently 'process' divorcing couples and whether the balance should be different. If there should be a different balance then what process or processes would best ensure it? As Davis *et al.* have pointed out in the final sentence of their book, 'Reform takes a long time: the first task of research is to provide an accurate description'.[28] If the debate about divorce in the future is not grounded in a clear idea of current divorce 'processing' it is difficult to assess the merits of mediation in the context of what it could replace and what clients want replacing. Yet productive debate about the role of mediation in divorce is often hindered by the lack of such a context.[29]

THE NATURE OF THE LEGAL PROCESS

Research has addressed the question of the role of law and of lawyers in the divorce process from a range of perspectives. This section will review, very briefly, research which has investigated what divorce lawyers 'actually do' and research which has tried to specify the norms – legal or otherwise – operating in the 'progress' of a divorce case.

A day in the life of a lawyer

Research in North America and the UK in the 1980s about the 'everyday' role of the general practice lawyer found it difficult to generalize. In the UK, Davis noted:

> In the course of this project[30] we discovered that … within the broad range of what might be regarded as appropriate (or at least, not negligent) work styles, there is a remarkable variety of approaches in response to (but not wholly matched with) an almost equally varied set of expectations.[31]

North American research also warns against analysing the work of divorce lawyers in simplistic 'either/or' terms such as formal or informal, lawyer or client control, rights or needs.

> Whatever utility it may have for forming rhetorical questions about legal reform, such binary thinking does not accord with the more complex realities of legal practice, which are often located not at one end or another of such polarities but in the dynamic interplay between them.[32]

One expectation is that the solicitor will act as 'a sounding board' for a client unsure of whether or not to seek divorce. Here she acts as a source of counselling and support and general advice, as well as specifically legal advice. Davis argues that traditional 'partisan' support is the type of emotional support people often seek when at their most vulnerable,[33] and some clients believed that their solicitors had been insufficiently controlling by outlining options but refusing to make a choice of options for them.[34] Skills and knowledge which are not part of legal discourse or 'traditional' training are already being utilized – albeit in patchy and varied fashion – by lawyers. McEwen *et al.* also stress the difficulty of providing 'clients with legal advice while addressing vitally important non-legal issues' yet perceive that this balancing act is 'at the heart of divorce lawyers' work'.[35] Thus, lawyers were observed to offer 'personal' as well as legal advice and to situate their advice in a context which includes their assessment of suitable living arrangements and of children's needs. Many lawyers expressed the view that mediation could be helpful to them by providing an emotional outlet for their client, an arena for working through the detail of contact and property arrangements and a forum in which to examine legal issues further. In addition, it gave the opportunity to restructure cases because initiating mediation 'moves the process along; forces the other side "to the bargaining table" or provides opportunities for exchanging information'.[36]

This is related to the most common complaint revealed by research – that of delay: 'It would appear that some solicitors are reluctant to actually *do* anything'.[37] Yet, 'Faced with a workload of some 200 cases, it is almost impossible to initiate or to monitor progress. The solicitor can only respond to immediate demands'.[38] Mediation as a better alternative would therefore need to provide 'emotional' benefits to a more consistent effective degree, to provide appropriate legal and general advice in a manner which clients feel better able to digest and act on, and to provide all within a tighter and shorter timescale. In addition, mediation research confirms that clients want to be told what to do in the new situation they find themselves in, or at least to be given guidelines for making decisions. To quote from recent UK research on comprehensive mediation:

> Both Mr and Mrs Clifford found mediation helpful, but the search for norms remained unsatisfied. Mrs Clifford said: '*We were trying to find out what was the norm. We wanted guidance but they said that as long as we were happy it was alright*'. Mr Clifford was searching for a norm concerning suitable property for bringing up the two children. '*So it was really a question of looking for norms for that...*'.[39]

At least one person in Walker *et al.*'s sample thought that solicitors were more knowledgeable about norms than mediators: 'My solicitor did know a lot more, saying "it is normal" or "it is usual" ... that made it so I didn't feel guilty'.[40] Such a comment also reveals how the layperson is not necessarily able to distinguish between legal and social norms.

The law's shadow

Research using an organizational framework specifically designed to delineate the most influential norms in the processing of divorce has reached conflicting conclusions. Mnookin and Kornhauser, in their seminal work[41] on the 'shadow of the law' argued that negotiated settlements on divorce are the result of bargaining within the framework of divorce law, but later research in the USA suggests that, in various crucial stages of negotiation, norms other than the legal, introduced either by the client or the lawyer,[42] are operating and sometimes determine outcome.[43] Ingleby's small-scale study in the UK[44] also led him to conclude: 'The strength of the informally created norms is such that they can override apparently inflexible law'.[45] The research done by Davis *et al.* examines some of these non-legal norms which they refer to as 'folk myths', very strongly held by some of their sample of divorcing spouses. For example, they cite the man's belief that the family's financial resources are his because he earned them, or the belief that conduct should have a bearing on the financial resolution.[46] These myths enshrine normative principles in 'lay' thinking about divorce, but reveal a gulf between these principles and the assumption underpinning legal doctrine.[47]

All this begs the question of why particular norms are 'chosen' by clients. A recent piece of US research has tried to remedy this deficiency by sketching out a framework of variables which must be part of an explanatory account[48] of the conditions which lead to the employment and dominance of either 'folk' norms or legal rules. Jacob uses a continuum which has a legal vocabulary of rights at one end and, at the other, an 'affiliative' vocabulary which 'emphasizes a web of interdependent relationships'.[49] He argues that the manner in which a problem is initially framed is evident in the choice of language used and precedes the choice of legal or social norms.

> If disputants have close friends who are lawyers ... it is more likely that they will obtain legal information from such sources *and it becomes more probable that they will resort to law*. However, not all people in such networks will promote a legalistic framing ... the probability that social norms will be used increases when contacts in their network speak the language of relationships and stress social norms [emphasis added].[50]

'Chance encounters' influence, but do not determine, the eventual choice of norms:

> 'One third of both those who initially chose a legalistic framework and a relational framework ultimately reported using the law in their negotiations; two-thirds of both groups reported not using the law'.[51]

Therefore, this type of research supports the suggestion that the shadow of the law is 'dimly' cast[52] but has obvious limitations in that it gives no clear picture of how 'intervening' variables operate.[53] It can conclude that people choose particular language because for them 'social norms governing parent–child relationships may be more significant than the legal norms of property entitlement' but not explain why, for them, social norms about children predominate over legal norms about property. It can state that those people who 'want' mediation[54] are 'unlikely to use a legalistic framework for articulating their dispute' but cannot explain why they should assume mediation will be 'better'.

Jacob's research is also difficult to interpret because social/folk norms are defined only as 'standards for conduct that are not referred to as legal standards' and which are seen as influential because 'peers demand conformity'.[55] So, in the divorce situation, he refers to social norms that 'commonly exhort both parents to avoid inflicting harm on their children'[56] but does not establish that this is a *social* norm in the sense that the avoidance of harm to children during divorce and separation is upheld as a guiding principle by a sufficient section of the general population for it to be labelled as such. Even if it is, its operation may be problematic because it is one of several conflicting principles or because what is meant by 'harm to children' is left sufficiently vague to render the principle difficult to implement in any prescriptive way.

As critics of informal justice pointed out throughout the 1980s, '[b]ecause Western capitalism is characterised by a high degree of normative dissensus and rapid change, norms must be imposed by informal institutions'.[57] Davis sums up the dilemma this creates for such critics, 'In heterogeneous societies, where there may well be no "community" of shared values, law is all we have left - but that law is bound to be unsatisfactory since it is not sustained by shared norms'[58] although he queries whether this critique can be applied to family disputes where a system of shared family values may exist.[59] However, this does not mean there exists a 'normative void'. Instead of being a social, familial or legal norm, the operative norms may be those which are part of professional knowledge which is not yet 'taken-for-granted' knowledge,[60] in particular that of family or marital therapy or that used by 'child welfare' professionals. The norm of 'avoidance of harm to children', evident in literature which promotes mediation and an agreed outcome as being 'for the sake of the children',[61] is one such norm, delineating what constitutes the best interests of the child in the divorce situation.

THE NATURE OF MEDIATION

Legal and non-legal communications

The above research indicates that lawyers perform a wide variety of 'mixed' roles[62] in a divorce process in which process and outcome are influenced by a range of legal and non-legal norms. The theoretical framework derived from the biological notion of autopoiesis[63] – DIY reproduction within a closed system – as applied to the operation of social systems[64] is productive in terms of a better understanding of the nature of these mixed roles. The focus is on systems of communication with unique procedures and criteria for arriving at 'truth'. Law is one such system of communication which cannot deal directly with the outside world but must, if confronted with 'truths' from other systems, reconstruct those non-law communications. There is no assumption that legal institutions always operate within a system of legal communications or, conversely, that mediation is a system of communications which is 'other' – that is, non-legal. Rather, this approach analyses the knowledge which is constituted within systems of communications, be they of science, law, economics or religion, and leads to an examination of the nature and limitations of a specified system of communications.

This theoretical approach has been used to analyse the way law and 'child welfare science' operate as separate and 'hybrid' discourses within and outside legal institutions.[65] As already noted, in relation to the area of divorce there is an apparent consensus within and across non-legal discourses about what is best for the children – notably their need for contact with both parents and the absence of parental conflict – but these truths about the welfare of the child are communications from medical science, and law must constitute them anew as legal communications[66] if law is not to lose authority over an area of decision making. The 'consensus' about the child's welfare is not the result of there being one 'unified' truth held by two or more systems of communication but, rather, because there is 'interference'. The impression is given that realities and normativities are being 'shared' with other discourses but, '[a]ll that results are simultaneous statements about the child and its problem, which, like parallel lines, never meet but must continue along their own path',[67] with resulting confusion and distortion of communications.

This reliance on reconstructing non-law truths has now put law at risk of having to reconstruct 'an image of itself which may cast serious doubt on its ability in practice to resolve conflicts in ways which promote children's welfare'.[68] The truth that conflict is harmful to children has been extended to the idea that the legal process itself is harmful to children – a development which places law in an 'epistemic trap'.[69] One way out of the trap has been to embrace mediation.[70] It is difficult to determine, however, whether this is resulting in the communications of mediation being 'enslaved' by law: the epistemic status of 'pure' mediation is far from clear. Three principal social discourses seem to have been involved in the development of mediation – an economic discourse and two medical discourses (concerned with therapy and child development)[71] – and evidence from the 1980s suggests that the medical elements were then dominant. However, mediation of all issues has so far been a relatively rare phenomenon in the UK although the current development of 'comprehensive' mediation,[72] the growing interest in the Family Mediators Association,[73] the inclusion of legal matters in the training of mediators and the increasing involvement of lawyers in mediation indicate a growing predominance of economic and legal communications. Mediation may, therefore, be operating using norms that 'belong' to law as well as to those branches of medical science such as therapy and child development which have very different processes and desired outcomes.

What is clear is that mediation does not *necessarily* provide different norms and end products – it may be different only in its settings and working methods. Certainly, mediators have been concerned about issues of 'site' (in-court or out-of-court), of the number and gender of mediators (co-working, man and woman teams), of the structure of appointments (clients seen together or separately, the length and number of appointments) and the qualifications and training of mediators. All these are of importance for efficient and effective mediation, and may shed light on the nature of 'interference', but they beg the question of the 'criteria' for efficiency and effectiveness. Such criteria depend again on the nature of the system of communications, the norms and 'semantic artifacts'[74] with which it operates and the types of outcome it promotes.

Mediation as a separate process

One starting-point to tackle these questions is in-house literature – that written to describe the techniques and procedures of mediation as mediators perceive and practise it. A currently influential text is Haynes' *The Fundamentals of Family Mediation*,[75] described in its preface as 'a cookbook for family mediators'. The previous version of this text[76] provided the model for many mediation services in the USA in the 1980s, and its author has recently trained mediators for five pilot projects of comprehensive mediation established and researched in the UK.[77] In his model of mediation the 'generic process' is seen to have nine stages: reorganizing the problem; choosing the arena; selecting the mediator; gathering the data; defining the problem; developing options; redefining positions; bargaining and drafting the agreement.[78] This generic process may include, at various stages, the use of a 'normalizing' technique.[79]

> Normal problems, after all, are solved normally. But clients often frame their problem as abnormal or as having unusual aspects. The mediator must convince them that theirs is a normal, resolvable problem.[80]

In order to achieve this normalization the mediator may need also to 'mutualize': 'When each person makes a strong case that is unilateral, the mediator attempts to reframe the issue as a mutual one'.[81]

Another important technique to move on the mediation process is the mediator's summary of what has happened so far:

> The summary drives the session .... The mediator does not summarise everything the clients say. He chooses to summarise what he believes is important'.[82]

Information regarded as non-useful, such as 'social talk', 'emotional and emotive statements' and 'legal and therapy questions' are ignored and instead the focus is on dialogue the mediator believes is 'relevant'.[83] This mediator approach is explained on the basis of a belief that people have both 'personal and professional prisms' for understanding events and that these may conflict. To decide which questions to ask as a professional mediator,

> [The mediator] constructs a hypothesis about what is happening in each session as a way of guiding him through the session. ... Different professions develop different hypotheses. ... A mediator develops a hypothesis about
>
> - the problem to be resolved through negotiations
> - the client's goals
> - their negotiating behaviour.[84]

These hypotheses therefore determine which issues are relevant to mediation and which should be summarized.[85]

Haynes' text prompts crucial questions about the process of mediation. Most couples attending mediation do so because they have been unable to resolve their dispute on their own: despite earlier optimism arising from sample of 'routine' divorce cases, research suggests that only a small minority of couples can negotiate easily or at all without third-party assistance.[86] What is the nature of that assistance? Such a question brings together concerns about control and the nature of the 'hypotheses' that mediators use and, in particular, what they perceive and convey as normal, what is made mutual and *how* they achieve 'normalization' and 'mutualization'.

A normalization process

Whilst Haynes' handbook deals with mediation of all issues, he makes the point that '[t]he mediation process is the same for parenting decisions as for support and assets'.[87] Discussion of the processes by which events are made mutual and normal will draw on UK research, based on the mediation of residence and contact issues.[88]

Mediators face clients with grievances: they complain about the behaviour or proposed plans of the (ex-)partner and are resentful that the other's actions have led to the current problems. A way of undermining such grievance is to construct as normal the content of the grievance. For example, the mediator response to mutual allegations in relation to the family finances during a mediation session was, 'It still sounds as though your separation's very, very raw' – a response implying that such conflict is both normal and understandable and the 'usual result' of attempts to live separately.[89] Conflict is also reframed by conveying the idea that it arises out of different perspectives which 'one often gets' because of the strong emotions being experienced and not because there really are conflicting facts, incompatible explanations and lies being told.[90]

> There are strong feelings from everybody here ... Everybody has been very hurt indeed and in a sense the children are in the centre of it aren't they?[91]

Greatbatch and Dingwall have referred to a process of 'selective facilitation' in relation to the choice of outcomes which they observed in their research.[92] However, more important is this same process in regard to the construction of problems to be addressed in mediation: the 'hypotheses' referred to by Haynes are the criteria by which mediators choose items to select or to ignore, thus remaking the problem to one which is amenable to a solution within mediation. At the same time this process constructs a very clear vision of what it is 'normal' for separating parents to do and feel. Indeed, in the USA the 'education' of parents about the 'normal' emotional and behavioural difficulties encountered in divorce and the way they should respond to their children's needs has become an art form. There are now many such 'orientation' programmes. In several counties of Kansas, for example, there is compulsory attendance for all divorcing couples at a two-hour programme entitled 'General Responsibilities of Separating Parents' or GRASP![93]

A mutualizing process

Parents in conflict about arrangements for their children often hold different views on who is responsible for the problem: mediators therefore seek to mutualize responsibility in regard to contact difficulties and the separation itself.[94] For example, one mother, who persisted in blaming her husband for the break-up, was told, 'Only when you can accept it's a mutual thing can you go into arrangements regarding the children'.[95] It was similarly explained to a father that, 'if you are saying that you can see a future where access is stopped and you cannot change to accommodate the possibility of it happening then you must take part of that destruction as being yours'.[96] In the same way, past and present burdens of parenting – perceived as unfair – were 'equalized'. So, for example, a mother's burden arising from the physical tasks of laundering, shopping and preparing for contact visits was balanced, and thereby made a mutual burden, by reference to the father's 'pain' at not seeing the children every day.[97] But conflict itself is also rephrased out of existence by reconstructing grievances as an expression of mutual concern:

> What I really want to get to is the concern you are both feeling about Robert and in a way it is taking the form of saying 'you did unsuitable things with him' ... You're both at it in that sense whereas you are both very worried about Robert.[98]

The result is that, at least in child-related mediation, the focus is on parental communication and trust, and the solutions are supported by a particular construction of what constitutes parental or spousal responsibility. This is very different from 'pure' legal procedures of examining past behaviours as the basis for present decisions or of concentrating on material matters. The alternative version of reality constructed in mediation may, therefore, be fragile. Mediators must persuade parents that it is supported by specialist knowledge which is 'scientifically proven' and, in modern societies, authoritative. Mediators know about and refer to such research and, in the USA, the pre-mediation education/orientation sessions aim to provide 'scientific' data so that such knowledge can begin to be accepted as 'normal' before mediation.[99] The UK is now following this lead with parent education packs being developed by two mediation services with funding from the Department of Health.[100]

JUSTICE: PERCEPTIONS AND SUBSTANCE

Parents at the beginning of the first session of mediation are not in agreement but may be so at the end: to what extent has this depended on the acceptance of norms proffered by mediators and lawyers? Or, to put it another way, Joan Kelly has referred to the ideas of clients new to mediation as being 'so off the wall'[101] and for settlement to occur there must be a transformation of such ideas to ones more acceptable to mediators. Walker *et al.* have referred to this shift in perception by clients as 'coming round' and comment that it 'is one of the most important processes in mediation'.[102] One question which this raises is whether clients and observers of mediation perceive this process and its outcome to be acceptable.

Acceptance of norms

Legal norms

Research reveals evidence of gender difference in the acceptance of legal norms by separating spouses. For example, men do not like legal norms in relation to finance and property[103] and woman are unhappy with the legal norms in regard to their children's contact with the 'absent' parent.[104]

The bigger issue, underlying the gender differences in the acceptability of particular legal norms, is that there are different conceptions of justice held by the parties to a divorce:

> We suggest that a central dynamic underlying fathers' dissatisfactions ... following divorce ... is related to perceptions of equity. ... equity is related to the moral idea of justice.[105]

The following comment, from a father who had attended out-of-court mediation, would bear this out:

> I find this whole system unsatisfactory. It's almost immoral in my opinion ... People are sort of actively encouraging the situation to exist where people separate .. To try and conciliate between right and wrong isn't necessarily the most moral thing to do.[106]

He expressed hostility to the very notion of mediation because of its apparent readiness to accept separation as 'normal', and focused on a desire for 'justice' to be part of the process which decides the practicalities involved in the end of a marriage. Many separating spouses do have a strong sense of being 'wronged' and need some form of 'justification'. Walker, for example, found parents who needed 'fault' to be acknowledged because the lack of condemnation by mediators was interpreted as condonation, perhaps even of domestic violence.[107] This criticism of the perceived lack of any sense of 'right and wrong' in mediation reveals a 'need' for those normative, moral judgements which are part of law's general function of delineating the legal from the illegal, the innocent from the culpable conduct.[108]

Yet this conception of justice – evident also in some of the folk myths delineated by Davis *et al.*[109] – will probably not be satisfied by the legal system. As two district judges recently pointed out, 'It is hard for many litigants to appreciate that all the court is trying to do is to be fair and equitable, not to make moral judgements'.[110] As a result, mediators may propose false dichotomies between the legal system and mediation. For example, Haynes comments that 'determining who was right or wrong about the past is the function of a judge, not the mediator',[111] yet judges refute that function in the area of divorce. Haynes' case for a future focus – to be supplied uniquely by mediation – is also, in practice, an approach no longer so alien to the courts.

> The wrongs of the past are unchangeable. Talking about the past does not resolve it; the dialogue simply reinforces the disputants' individual views of their joint past. Searching for solutions requires a future focus because the solution lies in the future.[112]

As Davis *et al.* point out:

> Another way of expressing the disjunction between private conceptions of financial justice and the framework provided by legislation and case law is to say that courts are loath to adopt a historical perspective ... lawyers and courts focus only upon the circumstances, needs and resources pertaining at the time of divorce. The legal construction is thus in the nature of a 'snapshot' view of justice, lacking any historical or relational dimension.[113]

To refer to Gilligan's influential work on the male and female 'voices' in legal and moral reasoning,[114] it is no longer possible to argue that the voice of law and legal practice is male and can be described unproblematically in terms of formal equality, fairness and rights. The practice of divorce law is now something else. Just as Daley has argued that '[t]he relational, contextual and concrete reasoning which Gilligan associates with the female voice *is* the voice of criminal justice practices',[115] it is possible to argue that the practice of divorce law also reveals the characteristics of the female voice. This highlights law's reconstruction and use of non-legal communications which diminish the difference between the legal process and mediation.

Daley's observation that, in criminal justice, this development has led to further danger for some victims, notably female victims of male violence,[116] is relevant in that mediation is also putting victims of domestic violence at risk.[117]

Non-legal norms

> ...Focus not on whatever conflict you have with the other parent; focus on your child, your children, and what's in their best interest.[118]

This focus on the child not only entails the promotion of a variety of norms about what constitutes their best interest[119] but also constitutes a norm itself. The good parent relegates his or her own interests to second place and does not oppose arrangements which put these norms into practice: the converse is that parents who do otherwise are not good parents. Smart's research revealed many women whose opposition to the father's plans for the children, based on years of caregiving, was rephrased as an expression of self-interest on their part because the 'caring about' of the father was placed more highly than her 'caring for'.[120] She argues that this leads to a situation where mothers 'have no legitimate voice unless they speak the language of equal rights [for fathers] or welfare [for children].[121] This 'silencing' of women is not only in relation to what they have said but also to what they might have said. Some clients, expecting the mutualizing and normalizing process to take place do not speak up:

> I just couldn't think straight ... I just didn't want to see him. He was so charming, that's really what got me. And I knew he was lying, but what was the point in saying anything – they'd just say I was being miserable and bitter.[122]

The problem is that the influence of those norms which silence the divorcing spouse depends on two factors: prior knowledge of 'child welfare' norms and prior experience of putting children first. Mothers, given that they are still usually the main caretakers of children, have had greater contact (either via child-care professionals or women's magazines) before approaching lawyers or mediators with the sort of child-focused advice which will produce the 'right' attitude in mediation. In addition there is some evidence that women might also be more receptive to such advice.[123] There are therefore gender differences in the acceptance of both legal and non-legal norms.

No alternative?

What becomes increasingly apparent is that law and mediation are not radical alternatives:[124] as Bottomley pointed out over a decade ago, 'The presentation of conciliation and litigation as opposites proves to be a false distinction'.[125] It is not therefore surprising that clients are unable to choose between using solicitors and mediators when given the choice: Walker *et al.* found that 78 per cent of the clients in their sample thought that solicitors had been 'helpful' in the settling of their disagreements, with 76 per cent finding mediators equally helpful.[126] Kelly's comment, above, about clients' ideas being 'so off the wall' was made in the context of sending clients of a mediation service to solicitors because they first needed 'educating' – presumably away from the 'folk myths' which hinder negotiation by both mediators and lawyers.

Walker *et al.* have recently argued that '[t]hc framework for negotiations has been the court and the law; now the framework is being provided by mediation and the law'.[127] What this might mean is that the negotiations of lawyers were previously constrained only by what the court would impose if asked to adjudicate, whereas the norms structuring negotiations are now those provided by mediators and lawyers. Yet, as we have seen, lawyers may not be operating within a purely legal discourse or mediators within a discourse external to law. The framework for negotiations could be presented as a relatively seamless web of norms in which both law and mediation are enslaving the truths of each other. Such a development is helpful if the required end-product is speedy settlement of their disputes by the parties to divorce: the operative norms are all encouraging movement – a coming round – in the same direction. In terms of the earlier analysis of both Fineman and Bruch, [128] familial ideology has 'won' hands down.

Yet parents do resist the combined normative pressure.[129] In interviews, after mediation women have shown anger at the way mediators have constructed as mutual or joint what they have never experienced as joint.[130] This may stiffen their resistance to settlement within mediation or lead to resentment afterwards[131] – neither being conducive to lasting agreement or perceptions of a just process. The apparently 'single voice' of lawyers and mediators can lead more effectively to settlement, but could lead to destructive feelings of injustice.

Mediation and domestic abuse

Although research reveals men who feel mediation is against their interests, most criticism of mediation has focused on the coercive nature of mediation in regard to women, especially mothers. The last decade has witnessed the production of a growing volume of feminist writing, critical of mediation and upholding the continued use of legal procedures to protect women against the injustices believed to result from informal negotiation between partners who have differential ability to control the process and outcome of mediation because of the structural inequalities between men and women in society. Some of these criticisms have not taken sufficiently into account the variety and complexity of the family situations subject to the change of divorce or, indeed, the effects of the changes on both the economic and personal resources of the participants. However these criticisms of a process which seems more easily to silence mothers and to persuade mothers to accept its norms[132] are now becoming particularly influential in relation to mediation where spousal abuse has occurred.[133] The existence of a violent relationship undermines the voluntary nature of mediation: the victim has no choice but to attend if the abuser wishes it and control by clients in mediation will mean control by the abuser: there will not be cooperation for mutual benefit, given that the victim is unable to articulate her own wishes. In addition, mediation may lead to an 'agreed' solution which endangers both the victim and her children.[134]

The debate now taking place both within and outside mediation services is whether and to what extent mediators can compensate for these power inequalities and, therefore, what types and effects of domestic abuse preclude the possibility of fair and safe mediation. Furthermore, it is now being acknowledged that those who have been abused will often be unable to admit the abuse to themselves or others, so making diagnostic screening of clients a necessity.[135] Such screening should not be viewed as an optional extra by mediators (or, indeed, by lawyers): there is a growing body of evidence from US research that the period of separation is a particularly dangerous time for the victims of domestic violence.[136]

This is no minority issue: US research indicates that 10–15 per cent of the women who use divorce mediation have been battered by their (ex-)husbands.[137] Nor is the fact that mediation is not compulsory in the UK (and there are currently no proposals to make it so) a cause for complacency. Many clients perceive their 'voluntary' attendance as being coerced and, if the proposals in the consultation paper reach the statute book, the regulations in regard to legal aid may force attendance at mediation.[138] This issue is therefore forcing practitioners and academics alike to rethink the arguments for and against mediation in the light of the more detailed research, both about the process of mediation and also the aetiology of domestic violence and spousal power, which has accumulated in the last decade. It is hoped that this will result in a much clearer examination of what mediation 'is' and of the differential use and influence of particular norms than this chapter has been able to achieve.

One result of this must be a discussion of how both mediation and the legal process can be used to protect the weaker party without fomenting conflict where that is not helpful and without making private those inequities and acts of abuse which should be publicly examined. The law can provide remedies (albeit still inadequate ones) for those unable to achieve – on their own or with the assistance of a mediator – a fair settlement and safe home but the current self-denying ordinance of the legal system has left a situation of too little real choice for many of those who decide to divorce. The pressure has been for the coming together of professionals around the 'problem' of settling children, property and financial matters on divorce. Whilst this has not occurred institutionally – hence the discussion about the place and funding of mediation services – the coming together has occurred, in large measure, at the level of the norms and parameters for negotiation by lawyers and mediators alike. I would argue that the benefits of this 'convergence' need re-examining. The legal process is far from perfect, and mediation has much to offer. What precisely each could uniquely offer and the benefits and disadvantages of each process 'properly' done is, however, still not clear.

NOTES

1. Judge Herrell in E. Welch, S. Herrell and D. Koch (1994), 'Judicial orientation', *Family and Conciliation Courts Review*, **32**, (3), pp. 299–305 at p. 301.
2. A lawyer quoted in C. McEwen, R. Maiman and L. Mather (1994), 'Lawyers, mediation and the management of divorce practice', *Law and Society Review*, **28**, (1), pp. 149–86 at p. 174.
3. A term used instead of mediation, especially in UK in the 1980s. 'Mediation' is now the commonly used term in most jurisdictions. One reason for the change to mediation is the confusion engendered by the similarity of 'conciliation' and 'reconciliation'.
4. They were made, respectively, by a judge in the Multomah County Mediation Programme (Oregon) and by a divorce lawyer in Maine.
5. Lord Chancellor's Department (1993), *Looking to the Future: Mediation and the Ground for Divorce*, Cm 2424, London: HMSO.
6. *Ibid.*, para. 7.7.
7. *Ibid.*, para. 7.22 See also Lord Chancellor's Department (1995), *Looking to the Future: Mediation and the Ground for Divorce*, Cm. 2799, London: HMSO, paras 5.3–5.9 and para. 5.21.
8. J. Walker, P. McCarthy and N. Timms (1994), *Mediation: The Making and Re-Making of Co-operative Relationships*, Newcastle University: Relate Centre for Family Studies, p. 30.
9. See the Robinson Report (1983), *Report of the Interdepartmental Committee on Conciliation*, London: HMSO.
10. *Op. cit.*, note 5 above.
11. See C. Piper (1993), *The Responsible Parent*, Hemel Hempstead: Harvester Wheatsheaf, pp. 7–11 for a fuller discussion of why mediation was perceived as a solution.

12 *Looking to the Future* (*op. cit.*, note 5 above), para. 4.5. See para. 4.4 for a summary of the results of research.
13 *Looking to the Future* (1995) *op. cit.*, note 7, para. 5.16.
14 See C. Piper (1994), '"Looking to the future" for children', *Journal of Child Law*, **6**, (3), pp. 98–10 for a review of research, not all of which stresses that divorce is 'bad' for children.
15 J. Kelly (1991), 'Children's post-divorce adjustment: effects of conflict, parent adjustment and custody arrangements', *Family Law*, **21**, p. 52; (1991), 'Mediated and adversarial divorce resolution processes: a comparison of post-divorce outcomes', *Family Law*, **21**, p. 382; also (1994), Address to joint meeting of the Solicitors' Family Law Association and Family Law Bar Association, Middle Temple Hall, London, 2 November.
16 Conversely, most of the beneficial effects had disappeared one to two years after separation, and some parents were more bitter after mediation than before.
17 A requirement under s.41 of the Matrimonial Causes Act 1973 (formerly s.2 of the Matrimonial Proceedings Act 1958 and now amended by schedule 12, para. 31 of the Children Act 1989).
18 See D. Greatbach and R. Dingwall (1989), 'Selective facilitation: some preliminary observations on a strategy used by divorce mediators', *Law and Society Review*, **23**, pp. 613–41; also M. Roberts (1990), 'Systems or selves? Some ethical issues in family mediation', *Journal of Social Welfare and Family Law*, pp. 6–17; *idem* (1991), 'The integrity of family mediation: a challenge from the professions', paper given at the meeting of the Law and Society Association, Amsterdam, 28 June; *idem* (1994), 'Who is in charge? Effecting a productive exchange between researchers and practitioners in the field of family mediation', *Journal of Social Welfare and Family Law*, (4), pp. 439–54; also Piper, *op. cit.*, note 11 above.
19 These figures are provided in *Looking to the Future*, *op. cit.*, note 5 above, at para. 7.13 which refers to 'conciliations' after pointing out the various methods used by court welfare officers.
20 *Ibid.*
21 G. Rose and S. Gerlis (1991), 'Conciliation for family finance', *Family Law*, **21**, pp. 92–3 at p. 92.
22 G. Davis and M. Roberts (1988), *Access to Agreement*, Milton Keynes: Open University Press, ch. 5.
23 B. Simpson *et al.* (1990), 'Client responses to family conciliation: achieving clarity in the midst of confusion', *British Journal of Social Work*, **20**, (4), pp. 709–35 at p. 562.
24 Piper, *op. cit.*, note 11 above, pp. 54–62.
25 Walker *et al.*, *op. cit.*, note 8 above, p. 1.
26 The most detailed account of the different emotional and practical stages within the process of 'uncoupling' is that of D. Vaughan (1987), *Uncoupling*, London: Methuen.
27 G. Davis (1988), *Partisans and Mediators: The Resolution of Divorce Disputes*, Oxford: Clarendon Press, p. 1.
28 G. Davis, S. Cretney and J. Collins (1994), *Simple Quarrels*, Oxford: Clarendon Press, p. 274.
29 *Looking to the Future* (*op. cit.*, note 5 above), for example, refers in pejorative terms to the unsuitability of the courts for resolving disputes and appears to present mediation as an alternative to the entire legal process. Yet there is no discussion of what the legal process currently 'does'.
30 'Conciliation in Divorce'; this analyses the work of solicitors in almost 300 cases.
31 Davis. *op. cit.*, note 27 above, p. 86.

32 McEwen *et al. op. cit.*, note 2 above, p. 149 (the research from which the second quotation in this chapter is drawn).
33 *Op cit.*, note 27 above, chs 8 and 9.
34 *Ibid.*, pp. 94–6.
35 *Op. cit.*, note 2 above, p. 150.
36 *Ibid.*, pp. 169–75.
37 Davis, *op. cit.*, note 27 above, p. 107.
38 Davis *et al.*, *op. cit.*, note 28 above, p. 257.
39 Walker *et al.*, *op. cit.*, note 8 above, p. 94.
40 *Ibid.*, p. 92.
41 R. Mnookin and L. Kornhauser (1979), 'Bargaining in the shadow of the law: the case of divorce', *Yale Law Journal*, **88**, p. 950.
42 Research on Dutch lawyers found, for example, that the objective was 'a reasonable divorce': J. Griffiths (1986), 'What do Dutch lawyers actually do in divorce cases?', *Law and Society Review*, **20**, (1), p. 135.
43 See, for example, A. Sarat and W. Felstiner (1986), 'Law and strategy in the divorce lawyer's office', *Law and Society Review*, **20**, p. 93; also H. Erlanger, E. Chambliss and M. Melli (1987), 'Participation and flexibility in informal processes: cautions from the divorce context', *Law and Society Review*, **21**, p. 585. This latter research was based on 25 informally settled divorce cases and found that the 'relative impatience to finalize the divorce' (p. 586) was a particularly strong non-legal factor.
44 R. Ingleby (1992), *Solicitors and Divorce*, Oxford: Clarendon Press. Using an in-depth study of the work of five solicitors drawn from different types of firms, Ingleby draws on Cain's (1979) work ('The general practice lawyer and the client: towards a radical conception', *International Journal of the Sociology of the Law*, **7**, pp. 331–54) in which she concluded that 'lawyers' characteristic and specific practice is *translation* into a discourse which they both use and create' (p. 352). Ingleby argues that there are often good reasons why solicitors cannot 'translate' their clients' chosen outcomes (p. 16), and that legal norms did not influence negotiations with any certainty. Rather, 'bargaining endowments' are created by other non-legal aspects of the dispute.
45 *Ibid.*, p. 144.
46 *Op. cit.*, note 28 above, p. 144. In many cases, however, the law in this area is imprecise, not 'inflexible', putting 'inside knowledge' of the legal system at a premium. Yet this dependence on the solicitor may also lead to distrust and cynicism on the part of the client – see Ingleby, *op. cit.*, note 44 above, p. 144.
47 See also Davis *et al.*, *op. cit.*, note 28 above at p. 72 for their reference to 'soft' legal knowledge.
48 H. Jacob (1992), 'The elusive shadow of the law', *Law and Society*, **26**, (3), pp. 565–90. He uses the organizational framework of 'naming, blaming and claiming' used by Felstiner *et al.* (1980–81, 'The emergence and transformation of disputes: naming, blaming, claiming', *Law and Society Review*, **15**, p. 631) in relation to the process of perceiving and resolving a problem. First, he refers to characteristics of the disputants – kinships. gender and preference for a particular type of outcome (pp. 568–9) – and, second, to 'intervening variables' (pp. 570–3), such as the employment of particular professionals and the degree to which the disputants 'activate social networks' of relatives and friends.
49 *Ibid.*, p. 568.
50 *Ibid.*, p. 571.
51 *Ibid.*, p. 579. In Jacob's sample, 42 of the 90 respondents (58 per cent) framed issues primarily in relational terms and 38 (42 per cent) in legalistic terms (p. 576).

52 *Ibid.*, p. 585. The importance of network has been noted in several studies of dispute processing and the role of advice in both legal and mediation processes is increasingly coming under scrutiny.
53 *Ibid.*, pp. 578–83.
54 *Ibid.*, pp. 568 and 569.
55 *Ibid.*, p. 567.
56 *Ibid.*
57 R. Abel (1982), *The Politics of Informal Justice: Comparative Studies*, **2**, London: Academic Press, p. 4.
58 Davis, *op. cit.*, note 27 above, p. 4.
59 Davis also discusses the 'strongly articulated view' (*ibid.*, p. 6) that gender differences undermine the possibility of such a consensus.
60 See P. Berger and T. Luckman (1966), *The Social Construction of Reality*, New York: Doubleday.
61 For example, see Davis, *op. cit.*, note 27 above, p. 80, for a discussion of the 'kids first' values evident at Bromley FMS and the contrast this makes with the North American schemes where such norms are not made explicit.
62 Any cursory examination of the topics covered by accredited trainers who are part of the burgeoning UK industry of providing Law Society Continuing Education courses reveals that practitioners perceive themselves as needing a wide knowledge base which includes skills and knowledge imparted by various non-legal professionals.
63 'Autopoietic systems are...systems that recursively produce their own elements from the network of their own elements' (G. Teubner (1989), 'How the law thinks: towards a constructivist epistemology of law', *Law and Society Review*, **23**, (5), pp. 727–56 at p. 736). By applying the notion of autopoiesis to social systems Luhman succeeds in resolving the paradox and tautology of self-reference, simply by stating that self-referentiality, far from being a problem, is an essential characteristic of organizational discourse (M. King and C. Piper (1990), *How the Law Thinks About Children*, Aldershot: Gower, p. 21).
64 See G. Teubner (ed.) (1988), *Autopoietic Law: A New Approach To Law and Society*, Berlin: Walter de Gruyter; also N. Luhman (1986), 'The autopoiesis of social systems' in F. Geyer and J. van der Zoven (eds), *Sociocybernetic Systems*, London/Beverley Hills: Sage.
65 King and Piper, *op. cit.*, note 63 above and rev. edn (1995), Aldershot: Arena; M. King (1991), 'Child welfare within law: the emergence of a hybrid discourse', *Journal of Law and Society*, **18**, (3), pp. 303–22; *idem* (1993), 'The truth about autopoiesis', *Journal of Law and Society*, **20**, (2), pp. 1–19.
66 Teubner, *op. cit.*, note 63 above, p. 745.
67 King and Piper, *op. cit.*, (rev. edn) note 65 above, p. 21.
68 King and Piper, *op. cit.*, note 65 above, p. 83.
69 See King and Piper, *op. cit.*, note 63 above, pp. 26–32 and p. 76. This is not to deny that, at another level of analysis, it is possible to argue, as does John Eekelaar ((1995), 'Family Justice: Ideal or Illusion? Family Law and Communitarian Values', *Current Legal Problems*, **48**, pp. 195–216), that this 'truth' is being used to argue for diversion from the legal process on grounds of cost. His argument that the language of *Looking to the Future* (*op. cit.*, note 5 above) is deliberately 'loaded' to give a negative view of the legal process for this purpose is therefore a valid one.
70 This is not the only possible way out of the trap. Michael King and I (*op. cit.*, note 65 above, ch. 8) argue that law could become more 'child-responsive'.
71 See *ibid.*, ch. 5, part III.

72 The Joseph Rowntree Trust has recently funded the setting up and research into five pilot projects of comprehensive mediation (see Walker *et al.*, *op. cit.*, note 8 above).
73 This is an organization which trains lawyers as mediators capable of mediating all issues. There are currently discussions between the FMA and the National Family Mediation with a view to further cooperation or merger.
74 See King and Piper, *op. cit.*, note 65 above, ch. 4.
75 J. Haynes (1994), *The Fundamentals of Family Mediation*, New York: Albany State University of New York Press.
76 J. Haynes (1981), *Divorce Mediation*, New York: Springer.
77 See Walker *et al.*, *op. cit.*, note 8 above, pp. 18–19.
78 Haynes, *op. cit.*, note 75 above, p. 1. The central stages may be repeated as necessary for each issue within particular mediation.
79 *Ibid.*, p. 8.
80 *Ibid.*, p. 9.
81 *Ibid.*, p. 11.
82 *Ibid.*, p. 18.
83 *Ibid.*, pp. 15 and 17.
84 *Ibid.*, p. 19.
85 *Ibid.*, p. 25. The remaining chapters of the book give detailed advice, including practicalities as well as the implications of intake procedures, sessions on financial and property arrangements, 'future parenting' (ch. 5) and a discussion of negotiating behaviour models.
86 Davis, *op. cit.*, note 27 above. In his 'Special Procedure' sample, Davis asked couples (interviewed in 1980) about their experience of trying to negotiate together: about 25 per cent of the sample had remained friendly, with little or no tension between them (p. 25); 31 per cent had not communicated and had not been at all amicable (p. 25); a middle group had had disagreements but had tried to behave in a civilized fashion (p. 25). *But*, in a later sample of interviewees (from the Conciliation in Divorce project) who were parties to contested legal proceedings, he found many couples who 'had no sense of there being a "middle ground" which might be tapped by a skilled mediator' (p. 26).
87 Haynes, *op. cit.*, note 75 above, pp. 68–9.
88 My research (*op. cit.*, note 11) was based on an out-of-court mediation service with close links with a probation service in the Home Counties.
89 Piper, *op. cit.*, note 11 above, p. 76.
90 *Ibid.*, pp. 68–9.
91 *Ibid.*, p. 75.
92 *Op. cit.*, note 18 above.
93 C. Roeder-Esser (1994), 'Families in transition: a divorce workshop', *Family and Conciliation Courts Review*, **32**, (1), pp. 40–9 at p. 40.
94 Piper, *op. cit.*, note 11 above, p. 85.
95 *Ibid.*, p. 87.
96 *Ibid.*, p. 90.
97 *Ibid.*, pp. 91–4.
98 *Ibid.*, p. 74.
99 L. Lehner (1994), 'Education for parents divorcing in California', *Family and Conciliation Courts Review*, **32**, (1), pp. 50–4 at p. 54.
100 See *Family Mediation* 1995, vol. 5, No. 1.
101 *Op. cit.*, (1994), note 15 above.
102 Walker *et al., op. cit.*, note 8 above, p. 97.

103 Davis *et al., op. cit.*, note 28 above. See also J. Arditti and K. Allen (1993), 'Understanding distressed fathers' perceptions of legal and relational inequalities post-divorce', *Family and Conciliation Courts Review*, **31**, (4), pp. 461–76 whose research in the US found that some men had very strong negative feeling about all things legal and perceived inequity in relation to all issues.

104 Piper, *op. cit.*, note 11, pp. 110–115; C. Smart (1991), 'The Legal and Moral Ordering of Child Custody', *Journal of Law and Society*, **18**, (4), at p. 485.

105 Arditti and Allen, *op. cit.*, note 103 above, p. 461. This research is based on a group of 87 'distressed' fathers drawn from a larger sample of 232 divorcing fathers.

106 Piper, *op. cit.*, note 11 above, p. 170.

107 J. Walker (1991), 'Divorce: whose fault? Is the Law Commission getting it right?, *Family Law*, **21**, pp. 234–7 at p. 236.

108 See King and Piper, *op. cit.*, note 65 above, ch. 1 for a discussion of the nature of legal discourse.

109 Davis *et al.*, *op. cit.*, note 28 above.

110 Rose and Gerlis, *op. cit.*, note 21 above, p. 92.

111 *Op. cit.*, note 75 above, p. 12.

112 *Ibid.*, p. 12.

113 Davis *et. al.*, *op. cit.*, note 28 above, p. 53.

114 C. Gilligan (1982), *In a Different Voice*, Cambridge, Mass: Harvard University Press.

115 K. Daley (1994), 'Criminal justice ideologies and practices: some feminist questions about justice' in N. Lacey (ed.), *A Reader on Criminal Justice*, Oxford: Oxford University Press, p. 227. She bases this analysis on her observation of the operation of the ethic of care in relation to some types of crime and victim-offender relations (p. 237).

116 *Ibid.*, p. 237.

117 See p. 81.

118 Welch *et al., op. cit.*, note 1 above, pp. 301–2.

119 See Piper, *op. cit.*, note 11 above, pp. 101–6 where mediator explanations of what the problem 'really' is reveal their norms in regard to the welfare of the child.

120 C. Smart *op. cit.*, at note 104 above.

121 *Ibid.*, p. 498.

122 Walker *et al.*, *op. cit.*, note 8 above, p. 92.

123 Piper, *op. cit.*, note 11 above, pp. 176–81.

124 E. Pickett (1991), 'Familial ideology, family law and mediation: law casts more than a shadow', *Journal of Human Justice*, **3**, (1), pp. 27–45.

125 A. Bottomley (1984), 'Resolving family disputes: a critical view' in M. Freeman (ed.), *The State, the Law and the Family*, London: Tavistock/Sweet & Maxwell, p. 183.

126 *Op. cit.*, note 8 above, p. 129. However, these averages are based on slightly more clients feeling that solicitors had been helpful in regard to child-focused mediation and fewer feeling them helpful regarding comprehensive mediation.

127 *Ibid.*, p. 131.

128 M. Fineman (1988), 'Dominant discourse, professional language and legal change in child custody decision-making', *Harvard Law Review*, **101**, pp. 727–74; C. Bruch (1988), 'And How are the Children? The Effects of Ideology and Mediation on Child Custody and Children's Wellbeing in the United States', *International Journal of Law and the Family*, **2**, (106). See also E. Havas (1995), 'The Family as Ideology', *Social Policy and Administration*, **29**, (1), pp. 1–9.

129 See Piper, *op. cit.*, note 11 above, ch. 7.

130 *Ibid.*, pp. 161–76.

131 Davis and Roberts, *op. cit.*, note 22 above, p. 305.
132 See, in particular, T. Grillo (1991), 'The mediation alternative: process dangers for women', *Yale Law Journal*, **100**, pp. 1545–610.
133 It is interesting that Daley (*op. cit.*, note 115 above, p. 237) has noted that the result of the inclusion of the female voice into the operation of the criminal law and sentencing has been 'continued harm and danger for victims', notably female victims of male violence.
134 F. Kaganas and C. Piper (1994), 'Domestic violence and divorce mediation', *Journal of Social Welfare and Family Law*, pp. 265–78.
135 See *ibid.*, pp. 272–3 for a review of this literature.
136 *Ibid.*, p. 267.
137 K. Fischer, N. Vidmar and R. Ellis (1993), 'The culture of battering and the role of mediation in domestic violence cases', *SMU Law Review*, **46**, (5), pp. 2117–74 at p. 2143.
138 *Looking to the Future, op. cit.*, note 5 above, paras 9.8 and 9.22.

5 Property and Money Matters

*Ruth Deech**

In the field of property and money matters there has been a significant shift away from private adjudication to administrative settlement – a shift that may well be permanent. The undoubted catalyst, or irritant, of the change has been the Child Support Agency (CSA), established by the Child Support Act 1991. This is not because the Agency has been very active in terms of quantity, nor because its operation is very profound as an intellectual matter; it is because its existence and the attendant publicity have thrown new light on topical issues, both political and legal. The existence of the CSA has thrown into relief:

1 the amount of public funding expended on single-parent families;
2 the advantages, or otherwise, of administrative settlements as opposed to judicial;
3 the extent of funds remaining for support of a spouse after assessment of children's needs;
4 the diminishing importance of the matrimonial home as an asset; and
5 the relationship between the different types of ancillary relief and their modes of determination.

It may be that future historians of family law will see the Child Support Act as the event that brought to an end the systems of private support of spouses and children, and the division of the home, that have prevailed during this century. Alternatively, it may one day be said that the Child Support Act was an experiment in mechanical determination that failed spectacularly.

The political agenda in the early 1990s in relation to family law was set by the government's pronouncements on 'family values' and 'back to basics'. It was never clear what was meant by these phrases, widely used though they were. They could be interpreted as meaning that the traditional

* Principal, St Anne's College, Oxford.

nuclear family should be supported, divorce rendered more unacceptable and deterred. The slogans could also mean that greater efforts should be made to force absent fathers to support their children and the children's mothers; or they could equally well mean that the formation of second families and the encouragement of conciliation and stable cohabitation were to be promoted. Whatever the political agenda, family matters, especially property and money, have been controversial and discussed in the media to a far greater extent than before. Nevertheless, there remain grave misunderstandings on the part of the public over certain basic issues. As the protests about the operation of the CSA unfolded, it became clear that the aim of the Child Support Act had never been sufficiently explained. Most commentators seemed to believe that the aim of the Act was to ensure that more money was available to single mothers whereas, in truth, its objective was to enable the taxpayer to recoup from the absent father more of the funds expended by the state on the single-parent unit. While the welfare of the child is the paramount aim of modern family legislation, this tended to be overlooked or underplayed in favour of the freedom of absent fathers and second wives to re-establish another happier, and more stable, union.

The social background is that single parents now form 18 per cent of all families with dependent children, and there are 1 500 000 single-parent families, of whom 33 per cent are divorced and 31 per cent single. The UK has the highest percentage of single parents in Europe, and only the USA has a greater proportion. State spending on single parents has risen to £6 billion and it is expected that 1.5 million single parents will be claiming social security by the year 2000. Currently, 30 per cent receive some maintenance from the father, but the average amount per child was only £16 per week in 1990 figures. In the same year, 70 per cent of single parents depended on social security but only 17 per cent worked full-time and 21 per cent part-time. In contrast, 20 per cent of married women with children worked full-time and 39 per cent part-time, probably reflecting the fact that it is easier for a married woman to find help with childcare while she works part-time than it is for the single mother. Of single fathers, 74 per cent worked.

In 1990 Relate estimated the additional cost to the taxpayer of single parenthood to be about £10 500 per divorce or separation, plus £3000 per year per employee in time off and sick leave. These costs include legal aid, social security and costs relating to children in care and in ill-health. With inflation, the cost per marital breakdown today could be estimated at around £20 000 per couple. Whatever system is used to estimate these costs, a sufficiently large burden undoubtedly falls on the taxpayer to worry a government set on cutting the tax bill and saving costs. Indeed, Baroness Thatcher had considered that a child support system modelled on the Australian one, and intended to recover some of these costs, would meet universal approval. Recently, media commentators have blamed the broken family for a wide range of social ills, including criminal behaviour, poor educational performance and ill-health and, at the heart of the complaints, lies the alleged inability of the single mother to cope in the absence of the unsupporting father.

THE CHILD SUPPORT AGENCY

The operation of the CSA was described in the first report of the House of Commons Social Security Committee as follows:

> The changes brought about by the Child Support Act are the most far-reaching social reforms to be made for forty years. The assumption that in broken marriages or partnerships taxpayers should assume financial responsibility for the first family is, at long last, challenged. The prime responsibility is placed where we believe it has always rested until recently, i.e. with the natural parents. In making this change a second fundamental reform is brought about. The essence of change was to move from a legal system dealing with child maintenance on a case-by-case, discretionary basis, to an administrative system which assesses all maintenance according to the same criteria, with the aim of achieving higher levels of maintenance.[1]

Legal negotiations over money and property are characterized as discretionary and flexible, and judges tend to say that individual circumstances vary too much for any formula to be applied. The disadvantages of the legal system, as recently analysed in *Simple Quarrels*,[2] are the uncertainty, expense and intrusiveness of investigation. The system is characterized, say the authors, by settlement and delay, whereas women, in particular, need a speedy order; men may well prefer delay, since they are likely to be the losers. By contrast, the CSA operates by a rigid formula.

The Act was preceded by a White Paper, *Children Come First* – a prophetic title.[3] Under the legislation, the operation of the new system starts with parents receiving state benefit, who are now compelled to make application under the Act. There are penalties on parents who do not comply with the request to disclose information. Inspectors have power to enter premises, to obtain information and access to records. The priority for the CSA is to recover funds, for the benefit of the taxpayer who is already paying for the support of the priority applicants. It was planned that, from 1997, collection of maintenance by the CSA would benefit all classes of applications, so that some families might actually receive more cash in hand. At present, however, most children subject to the Agency's formula will not see any extra cash because the state benefit that they receive will not increase; the state merely recovers money already paid out.

The CSA enforces its orders by garnishee, distress and committal. It is modelled largely on the Australian Child Support (Assessment) Act 1989. An important difference is that the latter legislation takes account of clean-break agreements already reached by the divorcing couple, whereas the English version has not done so, as will be seen. During the passage of the Act, much was made of the fact that unwilling mothers might be forced to name the fathers of their children and that they would be punished by reduction of benefits if they unreasonably refused to name him. In fact, according to evidence given to the House of Commons, only 22 mothers have so far unreasonably refused to name the father. However, once the Agency started to operate in April 1993, the main concerns changed; they began to relate to the formula used, its treatment of existing clean-break settlements, the costs of the father's travel to work and his visits to his children, debts resulting from the divorce or separation and the new costs assumed by the father in relation to his stepchildren. Rarely has the aftermath of a piece of legislation been so much at variance with the predictions.

The Matrimonial Causes Act 1973, s.25 (1), provided that, in ancillary relief, first consideration should be given to the needs of children, and this principle has been growing in importance over the last 20 years, culminating in the force of the CSA. Despite the provisions of the Matrimonial Causes Act, it had become clear that the levels of maintenance awarded to children were unduly low, and enforcement against absent fathers was too weak. At the same time, the importance attached to the maintenance of a spouse has diminished. The effect of the Child Support Act is that the court no longer controls the totality of ancillary relief because a significant part of it is beyond its control and is to be calculated by the Agency. At the time of writing, it seemed that the CSA assessment predominated by seizing the major part of the father's available income, leaving the court free, if involved at all, to order only a very small amount in most cases for the wife; the court's order took second place in size and importance to the CSA assessment.

Much of the criticism directed at the CSA has been misconceived: it never was the intention that the mother should receive extra cash, rather the primary objective was to relieve the taxpayer. Thus, quite logically, the CSA has given priority to cases in which the mother is in receipt of income support and where the father is known and already paying something towards maintenance. These priorities ensure the CSA an early success record. Its other successes have been obscured, but are undoubted: mothers, as well as fathers, will know the likely result of an assessment; similar cases will receive similar treatment; divorce bargaining can take place in the knowledge of the likely CSA assessment; the sums assessed can be uprated for inflation, and there should be prompt enforcement. Fewer than one in three single mothers received any maintenance at all for their children before the CSA came into existence, and this rate is bound to be improved. The Act may also have the effect of causing fewer fathers to lose contact with their children, even if the only reason is that he is being made to pay for them. The assessment will be a reminder to him of their existence and their needs and, it is to be hoped, this recognition will spread from financial support to involvement, where appropriate.

Rarely, however, has there been seen such a passionate, hate-filled and successful campaign against a piece of legislation. It brought to mind, in its intensity and breadth, the campaign against the poll tax, and it has been said that the CSA may become the domestic equivalent of the poll tax in its ability to make a government unpopular unless abolished or reformed. The same men, it seems, who campaign against the system of maintenance for ex-wives, have led the campaign against the Child Support Agency, even though it has a very different principle at its foundation. In this instance men have been far more successful, and this is puzzling. It would appear more logical and harmless to end maintenance to an ex-wife than to free men from responsibility for their children, yet the latter demand has caught the public imagination, with a great deal of unrestrained illustrated help from the press which has uniformly taken the side of the absent fathers in its coverage. The theme has chimed with attacks on the government's 'back to basics' policy. The grievances of the absent father have nearly always been presented as legitimate in the press, and the CSA assessment as inaccurate or too high, allegedly leading to the ruin of the absent father. On Valentine's Day 1994, assessed fathers with their second wives and children paraded through the streets of London, demonstrating against the effects of the Act. Virtually all absent fathers have been portrayed by the press as innocent victims. Their cause has been particularly articulately presented by the middle class, which has pointed out that, while (allegedly) feckless young men fathering children haphazardly on council estates were intended to be the target, the more responsible fathers, who were already paying something, have also been assessed.

After only eight months of operation, the House of Commons Social Security Committee investigated the working of the CSA, looking at complaints of excessive demands in disregard of settlements reached years earlier, intrusion by the Agency, and the (quite accurate) impression given that money was being saved for the government, not given to mothers. The operation of the Act had brought hate mail and death threats to the Agency offices; six suicides of absent fathers were alleged to be related to claims; 1000 men were disputing paternity by submitting to DNA tests, the costs of which have had to be reduced by the CSA; 11 000 single parents allegedly stopped claiming income support in order to avoid contact with fathers; and some men were even said to have sought artificial divorces in order to reduce the assessment. The formula was said to be unfair to second families. The Act was even labelled an affront to civil liberties in its procedure and by virtue of the fact that major details were left to delegated legislation and to Child Support Officers. The voice of the single mother, for whose sake this was partly undertaken, was not heard. This may be because she stands to gain very little personally from the Agency, but it is alarming that the fruits of many decades of research into the financial plight of the single mother and her child have been largely swept away by the recent protests of the absent fathers and their second families.

In October 1994 the Social Security Select Committee of the House of Commons reported that the National Audit Office had found that more than half of the CSA assessments had been found to be wrong. The critics placed greater emphasis on the cases of disputed paternity and inaccurate assessment than on the guiding principles of the Act – namely, relief of the taxpayer and the assumption of responsibility by absent fathers. The complaints had some basis in that there is no legal aid for appeals to tribunals against the assessments, and thus the frustration is likely to endure. The attacks on the Act focused on the Chief Executive of the Agency who resigned in the autumn of 1994.

The disruption centring on the Act may be the price that is paid for a high divorce rate amongst persons without sufficient private income to keep both a first and second family. It is also an illustration of contemporary uncertainty concerning the nature of fatherhood and men's responsibility and commitment to women and children. Many men feel aggrieved at being called on only to pay for their children without guaranteed access or, as they see it, equality in claims for residence orders, and they may also resent financially supporting the child's mother. This is a most surprising outcome, since the gestation period of the CSA was lengthy and extremely well researched and, at the time, there was no disputing the need to reassert fathers' responsibility and relieve the taxpayer. The Act remains a lesson in the fragmentation of family law adjudication.

A typical divorce case will now involve a property resolution, in or out of court, adjudicated maintenance for the wife and a separate CSA assessment. Different factors apply to each decision. The Child Support Act ends any choice of jurisdiction for the parent receiving state benefits and becomes the only avenue for child support, while those who are not state-supported still have a choice, although this may not last for much longer. A variety of factors and philosophies affects the different assessments: for example, all the factors listed in the Matrimonial Causes Act, s.25, may be taken into account in adjudication, but hardly any of them apply to the Agency assessment. When the Child Support Act was enacted the obvious question seemed to be, why can this not also apply to spousal maintenance? It ought to be easy and logical to extend the Act to spousal maintenance if its present unpopularity and problems of detail can be sorted out. However, it is quite likely to be argued that the unpopularity of administrative assessment, the lack of provision for appeals and the lack of fine-tuning have demonstrated conclusively that spousal maintenance must remain a matter of private law. This remains to be seen, but there is no denying that the current parallel application of administrative and private assessment is awkward.

THE CLEAN BREAK

The clash between the two systems is most clearly illustrated in the problems relating to the clean break. It seems that the Child Support Act has put an end to the desirability of the clean break (for example, the outright transfer of the matrimonial home to the wife), because a clean break settlement will not reduce the man's liability under the Child Support Act. This must mean that lawyers will advise ex-husbands to press for the sale of the former matrimonial home and the removal of their share of the capital, or some other more favourable and more liquid result, such as the immediate sale of the home or a *Mesher* order.[4] There is no longer any financial sense in trading off house transfer against nominal child maintenance orders. Nor is there any inducement to an ex-husband to pay the mother sufficient to enable her to manage mortgage instalments, because he still remains open to the full Child Support Act assessment. At the very moment when divorce could be said to have become 'non-interventionist', in line with the philosophy of the Children Act 1989, the Child Support Act has introduced methods that are highly directional and which ignore the independence of the spouses so carefully fostered by other recent Acts.

The leading case on clean break and the CSA is *Crozier* v. *Crozier*.[5] In this case the husband had transferred to the wife his half share in the matrimonial home; child maintenance had been deliberately excluded in the Registrar's order. A few years later the CSA ordered the husband to pay £29 per week for the child. The husband applied for leave to appeal against the clean-break consent order out of time. His argument was that he was being made to pay twice over because, in his view, the transfer of his half share in the home was to meet the obligations of child maintenance. The wife contended that she could come off state support if she could invest and keep the entire proceeds of the sale price of the home. Booth J noted that a consent order could only be set aside where there were new events that invalidated the basis on which the order was made. She held that the clean break governed the spouses but that, in relation to child maintenance, there was an ongoing parental responsibility to which the clean-break doctrine never applied. Although the parties to the clean-break order did not anticipate state intervention in the form of the CSA, the fact that Parliament had chosen a new administrative method by which the state could intervene to compel a parent to contribute to the maintenance of a child did not fundamentally alter the position as it stood at the date of the clean-break order, and the state was never bound by the agreement between parents. No new event had thus arisen, the only difference being that the parental continuing liability would be enforced by the Agency. This did not undermine the clean-break order, and the husband was refused leave to appeal.

Logical though this judgement is, it serves to remove any motivation on the part of the divorcing husband to reach a settlement of this sort with his wife, because he will know that, regardless of the value of the matrimonial home transfer, he will always remain liable to the CSA assessment.

The clean break has also been made less attractive by the judgement in *Richardson* v. *Richardson*[6] where it was held that, when an order for a prospective clean break is made – for example, that maintenance is to end at a certain future date – that date can be postponed unless the court made a specific order that it cannot be postponed under s.28(1A) of the Matrimonial Causes Act.

The ignoring of clean-break settlements by the CSA has been one of the most contentious points of dispute. This further illustrates how the existence of the CSA illumines contrasting principles in English law: on the one hand, the clean break as an appropriate order between adult parties, and on the other, priority for the financial interests of children and the relief of the taxpayer. As a result of the decision in *Crozier* it is likely that many fathers will apply to have existing child court maintenance orders revoked. It should be noted, too, that an ex-wife will receive some maintenance for herself as part of a CSA assessment, as up to £44 per week may be awarded for the carer. It is possible that the *Mesher* order may revive in popularity.

Initially, the House of Commons Social Security Committee suggested that, in a reform of the CSA, some account should be taken by the CSA of capital settlements made in divorce in lieu of child maintenance. However, the logic lies with *Crozier* for the following reasons:

1 a clean-break settlement cannot sensibly affect a CSA assessment, because the property transfer was between the husband and wife only and not expressly for the benefit of the children;
2 it would be difficult to calculate the notional income transferred to the wife along with the home;

3 the CSA allows the absent father to keep more of his income to reflect his new higher rehousing costs, where the house has been transferred to the mother;
4 the caring mother who has occupation nevertheless may have to assume mortgage debts as well, so that the transfer does not represent additional free income to her.

If the absent father had paid adequate child support in the intervening years between the house transfer and the CSA assessment, he might well have paid over more in maintenance than he lost in the value of his equity in the former matrimonial home. Nevertheless, the most recent reports are that the government has agreed to reform the CSA to enable assessment to take account of clean-break settlements made before 1993.

It is also likely that there will be reforms allowing the father's travel-to-work costs to be taken into account, and the CSA's plans to reassess absent fathers where the mother is not on social security from 1996 have been postponed. There are still no plans to allow appeals against assessment. Other reforms made are that the protected income of the second family has been raised from £8 to £30 per week, and a lower proportion of the father's assessable income is to be taken. The increased payments are being phased in. In late 1994 the Social Security Select Committee of the House of Commons recommended a simpler formula, taking more account of the father's ability to pay and allowing parents to keep a percentage of the maintenance recovered on top of state benefits. The recommended reforms, if implemented, go some way towards undermining the great plan of saving taxpayers' money and also represent a swing back in preference towards discretion and adjudication. In other words, the scheme to take the heat and expense out of maintenance orders by administrative settlements has been tried and has apparently failed.[7]

SPOUSAL MAINTENANCE

It seems clearer than ever that the system of private maintenance is insufficient in many ways. The divorce rate is higher amongst poorer and unemployed husbands. According to Haskey,[8] in 1984, 16 per cent of divorcing husbands had been previously divorced and had no money. Courts are now tending to allow the husband to maintain his present family rather than the discarded one, in direct contrast to the CSA's priority for the needs of the children from the first family over the support of the second wife and the stepchildren.

As we approach the twenty-first century there is still no agreed philosophy, role or justification of spousal maintenance. There are no social plans to help the single mother become self-sufficient. No further government assistance has been granted towards the building and financing of nurseries or to assist mothers in meeting the expense of other forms of child care. If men are unwilling, as demonstrated above, to spend a great deal of money on the maintenance of their children, how much less likely are they to want to spend on their ex-spouses? Davis *et al.*'s study, *Simple Quarrels*,[9] demonstrates that the parties' sense of justice and equality is totally ignored by settlements arrived at by courts and solicitors, even though the CSA method is equally as unpopular. Women sometimes receive more in maintenance than they think they should and the wish of the parties to bring in conduct as an issue in the size of assessment is ignored. Thus, many orders leave the parties with a lingering sense of injustice.

Again, in contrast to the CSA philosophy, lawyers and judges appear to conspire to manipulate legal orders in order to extract the most from the state by way of legal aid, income support, tax relief and council housing. We have not decided, as a nation, whether the care of the ex-wife is properly the responsibility of the ex-husband or of the state.

As described some time ago,[10] the maintenance system has fallen apart into three kinds of cases. The rich have a law unto themselves, vividly described by Mr Justice Wilson (a former QC with extensive experience in such cases) in his article 'Conduct of the big money case'.[11] Second, there is the middle range, the clean-break cases, now undermined by the CSA and the recession as it affects matrimonial homes, possibly with negative equity. Third and finally there are the social security cases, touched neither by adjudication nor by the CSA. The CSA has power under the Act to collect other forms of maintenance – for example, spousal maintenance – but this section is not yet in force and it seems unlikely that it ever will be, given the history of the CSA so far. Increasing numbers of cases[12] demonstrate that more of a man's assets are being used to pay for the child, leaving little for the wife. Incidentally, as 30 per cent of young people now proceed to higher education, their need for parental maintenance continues far longer due to the low levels of student grants, yet the support available through the CSA ends at age 18.

In *Mawson* v. *Mawson* the husband was assessed by the CSA to pay £569 per month – a sum greater than a court would normally order for a child. The matrimonial home was transferred to the wife, and the district judge ordered that as long as the husband paid the wife the CSA-assessed amount of £569 for the child he should pay the wife only £150 per month for herself. The wife appealed, seeking higher periodical payments for herself. Her appeal was dismissed with the comment that, even if the husband's income was set to decrease and the CSA assessment would likewise decrease, the CSA assessment would always determine the amount available for the spouse.

It would be understandable if, in an era of high unemployment and recession, the principal claim on a man's income was to be his children. That is contested, given the public attitude towards the CSA; yet, at the same time, there is no more desire or ability to pay high levels of spousal maintenance. Gradually the whole concept of maintenance of a family is fading and, despite the best efforts of the government, the first family is left, in a majority of cases, as a charge on the state.

PENSIONS

Recent developments in pension-splitting and property also illustrate the sensitivity of private law to the recession and the fall in house prices. Where once the matrimonial home was a valuable asset to be fought over, it may now represent a debt and a negative equity. Where once a husband's income could be counted on, unemployment has undermined this security for a wife. We appear to be in a situation where neither the administrative ordering of the CSA nor the private ordering of the court are popular or reliable and, although many women are reluctant to hear it, the message is one of 'fend for yourself'. Although it is not obvious why it should be argued that a wife has any entitlement to the private pension arrangements of her ex-husband, it has now been held that pension funds count as variable property entitlements.[13] The modern wife, aware of the high divorce rate, is, or should be, encouraged to seek independence and equality and will usually be economically active. There is no disputing that she can simultaneously hold responsibility for relationships, children and a career, and can make her own pension arrangements. Not to make her own pension arrangements could even be seen as negligent, or at least short-sighted. The arguments are even stronger in the case of multiple divorces, where any splitting of the husband's pension results in a negligible amount for each wife and jeopardizes the rights of the husband's eventual widow.

In the *Brooks* case, upheld by the Court of Appeal,[14] it was held that the potential benefits given to the spouse of an employee under his pension scheme are capable of rendering the scheme a post-nuptial settlement which can be varied in ancillary relief proceedings, but not if third-party rights are to be affected. It could therefore be argued that, if the husband has already married his second wife and she has acquired pension expectations, her rights might amount to third-party rights that should not be adversely affected.

In May 1993 a report, *Pensions and Divorce*,[15] recommended that a new 'pensions adjustment order' against pension schemes should be established. The report was submitted to the Pension Law Review Committee, which endorsed it. The *Brooks* case is perhaps rather narrow in view of this recommendation, because its finding depends on the terms of each particular pension arrangement and must not affect third parties. The judgement does not extend to ante-nuptial pensions, unless made in contemplation of marriage. In pension-splitting, the court will have regard to s.25 factors under the Matrimonial Causes Act, so it would be harder for young wives to win a rearrangement. It is currently more usual to achieve pension compensation by way of a lump sum or property adjustment orders.

PROPERTY

Immediately prior to the passage of the Child Support Act property law on divorce had reached a fairly stable and agreed state. It had become typical that, in a middle-class to low-income case, the matrimonial home was transferred to the wife, the husband's obligation to the children was minimal and it was quite likely that there would be no spousal maintenance, the wife and children availing themselves of income support. As has been seen, spousal maintenance has been threatened by the Child Support Act, and it will now be seen that the basis of the property settlement has likewise been undermined, if not destroyed. It now seems that child support will increasingly be determined by the (reformed) CSA whilst spousal maintenance is likely to be payable only to the wives of middle-and upper-income men. If spousal maintenance were abolished completely (not an unrealistic proposal), it might remotivate ex-husbands to transfer the matrimonial home to the ex-wife as part of a divorce settlement, especially if in future the clean break is to be taken into account in assessments made under the Child Support Act. It is very hard to argue today that a man's money should be available for anything other than his children and their welfare.

At present, three property laws are being administered side by side. There is 'pure' property law, if it may be so termed, reflecting the separate property rights of married men and married women as developed since 1882. It has been alleged that this law, now rarely applied, takes no account of the equality of women, the incidence of divorce and other social factors. Second, there is this law as applied between cohabitants, where it is affected by developments in divorce and in trusts and licences law. Third, there is the law as applied under s.24 of the Matrimonial Causes Act 1973, the section under which it is most likely that the house will be transferred to the wife on divorce. So, in effect, property law, bankruptcy, intestacy and pensions are all treated separately and will have different effects on the one couple. Marriage, death, divorce, cohabitation, single parenthood and bankruptcy may all result in different allocations and divisions, occupation and liquidity of the matrimonial home.

English property legislation of 1882 and 1925 coped appropriately with such property ownership questions as arose at the time of divorce. There was no substantial difficulty because the divorce rate was low, matrimonial fault was a determining factor, and very few members of the public and the divorcing population owned property in the early twentieth century. It was not until after the Second World War that both rates – those of divorce and property ownership – rose in parallel, and this was coupled with a feeling that wives deserved some sort of economic equality. Although few wives were economically active at that time, the participation rate began to grow and, even for those who stayed at home, there developed a belief that they had 'earned' a share in any assets available for distribution on divorce. Moreover, fewer judges were prepared to accept that there was unequivocal guilt and innocence on divorce such as to deprive a wife of her share of maintenance. Yet, technically, for the 'guilty' wife, no maintenance was payable, and she might also find herself homeless contrary to all principles of justice and the paramountcy of the welfare of the children.

Lord Denning was among the first to use separate property law flexibly to provide for women's needs, as he saw them, for housing and a share in the equity. He was open in expressing his scepticism in regard to total guilt on one side and innocence on the other in divorce and custody matters, and he emphasized in his judgements women's financial contributions, their independent status and children's needs for housing.[16]

The developments launched by Lord Denning affected divorcing couples and the development of the law of licences, trusts and estoppel. Once provision had been made by the Matrimonial Proceedings and Property Act 1970 for allocation of matrimonial property on divorce without dependence on strict property law, the Denning branch of this area of the law became redundant; it ground to a halt, or would have done had it not been taken up by the new and growing ranks of cohabitants, and had it not also left its mark on the continuing development of the parallel areas of property law.

The property law of related persons is now stable, if very artificial. Resulting trusts and common intention are said to exist where an agreement of a sort can be found. Proprietary estoppel is increasingly used to fill in gaps where justice seems to demand that the couple share the property even though no agreement can be discovered, and also to bridge the gap between contractual licences and resulting trusts. So keen are judges to do justice in these situations that there is a certain one-sidedness to the law in favour of women,[17] and sharing is enforced in cases where it is clear, to the average reader, that the man, at least, never had any such intention.

In many cases control and occupation of the home are far more valuable than a share in the capital or in the paper title, because to realize the capital and share it often means the destruction of the prime asset itself and its sale in a difficult market. Protected occupation under the Matrimonial Homes Act or by virtue of 'occupation' as understood in land registration law and the 1925 legislation are nearly always more readily available to a needy spouse or cohabitant than a legal share. Thus status may still be of more significance than contract in property law. At the same time, judges are concerned to uphold the main pillars of the 1925 property legislation by protecting third parties without notice, and they have become adept at reconciling the claims of the innocent occupier and the equally innocent third-party purchaser. The cases of *Williams & Glyn's Bank* v. *Boland*[18] and *Lloyds Bank* v. *Rosset*[19] established a great deal of security for the sole occupier of property who has made a contribution. *City of London BS* v. *Flegg*[20] marked something of a retreat because, in that case, it was held that a mortgage that happened to be executed by two legal owners, instead of one, was indeed effective to overreach the occupier. In *Cann*[21] it was found that actual occupation only occurred after the execution of the mortgage so that the equitable charge of the occupier arose subsequent to the right of the lenders. This and the previous judgement removed some of the security, but the Law Commission has proposed in its report *Trusts of Land*[22] that beneficiaries who have an equitable interest should not be overreached without their consent.

The mortgage is still of supreme commercial importance and tends to prevail over other debts and the possible right of the wife to occupy the home.[23] Courts still try to protect wives against themselves by a generous interpretation of undue influence or pressure. While it would be inappropriate to refer to all wives as the objects of undue influence, the courts nevertheless take great pains to ensure that a woman who is cooperating with her partner in the use of her home as surety for a loan receives independent advice and knows what she is doing: otherwise she will not be bound. In *Barclays Bank* v. *O'Brien*[24] it was held that a cohabitant may be at risk of emotional exploitation and that the lender should be aware that a surety might be set aside if the woman has not had independent financial advice. In this case the husband had misrepresented the effect of documents to his wife who signed them without reading them or having them explained to her. Although it was held that there was no presumed undue influence arising from the mere relationship of husband and wife, the facts could raise the likelihood. Although taking separate advice is a sensible step, it may be expensive and the wife may feel, after having received it, under just as much emotional pressure to sign on the dotted line as she did previously.

The emphasis on mortgages may seem unrealistic in the light of the very high rates of mortgage failure and repossession prevailing today. To make matters worse, social security can no longer be relied on to take over mortgage interest payments where the mortgage-holder has lost his or her job: recent years have witnessed a considerable cut-back in state support of mortgage interest payments. This will make it more likely that, on divorce, couples will lose their homes and less likely that a wife will be able to buy out her husband with a second mortgage. The slump in house prices and the stagnant market have continued for several years and have caused the decline of the traditional device of relying on the sale of the home at a convenient moment during the separation and divorce in order to realize the capital. This is particularly unfortunate, given that the Child Support Act also undermines clean break. House ownership – for so long the jewel in the crown of ancillary relief – has been changing from an asset to a liability now that so many couples find that their divorce coincides with negative equity and insolvency. House ownership peaked at 68 per cent in 1988 and has declined since then. Regardless of the fine developments in the law, on the whole favouring the wife, her claims and all the artistry that has gone into framing them and affording them may yet turn out to be worthless.

At the time of writing, there is a potentially even greater threat – namely, the weakening of legal advice in a reformed divorce law and its replacement by mediation. In a system where mediation is widespread, it is quite likely that women will not be made aware of the strength of their claim to a transfer of the home or a share in its value, as they tend to believe that they can leave the marriage with only what is theirs in strict property terms. It is only by the intervention of lawyers that property claims have been realized and developed by wives in recent years. Developments in this field may well come to a halt if couples are forced to mediate in the aftermath of separation. Cohabiting women have equally benefited by judges' tendencies to favour them and to believe that there has been a partnership and trust in cohabitation, such that sharing is inevitable. However, given that the median length of cohabitation is two years, judges and commentators have formed an unduly rosy view of the nature of the relationship of the cohabiting couple. The better approach (if any such approach is needed) might be to open up the possibility of legislation for unmarried couples, in order to test public opinion on the matter.

The division in opinion concerning the justice of cohabitants' claims is reflected in some uncertainty over the shares awarded in the cases. In *Springette* v. *Defoe*[25] the shares were held to have depended on the contribution to the purchase price and not on an uncommunicated belief. It was held in that case that a transfer into joint names that was silent on the question of beneficial ownership raised no presumption of joint beneficial ownership. In *Risch* v. *McFee*[26] a loan by a woman to a man gave her an increased share in circumstances that might have had a different result had the genders been reversed. In *Savill* v. *Goodall*[27] an agreement to share half and half prevailed over actual contributions in the determining of the shares. Thus cohabitants, unlike married couples, may find that their legal expenses in carving up the home are overwhelmingly great because of the uncertainty. Despite the arguments for fine-tuning raised by the unhappiness surrounding the CSA it is still hard to see why there should not be equal division of assets, or some form of community property regime, on the ending of a marriage. If that is logical, then it cannot apply in the same amount to cohabitants whose commitment and length of relationship is likely to be less.

A survey of property and maintenance on divorce in ten years' time is likely to find that spousal maintenance has been abolished; that absent fathers are paying child maintenance collected through income tax or in some other relatively painless form; and that private agreements are being reached over matrimonial homes. Yet such a report is unlikely to find reduced rates of unhappiness, divorce and legal expense.

NOTES

1 1 December 1993, para. 3.
2 G. Davis, S. Cretney and J. Collins (1994), *Simple Quarrels*, Oxford: Clarendon Press.
3 (1990) Cmnd. 1264.
4 [1980] 1 AER 126.
5 [1994] Fam. 114.
6 [1994] 1 WLR 186.
7 The Child Support Act 1995 introduced an element of discretion into the assessment of support. Child support appeal tribunals may make allowances for travel-to-work and other expenses, and for clean-break orders made before 5 April 1993.
8 J. Haskey (1984) 'Social class and socio-economic differentials in divorce', *Population Studies*, **38**, p. 419.
9 *Op. cit.*, note 3 above.
10 R. Deech (1982), 'Financial relief: the retreat from precedent and principle', *Law Quarterly Review*, **98**, p. 621.
11 Wilson, J. (1994), 'Conduct of the big money case', *Family Law*, **24**, p. 504.
12 For example *Mawson* v. *Mawson* [1994] 2 FLR 852 (Fam. D).
13 *Brooks* v. *Brooks* [1993] Fam. 322. [On which see, more fully, Masson, p. 113.]
14 [1994] 2 FLR 10.
15 Working Group of the Pensions Management Institute (1993), *Pensions and Divorce*; see now the Pensions Act 1995.
16 For an account of the process, see Lord Denning (1980), *The Due Process of Law*, London: Butterworths, parts 6, 7, 8.
17 *Pascoe* v. *Turner* [1979] 2 All ER 545; *Thomas* v. *Fuller-Brown* [1988] 1 FLR 237; S. Gardner (1993), 'Rethinking family property', *Law Quarterly Review*, **109**, p. 26.
18 [1981] AC 487.
19 [1991] 1 AC 107.
20 [1988] AC 54.
21 [1991] 1 AC 56.
22 Law Commission (1989), *Trusts of Land*, Law Com. no. 188, London: HMSO.

23 *Shipton BS* v. *Clayton* (1993) 66 P & CR 223; *Bristol & West BS* v. *Henning* [1985] 1 WLR 778; *Equity & Law Home Loans* v. *Prestidge* [1992] 1 WLR 137; *Paddington BS* v. *Mendelsohn* (1985) 50 P & CR 244.
24 [1994] 1 AC 180.
25 [1992] 2 FLR 388.
26 [1991] 1 FLR 105.
27 [1993] 1 FLR 755.

6 Right to Divorce and Pension Rights

*Judith Masson**

INTRODUCTION

The current proposals for divorce reform[1] recognize that divorce is no longer a remedy for a person whose marriage partner has broken the marriage contract, but a right of every spouse. Anyone who is dissatisfied with their marriage will be able to end it by following the required procedures. Recognition of divorce as a right has occurred not because divorce is good but because it is thought necessary to support the institution of marriage – without divorce there can be no remarriage[2] – and because attempts to control divorce have been ineffective and restrictions on it are no longer publicly acceptable. As a right, divorce should be equally available to all spouses. The law

> ...should not explicitly or implicitly, favour one of the spouses at the expense of the other simply because that spouse is husband or wife or male or female or chooses a particular role within the marriage.[3]

Neutrality between husbands and wives and between applicants and non-applicants is essential if divorce is not to penalize some who (or whose partners) wish to use it. A divorce law which is not neutral cannot support the institution of marriage, only the marriages of those who can divorce without adverse effects and of those who are ignorant of the pitfalls divorce may bring. Neutrality requires the continued enforcement of obligations created by the relationship, such as the care and support of children and the fair sharing of assets acquired through it. Where the spouses have taken decisions which lead to one becoming financially dependent on the other,

* Professor of Law, University of Warwick.

neutrality requires payment, either to maintain the dependent spouse or enable him or her to become self-sufficient once more.

WOMEN, WORK AND PENSIONS

Periods of dependence of one spouse on the other are a normal consequence of marriage in the UK. Although formal bars to married women working and beliefs that husbands should be providers and wives homemakers have been swept away, wives are less likely than their husbands to be economically active and more likely to arrange their employment to fit with domestic responsibilities. Martin and Roberts' study showed that women were economically active for only 65 per cent of their working lives.[4] That women's more limited participation in the labour market relates to marriage is clear from Gregory and Foster's study of the consequences of divorce. They found that, whereas 98 per cent of husbands were economically active at separation, this was true for only 62 per cent of wives; only 21 per cent of wives had worked full-time continually throughout their marriage compared with 70 per cent of husbands.[5] Twenty-five per cent of divorcing women had not worked during marriage; women with children under the age of 5 years were less likely to work.[6] Full-time work declined with family size so that 54 per cent of those with three or more dependent children had not worked full-time during marriage.[7] Part-time work was common amongst divorcing women; a third had never worked full-time, but only a minority of those with children under 5 or with more than three dependent children worked outside the home.[8] Although the ages and number of children have a demonstrable effect on women's employment, women without dependent children were less likely to be working than their husbands: 9 per cent had not worked during their marriage and a third had worked full-time for less than half their marriage.[9] The effect of spending periods outside the labour market continues after divorce; only 21 per cent of those who never worked during marriage were economically active three months after divorce and, of these, 4 per cent were unemployed.[10]

These working patterns have a marked impact on women's pensions. The state pension schemes (both the basic state pension and SERPS) take account of periods caring for children or invalids by providing Home Responsibilities Credits which reduce the number of years for which contributions must be made, but these pensions are low.[11] More valuable occupational pensions usually require contributions throughout a working life of 40 years for a full pension:[12] 10.7 million workers – 48 per cent of the working population – are members of occupational pensions schemes, but only 37 per cent of women workers are scheme members.[13] Women are less likely to be scheme members because of the types of work they do[14] and the fact that they work part-time. Only 16 per cent of part-time workers belong to pension schemes,[15] and many schemes are not open to part-time workers.[16] Women scheme members have lower pensions because their broken employment histories reduce their final salaries and the length of their scheme membership.[17] Those who do not have access to occupational pensions have been permitted (and encouraged) to take out private pensions since 1986.[18] The size of these pensions depends on the amount contributed, the administration costs and the performance of the investments bought. Women's lower earnings mean that they can[19] (and can afford to) contribute relatively little to a private pension. Charges may take up between 10 and 20 per cent of contributions[20] leaving comparatively little for investments. Taken together these factors mean that twice as many women as men – approximately two-thirds of the female population – will have an income below poverty level for their retirement.[21]

Where couples remain married the wife is protected from her pension poverty by partial dependence on the husband's pension. She will be able to enjoy a standard of living supported by the benefits earned through his contributions and employment. In the event of his death, in most cases, she will continue to receive income in the form of a widow's pension[22] which is usually half the retirement pension. If the couple divorces the former wife may obtain a maintenance order which can be paid from the husband's earnings or pension, but emphasis on making a 'clean break' means that few women do so.[23] If she does not, she may have no access to the benefits derived from contributions made during the marriage. Also, she will no longer be able to become the husband's widow and will thus lose the main avenue[24] for protecting her dependency in the event of his death. If divorce neutrality is to be achieved, systems must be developed which enable former wives to achieve an adequate pension.

Although it is more common for wives to be dependent on their husbands, there are families where roles are reversed. Since 1989 occupational pension schemes have been required to provide widower's pensions but only for service from 1988[25] and they cannot provide higher pensions to members because of their sex.[26] Consequently, the rights and remedies claimed for wives in order to achieve divorce neutrality should be available to husbands in appropriate cases.

Pensions have to be paid for. Current provision in the UK depends on a mix of employer's and employee's contributions and government subsidy derived from national insurance contributions and general taxation. Improving pensions for women requires increased contributions from them, their employers or from the government. Women's earnings make it difficult to make greater contributions and employers cannot provide better pensions for women than for men (or vice versa),[27] but there is room for improving women's pay and access to pensions during employment. The government's reluctance to increase taxation or national insurance to improve pensions is clear.[28] Indeed, the belated equalization of state pension ages at 65 has been devised to remove 'the last glaring inequality in our treatment of men and women'[29] and to cut costs.[30] It will lead to a substantial reduction in the size of the state pension for women who work beyond the age of 60 because they will no longer obtain enhanced pensions. They will, however, be able to claim Home Responsibilities Credits for three more years and count Family Credit or Disabled Working Allowance for the purpose of their SERPS pension.[31] Although there appears to be little scope for improving women's pensions without changes to their working lives, divorced women can be given better access to pensions earned by their husbands.

PENSIONS AFTER DIVORCE IN THE LATE 1990S

Twenty-five years of reports[32] have produced no agreement in the UK about the need for a system of compensating loss of pension rights or about the best method of making provision for this.[33] Although it seems likely that the most cost-effective solution would be to increase the basic state pension,[34] in the present political and economic climate this is also the least likely option. Whilst divorce legislation for England and Wales allows[35] and that for Scotland requires,[36] consideration of loss of pension when a court assesses maintenance or the reallocation of property, assets within pension schemes remain inviolate even against court orders. Moreover, it is a condition of the pension scheme's favourable tax treatment that pensions should remain inalienable.[37] Those dependent on their spouse's pension can only seek to avoid divorce, rely on the goodwill of their former spouse to make provision[38] or use the limited power of the divorce courts to obtain compensation from other assets.

In theory no one who has not committed a 'matrimonial offence'[39] can be divorced against their will if divorce would cause them 'grave financial or other hardship'.[40] In practice the courts have been reluctant to find that hardship, which will be compensated by means-tested, subsistence level state benefits, is sufficiently grave to justify continuing a marriage where a divorce petition has been filed relying on five years separation.[41] The refusal of divorce in such circumstances is seen as undermining the basic policy of enabling the empty legal shell of marriage to be destroyed and wasting resources by allowing a divorce application to be defended.[42] But women who are divorced and left pensionless after a long marriage consider themselves to have been doubly betrayed,[43] both by their former spouses and by the legal system which considers their hardship to be acceptable, or adequately compensated despite loss of pension rights.

Indifference to pension matters and ignorance of the details of employers' pension schemes is widespread.[44] Until the late 1980s many women and their solicitors seem to have been unaware of the impact divorce would have on their retirement income.[45] Divorce was most frequently linked to the loss of a widow's pension and seen as irrelevant to women intending to work full-time after divorce or expecting to remarry. The loss of access to other benefits such as the lump sum or secure income during the husband's retirement was largely ignored. Solicitors did not routinely seek to obtain a valuation of pension benefits;[46] thus, even where there were available assets, loss of pension was not effectively used as a bargaining counter.[47] Without access to the pension fund itself, the wife's loss of access to her husband's retirement pension and a widow's pension based on his contributions can only be compensated by giving a greater share of other assets from which she may make provision for her retirement by buying an annuity. The cost of annuities is high and increases as retirement draws near. This method of pension replacement is most successful if it occurs at a young age, but younger wives are less likely to be awarded a lump sum or to be able to raise capital from the former matrimonial home.[48]

In the OPCS study of the financial consequences of divorce only 5 per cent of wives obtained lump sum awards; lumps sums were more common for those with the longest marriages: 10 per cent of those married more than 25 years obtained them. Awards were low with only 1 per cent exceeding £25 000.[49] Unequal sharing of assets was unusual with two-thirds of couples taking approximately equal shares.[50] But in the minority of cases where the matrimonial home was sold, the wife took the larger share of the equity.[51] Nevertheless, the sums were small. In the majority of cases the available assets gave little scope for providing for the wife's future retirement. Where the wife obtained the larger share this was probably not intended to compensate for loss of pension. Rather, it reflected either greater needs resulting from day-to-day responsibility for the children, or the payment of capital in lieu of child maintenance.[52]

Even where the husband is willing to make provision or the court recognizes the need to do so, lack of access to the fund itself usually prevents the wife from being adequately compensated. Where a pension is already being paid it is not possible to divide the fund if the scheme has bought out its liabilities to the pensioner by purchasing an annuity. This would not prevent the pension itself being divided and a portion of it diverted to the member's former spouse. However, in the UK and in other jurisdictions which have not legislated for pension adjustment, this method cannot be used, and a maintenance order must be obtained against the pensioner because pensions trusts include a 'spendthrift clause' which prevents payment to anyone other than the scheme member.[53] Similarly, if the former husband fails to comply with a maintenance order, enforcement problems cannot be solved by an attachment order against the pension.

Requiring compensation for loss of pension without recourse to the pension fund can also be unfair on the payer. It has an adverse effect on his financial position immediately following the divorce leaving him pension-rich but poor in other respects. The spendthrift clause prevents him redressing this imbalance and releasing capital for the deposit on a house.

Where a divorcing couple are nearing retirement age it is sometimes possible to delay proceedings so that pensions are payable by the time the court considers the matter.[54] Deferment of the decision on pensions until the pension has become payable provided the basis for compensation in a number of jurisdictions before the development of sophisticated and flexible mechanisms for pension adjustment.[55] Deferment avoids the need to value the pension rights but creates other difficulties; in particular it fits poorly with the clean break. Neither party can be clear how they stand at the time of divorce and are thus in a poor position to make arrangements for their own retirement. Unless prevented from doing so, the payer spouse may make arrangements which adversely affect the former spouse – for example, by taking early retirement on a reduced pension or opting for better future benefits for a widow or widower. The task of the court is also more complex if it has to consider the extent to which the parties' current financial position results from their marriage. A wife's low pension may reflect the fact that she spent years caring for the children, but her pension might have been higher had she sought promotion, been prepared to move elsewhere for work or not belonged to a scheme which became insolvent and so on.

The court may be willing to include the future lump sum in the husband's available resources[56] in cases where the benefits provided under a pension scheme include a lump sum as is common in occupation schemes.[57] However, unless the application is adjourned until the pension lump sum is received or the court defers payment until the husband's retirement date, it will still be necessary for the husband to have other assets which he can use to satisfy the award. Where the lump sum is only available if the husband commutes some of his pension the court has no power to order him to take this step but could make an order which effectively forces him to do so.[58] These approaches may only be considered appropriate where the divorce occurs shortly before retirement.[59] They also can only provide a partial solution. Maintenance will normally cease on the husband's death; the lump sum may not be sufficient to provide a substantial pension,[60] but may provide some protection for the ex-wife against loss of support if the ex-husband dies before her.

A new approach to the pensions and divorce problem has recently been suggested. In *Brooks* v. *Brooks*,[61] District Judge Plumstead was persuaded to make an order varying the husband's pension trust on the basis that it was a post-nuptial settlement and variable under Matrimonial Causes Act 1973, s.24(1)(c). The decision was upheld by Ewbank J and a majority of the Court of Appeal[62] and now also by the House of Lords.

Mr Brooks, aged 64, was the sole shareholder of a building firm, D.E. Brooks Ltd. The company had ceased trading and owed £100 000 to Lloyds Bank, but provision had been made for a pension for Mr Brooks via the purchase of retirement annuities. The current value of these policies, £440 000, far exceeded the cost of providing the maximum pension which Mr Brooks could obtain under the Inland Revenue rules. The surplus would normally be repaid to the company and be accessible, after taxation at 40 per cent, to its creditors and to Mr Brooks. However, D.E. Brooks Ltd had ceased to exist, and an application to restore it to the register of companies would have been required before any money could have been repaid to it. Mr and Mrs Brooks had been married for 13 years, Mrs Brooks did not work (by her husband's wish) but was paid a salary by the company for nominal services. She was not a member of the company pension scheme although, had she been, her employment would have permitted the scheme to provide her with a small pension and lump sum. There were ample funds to make such provision from the pension scheme although, at the time of divorce, Mr Brooks apparently preferred repayment of the scheme surplus to the Inland Revenue[63] to a pension for his former wife. The court ordered a variation of the pension scheme trust to pay Mrs Brooks, from the scheme surplus, the maximum pension she could receive by virtue of her employment. This gave her an immediate pension of £2618 per annum, compared with £23 000 for Mr Brooks.

The decision in *Brooks* v. *Brooks* provided a creative solution which compensated the wife to an extent which would not have been possible without access to the pension fund. However, it will not provide a precedent for any but a tiny minority of cases. Even if every pension arrangement which potentially includes widow's or widower's benefits[64] could be construed as an ante-nuptial or post-nuptial settlement, as the wide interpretation by Ewbank J and the majority of the Court of Appeal suggests,[65] without legislation, the variation of a scheme to provide benefits for a former spouse would generally breach the scheme rules and Inland Revenue requirements. A scheme which provided such benefits for former spouses would not be able to continue to enjoy the advantageous tax regime open to other contracted-out schemes. Also, had the scheme not been in surplus, any variation of it would have required a reduction of Mr Brooks' benefit and breach the spendthrift clause in the trust. The arrangement was only possible in *Brooks* because the wife was an employee of the company, the scheme was in surplus and the Inland Revenue was willing to allow payment to her as if she had belonged to the scheme.

The decision to treat the scheme rather than the husband's rights as a scheme member, as a post-nuptial settlement was purely pragmatic and without principle. It enabled the wife to be compensated but the husband to retain his pension benefits intact. The share of the pension scheme allocated for the wife was not calculated by reference to the considerations in the Matrimonial Causes Act 1973, s.25 but using the rules for maximum benefit set out in the Finance Act 1970 and IR 12. In effect the wife's compensation was provided with 'someone else's money'.[66] Nevertheless the decision in *Brooks* is important because it clearly identifies the statutory changes necessary to enable pension adjustment to occur where the pension is not yet in payment. Legislation must operate on scheme rules to permit transfer of benefits in favour of someone who is not a member nor a dependent of a member; to allow charging, alienation and surrender of pension rights when required by a court order;[67] and the Inland Revenue rules must be amended so that compliance with a matrimonial order does not jeopardize the status of the scheme. Comparable changes would also be necessary to allow the transfer of private pensions irrespective of the terms of the contract.

All the methods of providing compensation for loss of pension, except that adopted in *Brooks,* fail to ensure that the recipient uses the assets transferred for her retirement. If she fails to do so she will become (more) dependent on state benefits. Thus the consequences of the lack of a system for sharing the pension fall primarily on the former spouse, but also on all taxpayers.

REFORM

Despite the recognition that pension rights are, for many peoples, the most valuable rights they will ever have,[68] that security in old age is crucial and that the UK divorce and pensions laws have failed to provide a system capable of compensating most spouses who suffer pension loss through divorce,[69] there is still considerable reluctance to solve this pensions problem. The Goode Committee on Pensions Law Reform broadly interpreted its terms of reference[70] and considered the topic of pensions and divorce but preferred to leave detailed consideration of the issue to a working party set up jointly by the Law Society and the Pensions Management Institute (PMI).[71] Members of this working party gave evidence to the Goode Committee and provided it with an early copy of the report. The Goode Committee endorsed the thrust of the working party's recommendations,[72] although their support was undermined by their acceptance of Treasury figures that pension-splitting would lead to a £500 million cash outgo from unfunded public sector schemes and their call for further detailed work on the subject. Peter Lilley, the Secretary of State for Social Security, undermined the case for reform further and ignored the work of the PMI in his statement to Parliament on the government's response to the Goode Committee. He announced a further major study on the effects of divorce on pensions to be completed by October 1995 and stated that 'it was far from clear that the problem is as large or the solution as simple as some have suggested'.[73] Considering the number of previous studies this looks conspicuously like a delaying tactic. It is clear that pension loss on divorce needs to be addressed even if only a minority of people are adversely affected by it. Knowing the size of the problem may help to design a workable system, but the solution must fit with the divorce process and be capable of applying to thousands of cases each year.

Government stonewalling has not succeeded. The introduction of the Pensions Bill to enact the Goode proposals, the equalization of pension ages and other changes has provided an opportunity for reform. A pressure group, Fairshares, lobbied for amendments to the Bill to require the courts to consider pension loss in all cases on divorce and enable regulations to be made which would permit reallocation of pension rights.[74] At the committee stage, Baroness Seear and Lord Meston also tabled amendments empowering the courts to adjust pension rights regardless of scheme rules.[75] The Minister for Social Security appeared uneasy about any change, particularly about giving the divorce court discretion over pension rights. Although he recognized that there were some difficult cases, he did not seem to view marriage as a partnership where decisions about lifestyle, having children and employment necessarily affect both spouses, preferring to see it as a relationship where each party makes career decisions which 'ought not to impinge on the other person's rights'.[76] Baroness Young's amendment received substantial and widespread support,[77] and this pressure seems to have forced a change in government policy. The minister finally acknowledged that there was a very real problem and announced that the government would consider amending the Matrimonial Causes Act 1973 to require the courts to place greater emphasis on pension rights.[78] It seems likely that government proposals will not provide for pension-splitting and will only take the more limited approach of requiring compensation from other assets, as in Scotland, or allowing decisions about pensions to be deferred until retirement.[79] A bill to provide for pension-splitting in marriages lasting twenty years or more was twice introduced under the ten-minute rule during the winter of 1994–95,[80] indicating an alternative restrictive approach to in this problem.

CRITERIA FOR A NEW SYSTEM

Before any system is designed for adapting pension rights on divorce, three fundamental questions must be answered. First, what is the nature of pension rights? Should they be considered as the property of the scheme member or are they merely contingent expectations which only become the member's property when the pension vests or the member retires? In Australia, the courts have resisted the notion that prospective benefits are property within the Family Law Act 1975[81] but many other states, particularly those with community property regimes, have come to regard such benefits as property. In the Member States of the European Union this point must be regarded as settled by Article 119 of the Treaty of Rome. The European Court has accepted that both members'[82] and survivors'[83] benefits in an occupational pension scheme constitute pay within Article 119. If pension benefits constitute pay, it is only logical to regard them as property, albeit property which cannot be used until some future date. Treating pensions as the property of a scheme member is problematic if he or she has not yet earned the right to receive a pension. Most schemes require membership for a period before benefits are secure: in some schemes, pension rights do not vest for ten or even twenty years.[84] If a person changes employment before the pension has vested he or she may not be able to continue membership of the scheme and may obtain no pension for that service. In the UK, the rules for contracting out of the state earnings-related scheme require pensions to vest and benefits to be preserved for those who leave a scheme, after two years. Those who leave before their rights are vested may reclaim contributions but limited benefits, equivalent to those in the state scheme (the guaranteed minimum pension) must be provided. Where a pension has not vested, the rights are likely to be of such little value[85] that it may be just to ignore them[86] or be possible to compensate by adjusting other assets.

Even if it is accepted that the pension is property, not all of it may be treated as matrimonial property. Where a 'community of acquests' regime operates the court will only have power to divide assets acquired during the marriage. This is the position under Scottish law but not in England and Wales under the Matrimonial Causes Act 1973. If this approach is taken, where the couple were married for a relatively short period the pension benefits acquired will be comparatively small. But the birth of children may prevent one party from being financially independent and acquiring pension rights for a long period. Access to pension rights acquired before marriage or after divorce could allow a more appropriate level of compensation for the dependent spouse. However, if this is allowed it could have the effect of undermining the payer's ability to provide adequately for their own retirement or even, in cases of serial marriage, transferring benefits between people who were never married to each other.

Second, if fair adjustment is to be made for loss of pension, the pension must be valued. If the court has to exercise any discretion, it will also need to know about any other pension assets the parties have so that it can reach a conclusion which is fair between them. Pension schemes can be divided into two types: defined benefit schemes where the rights to be received are fixed, usually in terms of a proportion of final salary and related to the number of years of service; and defined contribution schemes where the investment rate is fixed but the final pension depends on the success of the investments purchased. Defined benefit schemes pose the most difficult valuation problems until both the final salary and the length of service are known. The problem of valuation is avoided if reallocation requires only the determination of the share of the final pension to be paid ('earmarking') or if decisions are deferred until shortly before the retirement, but both these methods conflict with the clean-break approach. For this reason the PMI working party rejected 'earmarking' as the principal method of pension compensation on divorce, limiting it to cases where pension-splitting was not possible.[87]

Pension rights have to be valued to ensure that the pension scheme can cover its liabilities and if those leaving schemes before retirement are permitted to transfer to other schemes. Valuations for these purposes require actuarial calculations; actuarial values vary widely according to the assumptions used and the basis on which the calculation is made. There are two alternatives, estimating the benefits likely to be received by the member and calculating the proportion of these which relates to the current period of employment (the past service reserve or retirement value) and calculating the value of the employer's and employee's contributions (the cash equivalent or termination value). The former method usually produces the higher value and may be more accurate 'if the world unfolds as appears likely',[88] but can require the payer to compensate for loss of an asset which is greater than that which is finally received. Courts in Canada, the USA and England, awarding compensation for loss of pension, have preferred to rely on termination values.[89] This method has been endorsed by the Australia Law Reform Commission[90] and the PMI,[91] but in Scottish cases there has been greater reliance on the past service reserve.[92]

Actuarial services are expensive; unless there is a settled basis for assessing value, both parties to a divorce may each need to obtain their own valuation. In the UK there is such a basis for valuing pension benefits for those who leave schemes; scheme members are entitled to request the transfer value of their pension rights each year.[93] Consequently, many scheme administrators routinely calculate these values. The PMI accepted that the ease of producing transfer values and the agreement within the actuarial profession about the assumptions to be used for them[94] made this measure of value the most convenient and least costly for the purpose of property adjustment on divorce. However, research undertaken for the Goode Committee suggests that transfer values are currently a source of considerable dissatisfaction and viewed as unfairly low. Scheme administrators see this partly as a perception problem but acknowledge that there needs to be greater consistency in valuations and some improvement in transferred rights.[95] Transfer values are generally low when compared with the pension which would be received if the member had stayed in the scheme. In particular, discretionary increases of pension provided by the scheme do not have to be included in the calculation and inflation indexing is limited to 5 per cent.[96] Thus, if transfer values are to be used as the basis at divorce, the non-member, usually the wife, may be disadvantaged.

Further difficulties arise if only part of the period during which the payer belonged to a pension scheme is relevant. This will occur if the valuation occurs long after divorce or if the court has jurisdiction only over pension earned during the marriage. Unless there is a known value for the pension at the date of marriage, the value of rights accruing during the marriage must be estimated. A simple approach which views the pension as accumulating at the same rate each year allows the value of the pension accrued during the marriage to be calculated *pro rata* during the length of marriage. However, it has been argued that this accords too little weight to the years of service close to retirement when pension contributions are likely to have been greater. Nevertheless, the Canadian courts have rejected a wife's claim for a 'value added' approach because this required more actuarial assumptions and led to less precision.[97] The PMI recommended that the *pro rata* approach should be used for Scotland.[98] The alternative of valuing the pension at the date of marriage and again at divorce may not be impracticable, or less accurate, if there is a simple and agreed method of producing a valuation.

The third question is what power, if any, should divorce courts have over the pension scheme itself? Early attempts to compensate spouses of scheme members have generally treated the pension scheme as inviolate; any compensation has had to be found from the other assets. This avoids interfering with the relationship between the member and the pension scheme but does not enable retirement benefits to be provided; adequate compensation depends on the availability of other assets. This is the current position in the UK and in Australia. Second-generation systems, such as those in the USA and most provinces of Canada and South Africa,[99] allow for pensions in payment to be divided so that the former spouse receives their own pension cheque. These systems may defer the calculation of the spouse's share until payment can be made, or express it as a proportion of the final pension. At divorce, therefore, neither spouse can know the size of the pension to be received, and the non-member remains tied to the former spouse's pension scheme. The non-member needs protection against decisions, such as change of employment or postponement of retirement, which may affect the pension and continues to bear the risk of failure of the scheme. The inadequacy of such arrangements has lead to the introduction of a third-generation system in British Columbia;[100] a similar system has existed in Germany since 1976,[101] and was recommended for Britain by the PMI.[102] These arrangements, commonly referred to as pension-splitting, enable the court to divide the pension rights at divorce and allow the recipient to retain rights in their ex-spouse's scheme as if they were a former member of it or to transfer their pension rights to another scheme. The destination of the spouse's share must be a form of retirement pension and depends on the agreement of the trustees of the existing scheme. The PMI preferred transfer arrangements because of the burden to schemes of increasing the numbers of members with preserved pensions. However, unfunded schemes, such as the UK Civil Service Scheme, may prefer to offer limited membership to the ex-spouse because this avoids any immediate capital outflow. Currently, the majority of both public and private-sector schemes are willing to accept a transfer value and provide additional benefits for a person joining their scheme. In three-quarters of schemes the transfer value is used to provide additional years to the scheme.[103] If scheme membership is not an option, it is important to ensure that divorcees are able to purchase appropriate pensions without high commission charges and are protected from the pressure selling, poor advice and mis-selling which characterized the British private pensions market in the late 1980s.[104]

The British Columbian system does not allow any order or agreement which would leave the scheme member with less than 50 per cent of the rights he or she would have had. To do otherwise is seen as undermining the employer's interest in providing benefits for employees, reflecting the original notion of the pension as a reward for employee loyalty. Although the 50 per cent rule may be logical within systems which impose equal sharing it does not seem justifiable in other circumstances. It is also difficult to justify within a system like that in the UK where employers are not required to provide pensions, the pension is legally pay and employers must preserve pensions after relatively short periods of employment. Moreover, where many workers change jobs frequently and have preserved pensions in a number of schemes it would increase administration costs by requiring the division of each pension rather than trading off between them.

Where reallocation on divorce provides fixed rights for each party, after divorce, dependent wives appear to be worse off than their former husbands.[105] The 50 per cent rule similarly undermines the ability of the court to provide adequate compensation for a spouse who will be unable to acquire a pension in his or her own right for many years after divorce because of ongoing family responsibilities. This rule has a more adverse impact where division only operates on the pension which accrued during the marriage, as is the case in Ontario[106] and, normally, under the Family Relations Amendment Act 1994 in British Columbia.

If the pension benefit can be split, should a court order be required before this can occur? Requiring a court order, even a consent order, could place a burden on the courts and also runs counter to the trend of facilitating private ordering and the proposals for divorce reform[107] which suggest a more limited role for courts and lawyers. Nevertheless, the PMI recommended that pension adjustment should only be available under the authority of a court order[108] so that the obligations of scheme members would be clear.

The British Columbian system makes pension-splitting available but allows the parties to provide compensation for loss of pension in other ways. This parallels the treatment of other assets and gives the parties and the court the greatest flexibility to find a settlement. Similar benefit-planning in relation to obligations to children is generally restricted: for example, in the UK it is not possible to exclude the operation of the Child Support Act 1991. Allowing the parties to trade off between assets with no adjustment to pensions so that the recipient, usually the wife, remains unprovided for in her retirement, ignores the interest the state has in ensuring that everyone has an adequate income for their retirement. Arguably, the provision of a retirement income is more important than flexibility. This would suggest that not only should pension-splitting be made available but that it should be the only way of compensating pension loss when the pension is not in payment.

Even after these fundamental questions have been answered there are a number of other matters which need to be considered. Orders for pension-splitting, earmarking or compensation via other assets could be viewed as capital orders or orders for maintenance. Whichever method is used, the aim is to provide income for retirement although the form of the order might determine whether it was variable or could be made subject to the legal aid charge. The need for both parties to make additional pension provision on the basis of the arrangement made at divorce suggests that variation should not generally be permitted. The legal aid charge could only be imposed if the spendthrift clause was overridden. There is no reason why legal costs should be privileged in this way, particularly when a maintenance award would not be. The need for reform was recognized, at least in part, because of the hardship suffered by those who were pensionless after divorce. Does this necessitate some retrospective provision? The case against variation is also a case against retrospection, except in extreme cases. But unless there is some provision for those who divorce prior to the introduction of any new system there is a danger that divorce proceedings would be temporarily paralysed. The power in the Matrimonial Causes Act, 1973, s.23(1) to make orders at the time of divorce 'or at any time thereafter' has been held to allow a petition to be varied so that the court could grant a lump sum or property adjustment order even though there was no power to do so when the divorce was granted.[109] A similar provision for pensions adjustment could allow limited retrospection because variation of the petition will not be allowed unless there is a reasonable prospect that the substantive order would be granted.[110] The PMI recommended that pensions adjustment orders should only be available for those divorcing after a specified date which could be shortly before implementation. However, this would avoid the problem of paralysis but also prevent any retrospection.[111]

The availability of pension-splitting may be thought unjust if it is limited to those who divorce. If the wife relies on the husband's pension, even though she may be entitled to a widow's pension of half the amount on his death, she has no right to a share of this during his lifetime. Therefore, when the husband requires residential care, the whole of his pension may be used to pay for this, leaving the wife destitute apart from her right to claim income support. Local authorities have a discretion to allow a person in residential care to keep part of their pension to meet their obligations,[112] but other claims on local authority resources may mean that they cannot afford to be generous.[113] Continuation of this state of affairs after the introduction of pension adjustment could create an incentive for the elderly to divorce. Age Concern and others are lobbying[114] for changes which recognize the wife's right to half the pension but these are currently being resisted by the government. An alternative solution would be to recognize that any pension acquired during marriage is jointly owned by the scheme member and his spouse. A proposal based on this concept was made by Michael Meacher in 1990;[115] joint ownership is the basis for division of pensions in some states with community property regimes. Changing the design of pensions is another option. The PMI canvassed opinion on redesigning pensions so that each person builds up two funds – one for themself and one for their spouse – but found little support for it.[116] It seems unlikely that such a radical solution, which could remove the need for courts to adjust most pensions on divorce, will be introduced.

CONCLUSION

Provision for pension after divorce in the next century demands a third-generation system which requires the splitting of pensions rather than a trade-off with other assets. The new system should give the parties and the courts the maximum flexibility about the amount of pension transferred but not allow variation after an order has been made. This will ensure the fairest arrangements between the parties whilst recognizing the state's interest as a regulator, rather than a provider, of the main source of income for retirement. Although the reallocation of pensions is likely to be felt less severely than the changes introduced by the Child Support Act 1991, it is unlikely to be popular amongst men and second wives who may face a decline in their retirement income. Nevertheless, attempts to avoid or conceal the necessary changes by allowing compensation from other assets are likely to be unsuccessful in the longer term. Other systems will not ensure adequate support for formerly dependent ex-wives; neither can they be demonstrated to be fair because the scheme member retains the benefits of the tax regime applying to pension assets. Consequently, they are unlikely to remove the pressure for further reform. English law needs to move directly to a thorough, consistent and comprehensive scheme for splitting pensions so that those who are dependent on their spouse's pension can also exercise the right to divorce.

POSTSCRIPT

The House of Lords confirmed the decision of the majority of the Court of Appeal in *Brooks*.[117] Pension provision which was intended to support both the scheme member and a spouse was a marriage settlement which could be varied on divorce.[118] This paves the way for pension-splitting in a wide range of pension schemes[119] without any requirement for a scheme surplus,[120] but subject to Inland Revenue approval. So far the Revenue has limited approval to cases where the wife has been employed by the husband's employer and has qualifying earnings but no pension in her own right.[121] Lord Nicholls acknowledged that legislation was still required to make pension-splitting generally available.[122]

The Pensions Bill reached its final stages shortly before the decision in *Brooks* was published.[123] Despite intense lobbying the government refused to support a scheme for pension-splitting[124] but it finally agreed to make provision for earmarking[125] so that the courts could make deferred orders for maintenance or a lump sum, and pension scheme managers or trustees could be required to make payments from a member's pension to a former spouse.[126] Regulations will provide for spouses to have information about scheme member's rights and for the valuation of pensions.[127]

The size of the payment is likely to remain uncertain until the date of retirement; orders even for lump sums will be variable.[128] Pensions against which orders have been made will need to be tracked to ensure that the order is modified and applicable to any arrangement which accepts a transfer of the pension.[129] Payments will only be made whilst the scheme member receives a pension, the former spouse's retirement income will thus be linked to the date of the member's retirement. If the scheme member dies, the former spouse will not be entitled to a share of the widow's or widower's pension.[130] Payments will be treated for all purposes as payments by the scheme member and will therefore be taxed as his income.[131] Those divorced before the provisions are implemented will not be able to benefit from them.[132] These provisions do not provide a simple and comprehensive arrangement which can ensure fair compensation in all cases but create a complex and costly[133] mechanism which will leave the majority of wives without security in retirement.

The government failed to listen to the advice of those who had considered ways of making provision for pensions on divorce and to consider the need for a system which could operate largely within a framework of private ordering. The combined effect of a decision in *Brooks* and the Pensions Act 1995 is to create a set of rules which may be fair to some, but whether they are will depend on the happenstance of the spouses' working lives, and particularly their simultaneous retirement and death, the willingness of the pensioned spouse to cooperate, the good offices of the Inland Revenue and the negotiation and advocacy skills of the spouses' lawyers. Pension funds will not be able to obstruct fair settlements[134] on divorce but the Inland Revenue, the courts and those with pensions can continue to do so.

NOTES

1 Lord Chancellor's Department (1993), *Looking to the Future,* Cm. 2424; Law Commission (1988) *Facing the Future,* Law Com. 170; Law Commission (1990), *The Ground for Divorce,* Law Com. 192.

2 *Looking to the Future, op. cit.*, note 1 above, para. 3.2.

3 Australia Law Reform Commission (1987), *Matrimonial Property*, ALRC 39, Canberra, para. 350. The Commission recommended against pension-splitting but later published a consultation document on pension-splitting, ALRC (1992), *The Treatment of Superannuation in Family Law.*

4 J. Martin and C. Roberts (1984), *Women and Employment: A Life Time Perspective*, London, DOE/OPCS, table 9.3

5 J. Gregory and K. Foster (1990), *The Consequences of Divorce*, London: OPCS, tables 3.10, 3.11 and p. 38.

6 *Ibid.*, table 3.14.
7 *Ibid.*, table 3.15.
8 *Ibid.*, tables 3.6, 3.7, 3.10 and 3.11.
9 *Ibid.*, table 3.14 and p. 49.
10 *Ibid.* p. 47.
11 Prior to the Social Security Act 1988, SERPS pensions were based on the 'best 20 years' of contributions and thus provided more generous compensation for those with a broken work record. Despite the low level of benefits, SERPS is still the best pension arrangement for many low-paid workers who do not have access to an occupational scheme: S. Davies and S. Ward (1992), *Women and Personal Pensions*, London: HMSO, table 9.4.
12 The maximum benefit payable by an approved occupation scheme is set by the government using a formula based on 40 years' service, see Inland Revenue, IR12.
13 Government Actuary's Department (1994), *Ninth Survey of Occupational Pension Schemes 1991*, London: HMSO, table 2.3.
14 J. Masson (1985), 'Women's pensions', *Journal of Social Welfare Law*, pp. 319, 327.
15 Government Actuary, *op. cit.*, note 13 above, para. 2.16.
16 Masson, *op. cit.*, note 14 above. But following the decision of the European Court in *Vroege* v. *Fisscher*, *Financial Times*, 4 October 1994, part-time workers may have a right to backdated membership providing they make the necessary contributions.
17 In 1983 it was calculated that, whereas men made pension contributions for 41 years, women did so for only 24 years and mothers for 22 years: H. Joshi and S. Owen (1983), *How Many Pensionable Years?*, Government Economic Service Working Paper no. 65, London: HMSO.
18 Social Security Act 1986, s.1. Members of SERPS received a subsidy for taking out personal pensions to replace SERPS.
19 There are Inland Revenue limits on the maximum size of contributions to a personal pension which vary with age. For a person under 35, 17.5 per cent of earnings may be invested this way. See Davies and Ward, *op. cit.*, note 11 above, p. 100.
20 *Ibid.*, p. 31. Calculations based on a normal contribution of 5 per cent of pay.
21 Davies and Ward, *op. cit.*, note 11 above.
22 If the husband had a private pension he may have chosen not to provide a widow's pension.
23 S. Edwards *et al.* (1990), 'The continuing saga of maintaining the family after divorce', *Family Law*, **20**, p. 31.
24 She may still be able to make a claim under the Inheritance (Provision for Family and Dependants) Act 1975.
25 Social Security Act 1986, s.9(6).
26 *Barber* v. *Guardian Royal Exchange Group* [1991] QB 344.
27 Such payments would breach Article 119 of the Treaty of Rome, *Barber* v. *Guardian Royal Exchange Group* [1991] QB 344.
28 The ending of the links with earnings for pensions uprating will approximately halve the value of the basic retirement pension by 2030. See V. Fry, S. Smith and S. White (1990), *Pensions and the Public Purse*, Institute of Fiscal Studies, Report Series no. 36.
29 Peter Lilley, Secretary of State for Social Security (1993), Foreword to *Equality in the State Pension Age*, Cm. 2420, London: HMSO.
30 *Ibid.*
31 *Looking to the Future*, *op. cit.*, note 1 above.
32 Law Commission (1969), *Report on Financial Provisions in Matrimonial Proceed-*

ings, Law Com. no. 25; Occupational Pensions Board (1976), *Equal Status for Men and Women in Occupational Pension Schemes*, Cmnd. 6599; Law Commission (1980), *The Financial Consequences of Divorce: The Basic Policy*, cmnd 8041; Law Commission (1981), *The Financial Consequences of Divorce*, Law com. no. 112; Lord Chancellor's Department (1985), *Occupational Pension Rights on Divorce: A Consultation Paper*, London: HMSO; Michael Meacher (1990), *Pensions, Couples and Divorce, Consultation Paper*, London: Labour Party; Law Society Family Law Committee (1991), *Maintenance and Capital Provision on Divorce*; H. Joshi and H. Davies (1991), *The Pension Consequences of Divorce*, London: Centre for Economic Policy Research, discussion paper no. 550; Pensions Management Institute (1993), *Pensions and Divorce*; Pensions Law Reform Committee, Goode Committee; (1993) *Pensions Law Reform*, Cm. 2432. Further research has been commissioned by the government: see *Hansard, Lords* vol. 560, col. 1046, Pensions Bill, 2nd reading, Lord Mackay of Ardbrecknish.

33 The different constructions of the problem and its solution are discussed in J. Masson (1993), 'A poor and lonely old age' in A. Bainham and D. Pearl (eds), *Frontiers of Family Law*, Chancery Law Publishing, p. 161.

34 Joshi and Davies *op. cit.*, note 32 above, p. 76.

35 Matrimonial Causes Act 1973, s. 25(2)(h).

36 Family Law (Scotland) Act 1985, ss. 9(1)(a), 10(5).

37 Inland Revenue, IR 12. Pension scheme trusts include terms which preclude payment except on retirement and to members or qualifying dependants.

38 For example, a person could agree to pay over a portion of any lump sum provided on death in service or retirement.

39 The fault-based facts in the Matrimonial Causes Act 1973, s.1(2) may be broader than the old matrimonial offences, but a person whose behaviour is unimpeachable could not be divorced.

40 Matrimonial Causes Act 1973, s.5(1).

41 Where the court has found grave financial hardship divorce will be granted if the petitioner can make adequate proposals for relieving it, see *Le Marchant* v. *Le Marchant* [1977] 3All ER 610 CA.

42 *Looking to the Future*, *op. cit.*, note 1 above, paras 6.57, 6.60.

43 H. Cohen, Hansard *Commons*, vol. 253, col. 365, 1st reading debate of Divorce (Pensions) Bill, 25 January 1995.

44 *Pensions Law Reform*, 1993 Cm. 2342, vol. II *Research* p. 105.

45 J. Masson (1986), 'Pensions, dependency and divorce' *Journal of Social Welfare Law*, pp. 343, 352. It is not clear that this issue was discussed by solicitors with the divorced people in Gregory and Foster's study *op. cit.*, note 5 above, p. 138. Family law texts did not discuss this issue. Loss of pensions on divorce was said to lead to the use of judicial separation but there were few such decrees, S. Maidment (1982), *Judicial Separation: A Research Study*, Oxford: Centre for Socio-legal Studies, p. 52.

46 From 1986 a scheme member or their spouse was entitled to information about the scheme; Occupation Pension Schemes (Disclosure of Information) Regulation 1986 (SI No. 1046).

47 Cf. the position in Scotland, F. Wassoff *et al.* (1990), *The Impact of the Family Law (Scotland) Act 1985*, Edinburgh: Central Research Unit, Scottish Home and Health Dept.

48 Equity release plans, which were a popular method of boosting retirement income in the 1980s, are now considered inadvisable except for the very elderly because investment incomes may be inadequate to pay interest charges.

49 Gregory and Foster *op. cit.*, note 5 above, p. 136.
50 Gregory and Foster, *op. cit.*, note 5 above, table 6.59.
51 *Ibid.* The main value of the share received on sale of the home was £10 200 by wives and £8500 by husbands (1984 prices).
52 Although the legal obligation to maintain children continued beyond divorce, parties might arrange their finances with the intention that payments from the absent parent would stop. The introduction of the Child Support Scheme in 1993 led to such arrangements being superseded by the requirement to pay child support and consequent attempt to set aside previous orders, see *Crozier* v. *Crozier* [1994] 1 FLR 126.
53 See R. Ellison (1991), *Pensions and Divorce*, London: Pensions Management Institute, para. 6.4.
54 Delaying the divorce decree also has the advantage of prolonging the period during which the wife can rely on the husband's contributions for a state retirement pension.
55 For example in Ontario prior to the Family Law Act 1986, and also in Australia where contingent interest in a pension fund is not regarded as property. See R. Ingleby (1990), 'Superannuation and divorce' *Australian Law Journal*, **64**, pp. 244–65 and *Crapp* v. *Crapp* [1978] 32 FLR 286.
56 But they will not do so where the payment will arise in the distant future or its receipt is uncertain. *Milne* v. *Milne* [1981] 2 FLR 286 C.A., *Roberts* v. *Roberts* [1986] 1 WLR 437.
57 The Inland Revenue maximum for a lump sum on retirement at normal retirement date is 3/80ths final salary per year of service. See IR12, para. 8.1.
58 See Ellison, *op. cit.*, note 53 above, pp. 9–10; R. Ellison and C. Meltzer, *Family Breakdown and Pensions* (forthcoming).
59 *Milne* v. *Milne* [1981] 2 FLR 286 C.A.
60 For example in *Griffiths* v. *Dawson* [1991] 2 FLR 315 the cost of an annuity to replace the loss of the wife's/widow's pension was £25 000, some £7500 more than the court thought the wife would have been awarded from the husband's pension lump sum.
61 *Brooks* v. *Brooks* [1993] 2 FLR 491.
62 [1994] 2 FLR 10.
63 Expert evidence was given that the Inland Revenue would accept such an arrangement, at p. 16, although under this arrangement the Inland Revenue effectively paid 40 per cent of the cost of providing Mrs Brooks' pension. If the company were not restored the whole of the cost fell on the Crown which would otherwise receive the money in *bona vacantia*.
64 Contracted-out schemes must provide such benefits.
65 Hoffman, LJ dissented, but his reasoning would allow a pension arrangement which provided dependants' benefits to a widow as of right to fall within the definition of a nuptial settlement at p. 25–26.
66 Per Hoffman, LJ at p. 26.
67 This was the approach taken in the USA under ERISA (the Employee Retirement Income Security Act 1974) and the Retirement Equity Act 1984 which allows state family courts to make 'qualified domestic relations orders' (QDROs) ordering payment of a portion of the pension to a former spouse. See M.E. Park (1986), 'The division of private pensions in divorce actions since the Retirement Equity Act of 1984', *Clearinghouse Review*, **20**, p. 9.
68 The Report of the Pension Law Review Committee (1993) *Summary*, (Chairman R. Goode), London: HMSO.
69 *Pension Law Reform*, (1993), *op. cit.*, note 44 above, para. 4.16.1.

70 Goode Report, *op. cit.*, note 68 above, p. 5.
71 Pensions Management Institute (1993), *Pensions and Divorce*, London: Pensions Management Institute, based on a one year study financed by the Joseph Rowntree Foundation.
72 *Op. cit.*, note 69 above, para. 4.16.14–16.
73 Hansard *Commons*, vol. 245, col. 366, 23 June 1994. The survey will partially duplicate the work done by Gregory and Foster for the OPCS.
74 Amendments 166 and 192 set down for the committee stage by Baroness Young.
75 Amendments 192A.
76 Hansard, *Lords*, vol. 561, col. 929, Lord Mackay of Ardbrecknish.
77 Hansard, *Lords*, vol 561, cols 918–941, 20 February 1995.
78 Hansard, *Lords*, vol. 561, col. 939.
79 *Financial Times*, 9 March, 1995, p. 1.
80 The Pensions (Divorce) Bill, Hansard, *Commons*, vol. 248, col. 1353, 1 November 1994; vol. 253, col. 365, 25 January 1995, Harry Cohen, MP.
81 Ingleby, *op. cit.*, note 55 above, p. 252.
82 *Barber* v. *Guardian Royal Exchange Group* [1991] 1 QB 344.
83 *Ten Oever* v. *Stichting Bedrijfspensoen funds* [1993] IRLR 601.
84 Under German law some pensions do not vest for 10 years. See K. Scheiwe (1994), 'German pension insurance, gendered times' in D. Sainsbury (ed.), *Gendering Welfare States*, London: Sage, pp. 132–49. In the USA, pensions for federal employees vest only after 20 years.
85 Depending on the measure of value – see below.
86 The Pensions Management Institute recommended a *de minimis* rule which would have excluded such pensions from their pension-splitting scheme, *op. cit.*, note 71 above, para. 15.14.
87 PMI, *op. cit.*, note 71 above, paras 17.5–17.11.
88 Per Chapnik J. in *Salib* v. *Cross* (1994) 15 OR (3d) 521,533 (Ontario).
89 *Kurz* v. *Kurz* (1989) 443 NW2d 782 (Michigan); see also I. Baxter (1993), *Marital Property Cumulative Supplement,* Illinois: Clark Boardman Callaghan; *Salib* v. *Cross* (1994) 15 OR (3d) 521; *H* v. *H (Financial provision: capital assets*) [1993] 2 FLR 335.
90 ALRC, *op. cit.*, note 3 above, p. 173 and s. 71c (2).
91 PMI, *op. cit.*, note 71 above, paras 15.8, 15.11–15.12.
92 *Bannon* v. *Bannon* [1993] SLT 999.
93 Occupational Pension Schemes (Disclosure of Information) Regulations 1986 SI No. 1046.
94 See Retirement Benefit Schemes Transfer Values (GN 11).
95 Cm. 2342, vol. II, ch. 12.
96 The PLRC reviewed issues relating to early leaving and recommended no major changes. See summary, pp. 19–20. The government endorsed the current approach; see *op. cit.*, note 68 above. *Security, Equality, Choice: The Future For Pensions*, cm. 2594, London: HMSO, para. 1.32 et seq.
97 *Ramsey* v. *Ramsey* (1994) 111 OLR (4th) 312 at 317 (Saskatchewan) Cf. *Best* v. *Best* (unreported) Ontario Court of Justice (1993). It is not clear why there should be less precision if the same assumptions are applied to the two dates.
98 PMI, *op. cit.*, note 71 above, paras. 15.4 and 15.8.
99 Divorce Amendment Act 1989; the Act only enables the court to make an order against the pension fund where alternative arrangements are impossible or inappropriate, see Ellison and Meltzer, *op. cit.*, note 58 above.

100 Under the Family Relations Amendment Act 1994.
101 See B. von Maydell (1988), 'Credit-splitting [*versorgungausleich*] at divorce' in M.T. Meulders-Klein and J. Eekelaar (eds), *Family, State and Individual Economic Security*, Brussels: Kluwer, ch. 42; K. Scheiwe, *op. cit.*, note 84 above.
102 *Supra*, n.71 p. 52.
103 *Ninth Survey by the Government Actuary 1991* (1994), London: HMSO, table 11.4.
104 See Treasury and Civil Service Committee (1993–94), *Financial Services Regulation*, HCP 236, London: HMSO, especially the evidence of the Consumer's Association; *Pension Transfers Report to SIB by KPMG Peat Marwick*, (1993) London: Securities Investment Board, and *Which?*, August 1993, p. 13.
105 See L. Weitzman and M. Maclean (1992), *Economic Consequences of Divorce*, Oxford: OUP.
106 Pension Benefits Act 1987 (Ontario); a change has been recommended enabling the non-member to receive up to 50 per cent of the whole of rights, see Ontario Law Reform Commission (1993), *Report on Pensions: Valuation and Division*, Toronto: Ministry of Attorney General.
107 *Looking to the Future*, *op. cit.*, note 1 above.
108 PMI, *op. cit.*, note 71 above, para. 20.2.
109 *Chatterjee* v. *Chatterjee* (1976) 1 All ER 719.
110 *Chatterjee* v. *Chatterjee* (1976) 1 All ER 719, 725 per Ormrod LJ.
111 PMI, *op. cit.*, note 71 above, para. 20.10.
112 Hansard, *Lords*, vol. 561, col. 962.
113 Hansard, *Lords*, vol. 561. col. 961, example from the Alzheimer's Disease Society.
114 Pensions Bill Amendment 182B introduced at the committee stage by Baroness Hollis; Hansard, *Lords*, vol. 561, col. 960.
115 Meacher, *op. cit.*, note 32 above.
116 PMI, *op. cit.*, note 71 above, para. 10.12.
117 [1995] 3 All ER 257.
118 *Ibid.*, *per* Lord Nicholls at p. 265 h-j but '[i]t would be difficult to conclude that a scheme under which benefits were payable exclusively to the scheme member was a marriage settlement….'
119 *Ibid.* Although, at p. 267h, Lord Nicholls stated *obiter* that multi-member scheme pensions could not be split this does not appear to be the case providing Inland Revenue approval is obtained so that other members' interests are not prejudiced. *Pilkington* v. *Pilkington* (below) involved a multi-member scheme.
120 The original order was varied so that Mrs Brooks obtained her pension in priority to her husband leaving him the burden of sorting out the mess arising from the deregistration of the company.
121 See *Pilkington* v. *Pilkington* (unreported) Blackburn County Court, 1994 [1995] Fam. Law 264.
122 [1995] 3 All ER at p. 267h.
123 Pensions on divorce was considered at Committee Stage in the Commons on 22 June 1995 (Standing Committee D). The opinion in *Brooks* was delivered on 29 June 1995.
124 Amendments to allow pension-splitting were drafted by the Law Society with the PMI and tabled by Donald Dewar MP but not pressed to a vote, *Hansard*, Standing Committee D, col. 814, 22 June 1995. The government maintained throughout that pension-splitting was too difficult and too 'expensive' in terms of lost revenue and payments from unfunded public sector schemes.
125 Pensions Act 1995, s. 166 adding ss. 25B, 25C and 25D to Matrimonial Causes Act 1973; s.167 makes comparable provision for Scotland.

126 Matrimonial Causes Act 1973, ss. 25B(4), 25C(3). The court may order a scheme member to exercise a power to commute benefits, s. 25B(7).
127 Matrimonial Causes Act 1973, s. 25D(2).
128 Matrimonial Causes Act 1973, ss. 25C, 31(2)(dd).
129 Matrimonial Causes Act 1973, s. 25D. It appears that the government were unclear how this would be arranged at the time the provisions were debated, *Hansard*, Standing Committee D col. 807, 22 June 1995.
130 Matrimonial Causes Act 1973, s. 25B(4). Maintenance payments can only be ordered from pension which becomes due to the party with the pension rights.
131 Matrimonial Causes Act 1973, s. 25B(6).
132 Pensions Act 1995, s. 166(6) but it is presumably open to a person who has not sought the variation of a marriage settlement to seek leave to amend their petition or pursue a Brooks-type award.
133 The Under-Secretary of State for Social Security. James Arbuthnot MP acknowledged that the main costs arose from operating deferred maintenance orders, *Hansard*, Standing Committee D col. 801, 22 June 1995.
134 Pensions Act 1995, s. 166(5)(d).

7 Divorce and Ethnic Minorities

*Rhona Schuz**

INTRODUCTION

Structure

The main reason that a separate consideration of divorce in relation to ethnic minorities is justified is because most ethnic minorities have their own forms of dissolving marriages which are either religious or customary. This chapter will be restricted to such communities. The introduction includes a brief description of the divorces involved. The term religious divorces will include, where appropriate, customary divorces.

In the second part, the problems which may arise in England as a result of the existence of such forms of divorce are divided into three categories:

1 the position of members of ethnic minorities who wish to obtain a divorce in the UK;
2 the problem of remarriage where a secular, but not a religious, divorce has been obtained;
3 the recognition of religious divorces.

The third section of the chapter examines the policy basis of the present rules governing the recognition of religious divorces in the light of the historical development of the rules, and analyses whether the present rules in fact further the policies which underpin them. The final part of the chapter examines various proposals for reform, including a discussion of the likely impact of the Law Commission's proposals.[1]

* Lecturer in Law, Bar-Ilan University, Israel.

Religious and customary divorces

The different types of divorce[2]

Religious and customary divorces can be divided into three categories: judicial or quasi-judicial; consensual and unilaterial.

In the context of the ethnic minority communities in England, the most relevant divorces are Muslim, Hindu and Jewish divorces.[3] Whilst judicial divorce is available for Muslims and Hindus in India,[4] extra-judicial divorce is still widely practised both on the Indian sub-continent and amongst the immigrant community in the UK. Both religions provide for consensual divorces. However, amongst Muslims the use of the unilateral *talaq* by the man is still prevalent and recognized in Muslim countries, although some countries have added procedural requirements;[5] by contrast, non-consensual Hindu customary divorces have not generally been recognized.[6]

In Jewish law, only consensual divorce has been recognized since the decree of Rabbi Gershon in 1028. Outside Israel, it is clear that the Rabbinical court merely supervises the procedure for the consensual delivery and acceptance of the bill of divorce (the *get*).[7] In Israel, Jews are obliged to obtain a divorce under the auspices of the Rabbinical courts, which are part of the state court system, causing some to suggest that the divorce is therefore judicial. However, the better view is that the dissolution of the marriage is still effected by the act of the parties in delivering and receiving the *get* rather than being granted by the court.[8] The preparation, and the handing over, of the *get* are legal, rather than religious, acts and no affirmation of belief or faith is required. Indeed, the *get* may be delivered or/and received by duly authorized agents of the spouses.

Other examples of ethnic minority divorces which have been considered by the English courts are Thai consensual divorces[9] and divorces granted by customary tribunal in Ghana.[10]

How many religious/customary divorces?

It is not possible to produce any kind of reliable figure as to either the number of religious/customary divorces carried out or subsequently relied on in England and Wales.[11] In relation to the former category, with the exception of Jewish divorces,[12] the involvement of a religious authority, which might keep records, is not required. As we shall see below, such an extra-judicial divorce effected in the UK has no legal effect and, if the parties wish to have their divorce recognized for civil purposes, they will be forced to obtain an English judicial divorce or to effect a religious/customary divorce abroad which satisfies the English recognition rules.

In relation to the latter option, it was estimated that, in 1971, 150 marriages per year took place after extra-judicial divorce.[13] However, even leaving aside the fact that due to large-scale immigration from the Indian subcontinent the number would probably have risen, this figure represents merely the tip of the iceberg since it only deals with those getting remarried in England. It does not include cases where the validity of the first marriage is brought into question other than in connection with a remarriage. For example, one party may try to obtain a divorce in an English court or to claim maintenance or the right to inherit on the intestacy of the other party on the basis that the extra-judicial divorce is not recognized. Also excluded are cases where a spouse has remarried abroad after an extra-judicial divorce and the validity of the remarriage is relevant for purposes of immigration, taxation, social security et cetera.

THE LAW

Obtaining a Civil Divorce in the UK

Jurisdiction

The English court may entertain a petition for divorce provided that either party is domiciled or has been habitually resident in England and Wales for one year at the date of institution of proceedings.[14] Whilst immigrants will not obtain a domicile of choice in England unless they intend to remain in England and Wales indefinitely, they will become habitually resident if they intend to reside in the country for a settled purpose.[15]

Ground for divorce

The ground of irretrievable breakdown and the five facts which provide evidence thereof are discussed elsewhere in this volume. However, the ethnic background of the parties may be of considerable significance in determining whether one of these facts is satisfied. In particular, the 'behaviour' test clearly must be applied taking into consideration the particular circumstances of the marriage. Thus, it will be relevant, for example, to ascertain whether the behaviour complained of is part of the culture of the community to which the parties belong.

Where the marriage to be dissolved is polygamous there may be some difficulty in applying the facts which are designed for monogamous marriages. In particular, sexual intercourse with another wife will not be considered adultery.[16] However, depending on the circumstances and the expectations of the parties, the taking of the second wife may constitute 'behaviour' such that it is no longer reasonable to expect the petitioner to live with the respondent.[17]

The hardship bar

In a few cases,[18] female respondents from ethnic minorities have tried to invoke the hardship bar under s.5 of the Matrimonial Causes Act 1973, which is available where the petition is based on five years' separation. They have argued that, because divorce is not accepted within their community, they will be socially ostracized if the decree is granted and that this would cause them grave hardship. In no case has this defence succeeded, although the judgments leave open the possibility that in appropriate circumstances a decree may be refused.

Religious Bars to Remarriage

Where a civil divorce is obtained, the parties are free to remarry in the UK notwithstanding that they have not obtained a religious divorce in accordance with the customs of their community. This phenomenon gives rise to serious problems,[19] particularly in the Jewish community.[20] The husband might obtain a civil divorce but refuse to grant his wife a *get*.[21] He then remarries in a civil registry office but the wife, who wishes to adhere to Jewish law, is unable to remarry and is referred to as an *agunah* (a 'chained' wife).

There has been considerable debate within the Jewish community as to how to solve the problem internally.[22] At present, the London Rabbinical authorities are considering the insertion of a clause into the marriage contract which obliges the parties to submit to a Rabbinical tribunal if the marriage breaks down and requires the husband to continue to meet his obligations to his wife in accordance with religious law, even if civil proceedings are instituted in respect of the marriage.[23] However, the effectiveness of such a clause would depend to a large extent[24] on the willingness of the secular courts to enforce it.[25] It is submitted that provided that the contractual obligation is sufficiently clear, the only problems[26] with such enforcement are that there are no effective sanctions for breach of a court order[27] and that, if inappropriate coercion is used, the resulting *get* will be invalid in Jewish law[28], which defeats the whole purpose of the clause.

It is argued that the secular courts ought to be prepared to do everything possible to aid the chained spouse for two reasons. First, the civil law, by its willingness to dissolve marriages which were contracted under Jewish religious law, other than in accordance with that law, exacerbates the problem inherent in the consensual nature of Jewish divorce.[29] Second, 'it is the duty of the Court to ensure that appropriate orders are made fully effective not only in theory, but in fact'.[30] Until the religious divorce is obtained, the civil divorce is not fully effective because, in reality, one party is unable to remarry.

However, in the absence of an appropriate enforceable contractual obligation, the scope for the civil court to help seems to be limited to indirect measures directed towards persuading the recalcitrant spouse to cooperate. In *Brett* v. *Brett*,[31] the court ordered the husband to pay an increased lump sum if a *get* was not delivered within three months.[32] The difficulty with this solution is twofold. First, not all husbands are in a financial position to comply with such an order. Second, care has to be taken to ensure that the resulting Jewish divorce is not invalid because it was obtained under coercion.[33]

A court could refuse to make a decree absolute, under the hardship bar in the Matrimonial Causes Act 1973, s.5, in cases where the petitioner has refused to remove a religious barrier to the remarriage of the respondent. This solution is currently limited to the relatively few cases where divorce is obtained on the basis of five years' separation. Also, it may be difficult to prove that it is the *civil divorce* which is responsible for the hardship, since the wife's inability to remarry is caused by the husband's refusal to grant a *religious divorce*. On the other hand, it may be argued that the hardship comprises the injustice of enabling the husband to remarry whilst he refuses to allow such a right to the wife. Such a solution would only be effective where the husband is himself concerned to remarry or to obtain a civil divorce for other reasons.

Reforms which have been proposed to deal specifically with the problem of the chained spouse will be discussed in the final section of this chapter.

Recognition of Religious Divorces

Recognition of all divorces, annulments and legal separations (hereinafter referred to as divorces) other than those granted by an English court is now governed by the Family Law Act 1986, Part II, which (subject to saving provisions) supersedes the common law rules for recognition and the Recognition of Divorces and Legal Separations Act 1971.[34]

Divorces obtained in the UK

Before 1973 extra-judicial divorces obtained in the UK were recognized provided that the parties were domiciled abroad and the divorce was recognized by the law of the parties' domicile.[35]

However, s.16(1) of the Domicile and Matrimonial Proceedings Act 1973, which is reenacted by s.44(2) of the Family Law Act 1986, reversed this position by providing that:

> ...no divorce or annulment obtained in any part of the British Isles shall be regarded as effective in any part of the United Kingdom unless granted by a court of civil jurisdiction.

Overseas divorces

There are two sets of rules for determining whether an overseas divorce will be recognized, depending on whether the divorce is obtained by means of judicial or other proceedings (to be referred to as 'formal divorces') or without such proceedings (to be referred to as 'informal divorces'). There is no statutory definition of proceedings. Whilst there would not seem to be any problem in ascertaining whether there have been judicial proceedings, difficulty may arise in determining whether the steps involved in obtaining an extra-judicial divorce are sufficient to constitute 'other proceedings'.

The most helpful guidance to emerge from the case law can be found in the speech of Oliver LJ in *Chaudhary* v. *Chaudhary.*[36]

> in the context...of a solemn change of status, [proceedings] must import a degree of formality and at least the involvement of some agency, whether lay or religious, of or recognised by the state having a function that is more than simply probative, although *Quazi* ... clearly shows that it need have no power of veto.

Applying this definition,[37] it is clear that a Pakistani Muslim Family Ordinance *talaq*,[38] a Jewish *get*[39] and a Ghanaian customary arbitration tribunal divorce[40] are obtained by means of proceedings; whereas classical Muslim law 'bare' *talaqs*,[41] other non-judicial Muslim divorces and Thai consensual divorces are not so obtained. Into which category Hindu and African and Asian customary divorces fall must be decided in each individual case, depending on whether a state-recognized third party, such as a recognized *panchayat* or tribal elders, is involved.

Recognition of informal divorces[42] is more restrictive than that of formal divorces[43] in three principal ways. First, there are fewer jurisdictional bases available.[44] Second, in relation to formal divorces there is no restriction on the connection of the parties with the UK whereas informal divorce will not be recognized if either party has been habitually resident in the UK for more than 12 months. Third, informal divorces are more likely to be refused recognition on the basis of public policy.[45]

Transnational divorces

Transnational divorces are those obtained by means of steps taken in more than one country. In *R* v. *Secretary of State for the Home Department ex p. Ghulam Fatima*[46] (hereinafter referred to as *Fatima*), the question arose whether a *talaq* obtained in accordance with the provisions of the Pakistani Muslim Family Law Ordinance could be recognized under the Recognition of Divorces and Legal Separations Act 1971, where the *talaq* itself was pronounced in England and all the subsequent steps took place in Pakistan. The House of Lords held that the divorce was not an overseas divorce because the wording of the statute[47] indicated that a divorce would only be treated as an overseas divorce where all proceedings took place in the same foreign jurisdiction. Recently, Wall J in *Berkovits v. Grinberg (Attorney-General Intervening)*[48] held that, despite the changed wording, s.46(1) of the Family Law Act 1986 was to be interpreted in the same way and thus the transnational *get*, which had been written in England but delivered to the wife in Israel, could not be recognized. With respect, most of his Lordship's reasoning is not very convincing. In particular,[49] his conclusion that

> it cannot have been the intention of Parliament…to have legislated for the recognition of transnational divorce whilst, at the same time, denying the right of a spouse so divorced to seek relief under Part II of the 1984 Act[50]

is flawed because we know that Parliament did legislate for recognition of informal divorces whilst denying the parties relief under the 1984 Act (see discussion below).

There are dicta in the *Fatima* case which suggest that even if the transnational *talaq* had fitted within the scheme of the 1971 Act, it would have been refused recognition on public policy grounds because it was effectively a 'mail order' extra-judicial divorce obtained in England, which was contrary to the policy of what is now s.44(2) of the Family Law Act 1986.[51] However, doubt has been cast on the validity of such policy considerations because a rich man could avoid the effects of the decision by flying to Pakistan to pronounce *talaq* there.[52] In any event, there seems to be no reason why public policy should prevent recognition of a transnational *talaq* where the *talaq* is pronounced in a third country, at least where the latter recognizes such a divorce.

In *Berkovits v Grinberg*[53] Wall J expressly stated that there were no policy reasons for refusing recognition of the *get* in this case. However, he held that his interpretation of the statute should not be influenced by policy considerations.

THE POLICY BASIS OF THE RULES GOVERNING RECOGNITION OF RELIGIOUS DIVORCES

The current rules relating to the recognition of religious divorces can best be understood by looking at the historical background.

The common law

Since the size of the population professing any faith other than Christianity was, until relatively recently, very small, the common law hardly ever had to contend with the problem of how to treat religious divorces. There was a small Jewish community in England before their expulsion in 1290; Jews returned in the seventeenth century. However, whilst there is evidence that Jewish marriages were recognized by the courts,[54] there is no real evidence as to how Jewish divorces effected in England were treated.[55] Lord Hardwicke's Marriage Act of 1753, which introduced civil marriage requirements, specifically provided for the civil recognition of Jewish and Quaker marriages. However, there is no parallel reference in the Matrimonial Causes Act 1857, introducing civil divorce. Religious divorces effected overseas seem to have simply been treated like any other form of overseas divorce, which would be recognized if obtained in place of the domicile.[56] This rule was later extended to allow recognition where the divorce was *recognized* by the law of the domicile.[57] This extension made it possible to recognize religious divorces effected in England by foreign domiciliaries.[58] The universality of the principle that status is determined by the domicile seems eventually to have overridden those internal policy considerations which would not recognize such divorces.[59] Although there was always a residual discretion to refuse recognition where this would be contrary to public policy, the fact that the extra-judicial divorce took place in England does not seem to have been a reason for invoking this discretion.

Perhaps what is surprising is that, unlike in the case of the validity of a marriage where, notwithstanding the domicile principle, the formalities have to comply with the *lex loci celebrationis*, there was no reference to the *lex loci divortii*.[60] Similarly, the application of English civil law in all divorce cases heard in England seems to have been an inevitable result of the domicile principle, since the courts originally only took jurisdiction in cases where the parties were domiciled in England and Wales. Hardly surprisingly, since English society was essentially homogenous, there was no suggestion that the English *lex domicili* might itself give effect to the parties' own religious law.[61]

Thus, the treatment of religious divorces, wherever taking place, was, at common law,[62] determined by the general rules of private international law which were not informed by specific domestic law policy considerations.

Under statute

The Recognition of Divorces and Legal Separations Act 1971 was enacted to give effect to the Hague Convention on the Recognition of Divorces and Legal Separations 1970. The main purpose of this Convention, and the main reason for the UK's ratification thereof, was to avoid limping marriages.[63] In order to achieve this, the 1971 Act widened the traditional jurisdictional links even further than was necessary to comply with the Convention.

However, the Convention and the English legislation giving effect to it only applied to divorces obtained by means of judicial or other proceedings. This meant that only those religious groups whose divorces came within this definition benefited from the liberalization. On the other hand, since the domicile principle was saved by the 1971 Act, the basis for the recognition of informal religious divorces remained largely unchanged.

However, the occasion of the enactment of the 1971 Act,[64] together with the increase in the size of the ethnic minorities, led to an examination of policy in this area and resulted in the enactment of restrictions on the validity of religious divorces in the Domicile and Matrimonial Proceedings Act 1973. In the Family Law Act 1986, which amended the 1971 Act, these restrictions were intensified. The 1973 and 1986 provisions will be examined in turn.

Domicile and Matrimonial Proceedings Act 1973 s.16.

We saw above that s.16(1) of this Act provided that extra-judicial divorces taking place in the UK could no longer be recognized. The policy behind this reform can be found in the speech of Lord Simon of Glaisdale in the House of Lords' debate.[65]

> [T]he purposes of this clause is to prevent persons habitually resident in this country from being non-judicially divorced by reason of our rules of common law. It arises mainly in respect of Islamic divorces by instant repudiation, and it

> was conceived to be a hardship that we should be compelled by our rules of international law to recognise the repudiation of a perfectly innocent wife and allow the safeguards of judicial divorces in the country to be by-passed. For example, a wife could be left in this country without any means and thrown on the meagre resources provided by the taxpayer.

There was concern that Muslim men would evade the new prohibition by taking day trips to Calais and pronouncing *talaq* there. Thus, an additional subsection was added, denying recognition to extra-judicial divorces obtained abroad if both parties had been habitually resident in England for one year, unless the court was obliged to recognize them under the rules based on the Hague Convention on Recognition of Divorces and Legal Separations.[66]

Family Law Act 1986

The Family Law Act 1986 extended the restrictive approach introduced in 1973 by reducing the range of jurisdictional connections between the parties and the country where an informal divorce was obtained and thereby extending the difference between the recognition rules for formal and informal divorces.[67] This outcome is particularly striking as it involved rejection of the Law Commission's[68] recommendation to remove the distinction between different methods of divorce on the basis of the degree of formality of the acts involved in obtaining them.[69]

The government's reasons are provided by the Lord Chancellor in the House of Lords:

> We cannot accept this wide recommendation. There are public policy elements here. Such divorces are informal, arbitrary and usually unilateral. More importantly there is often no available proof that what is alleged to have taken place has taken place at all. In addition, these divorces are almost exclusively obtained by men and therefore discriminate against women. Finally, particularly where the wife is resident abroad, such divorces provide little or no financial protection for the wife and family.[70]

I suggest that four different policy objectives for restricting recognition of religious divorces can be distilled from the two extracts quoted:

1 to ensure that divorces are only recognized if there is proper evidence that they have been obtained;
2 to prevent discrimination against women by informal divorces;
3 to protect the wife and family against any hardship which may be caused as a result of the divorce;
4 to prevent evasion of English domestic law.

Analysis

We will now consider whether the current restrictions on the recognition of religious divorces do actually further these policy objectives.

Proof

It is beyond doubt that effect cannot be given to any divorce unless there is adequate proof that the divorce has been obtained. The courts have always been able to refuse recognition to any informal divorce where they are not satisfied on the balance of probabilities that the divorce in fact took place. Furthermore, an additional probative safeguard has been added by the conferring of discretion to refuse to recognize an informal divorce where there is no official document certifying that the divorce is recognized by the country where it was obtained.[71]

It is not clear why the narrowing of the available jurisdictional connections or the requirement that neither party be habitually resident for one year in the UK should solve the problem of proof other than by arbitrarily minimizing the situations in which informal divorces may be recognized.

Anti-discrimination

Whilst preventing discrimination against women may be a laudable aim, it is unclear whether it is either an appropriate or realizable objective in this context.

First, the law provides for selective application of such policy because foreign *formal* unilateral judicial or extra-judicial divorces are recognized on a liberal basis, even if they can only be obtained by men. Second, the application of the policy is inappropriate in relation to divorces obtained abroad, because it is inconsistent with the general private international law principle of recognizing foreign judgments and decrees without examining the merits thereof.

The objective itself is unlikely to be realizable because non-recognition will not actually prevent the discriminatory practice. Usually, it will simply force the husband to obtain a secular divorce as well. Otherwise, all that non-recognition can do is to protect the wife from the civil consequences of a foreign divorce, which will be discussed below. Where the parties are living in England, there is, in theory, little discrimination because the wife can obtain a civil divorce without any real difficulty although, in practice, this may not be a viable option for her if her local community disapproves of such action.

Conversely, it may be argued that it is important for the law to be seen not to be condoning practices which discriminate against women, especially where the divorces are obtained on home territory. The anti-discrimination objectives may be seen as part of an overall policy of education aimed at eliminating sexual discrimination. However, this policy also has to be balanced against that of removing religious discrimination. The pursuance of a policy of social engineering may not justify prejudicing individuals for complying with the dictates of their religion.

In any event, it must be remembered that not all religious divorces discriminate against women, and that many are based on mutual consent.

Protection

Because, prior to 1984, the issue of recognition of foreign divorces frequently[72] arose in the context of the wife's claim for financial provision from the husband, parliamentary debate has generally focused on financial protection. If the foreign divorce was recognized, the English court could not make any ancillary orders. However, this situation was rectified by legislation,[73] and the court is now empowered to make an order for financial provision following a recognized *formal* divorce on the same basis as after an English divorce.[74] Of course, this does not solve the problem for the wife who is divorced informally: because Parliament has decided to deny her the opportunity to claim financial relief, she may apparently still be in need of financial protection if the divorce is recognized.

However, an examination of the legislative history of the 1984 Act reveals no express discussion of the exclusion of informal divorces. The explanatory note to clause 1 in the draft Bill appended to Law Commission Report No. 117 states that

> ...the references to 'judicial or other proceedings' covers cases where the marriage has been terminated extra-judicially (for example by *talaq*): cf. Recognition of Divorces and Legal Separations Act 1971.

From the Working Paper preceding that report[75] it seems that the Law Commission had in mind all types of *talaq*s. In particular it should be noted that the Law Commission's work preceded the decision in *Chaudhary* v. *Chaudhary*.[76] Bearing in mind that the Law Commission later recommended the abolition of the distinction between formal and informal divorces,[77] it seems that the restriction of the court's powers to formal divorces under Part III of the 1984 Act, did not reflect the intention of the Law Commission whose recommendations were accepted by Parliament without any discussion on this point. Indeed, Gordon[78] suggests that the phrase should be interpreted in the light of the circumstances at the time of its enactment and that it should not be accorded the same interpretation as the like phrase in the Family Law Act 1986. With respect, given the courts' attitude to informal divorces in the past, such an outcome is unlikely.

Even if it can be assumed that non-recognition might be justified to ensure that the wife can obtain financial relief, this rationale cannot apply to cases where the wife does not need financial protection – for example, where the husband is not in a position to make financial provision or the wife has more assets than the husband.

It is also difficult to see how non-recognition of the religious divorce can protect the wife in non-financial ways. Non-recognition cannot force her husband to return to her and, indeed, she will be considered by her community as divorced. More crucially, non-recognition, far from protecting the respondent, may actually be prejudicial to her,[79] both financially and in other ways, if she wishes to remarry.[80]

Evasion

Evasion of what? Religious divorces may seem to allow evasion of both the procedures and substance of English divorce law, as well as of financial responsibilities.

1 *Procedures*: Under the 'special procedure' which applies in nearly all undefended divorces, there is no judicial hearing and only minimal scrutiny of the petitioner's allegations. The respondent's right to defend him or herself is often merely illusory.[81] Thus, it is difficult to see what procedural safeguards are evaded by obtaining an extra-judicial divorce provided that there is adequate proof of the divorce.
2 *Grounds*: Whilst the irretrievable breakdown of the marriage has to be evidenced by one of the facts listed in Matrimonial Causes Act 1973 s.1(2), these no longer provide any major obstacle to most couples. Where the parties agree, they can obtain a divorce after two years' separation. Where there is no agreement, in many cases it will be possible to satisfy the behaviour fact,[82] if there is no adultery. Thus, in practice, the present law allows most spouses to get divorced virtually at will. With the exception of cases where separation is relied on, the time taken depends on the speed of the courts rather than on any in-built safeguard. If the Law Commission's proposals are enacted it will be possible for either spouse to obtain a divorce effectively by repudiation. The major difference will be that the divorce will only become effective after a one-year 'cooling-off' period has elapsed. Since this period is a crucial part of the proposed new system, the argument that extra-judicial divorces evade domestic law requirements would be more cogent than in relation to the present law.

3 *Financial obligations*: This would seem to be the corollary of the desire to protect the wife, which we have discussed above. The solution to 'evasion' found in relation to overseas formal divorces[83] could equally be applied to informal divorces and to extra-judicial divorces obtained in the UK. Thus, the problem could be dealt with directly without compromising the objective of preventing limping marriages.

Evasion by whom? Evasion connotes not merely that the divorce does not comply with the safeguards of English law, but also that in fact it *ought* to do so. Clearly we recognize foreign formal divorces and some informal divorces whether or not they are consistent with the requirements of domestic law. Thus, we need to identify which divorces *ought* to be obtained under English law.

At common law, the determining connection was that of the domicile. Thus, spouses not domiciled in England were not expected to use the English system even if they wished to obtain the divorce in England. However, following the 1973 and 1986 enactments, two changes have been made to this policy. First, all persons who wish to obtain a divorce within the UK are required to use the courts to do so. Second, all those who have been habitually resident in England for one year are expected to use the English system in preference to obtaining an informal divorce abroad.

We will consider each of these in turn:

1 *Divorces within the UK*: Whilst it may seem reasonable[84] for the state to regulate the procedure for all changes of status taking place within its boundaries, it does not in fact do so in relation to marriage. Thus, marriages of Jews and Quakers are governed by the rules of these respective communities, subject to civil registration requirements and the eligibility of the parties according to the civil law.[85] Members of other religions may get married in a registered building in their own form provided that this includes the express consent by the parties to marry.[86]

Arguably, there is a significant distinction between marriage and divorce: policy requires that the former be encouraged and the latter be discouraged. Thus, the state is justified in imposing its own restrictions on divorce. Whilst this argument may have been convincing in the past, it is difficult to support in the light of the present liberal divorce law and the conversion of the task of terminating marriages from a judicial to a largely administrative function. Apart from in the case of unilateral repudiation, religious forms of divorce may provide more safeguards than the civil system.[87]

2 *Informal divorces abroad*: It seems ironic that it is now considered to be evasion for those habitually resident in England to obtain an informal

divorce in the country of domicile since, at common law, domicile was the only basis for divorce jurisdiction. Furthermore, why should a petitioner who is not habitually resident in the UK be expected to obtain a divorce through the English court rather than a religious informal divorce in the country of domicile where he is still living merely because the respondent is habitually resident in England?[88]

It should be reiterated that the anti-evasion policy is selective because it only applies in relation to informal divorces. It is not clear why the Indian Muslim who pronounces a bare *talaq* in India, where it is recognized, should be considered to be evading English law requirements any more than his Pakistani neighbour who returns to Pakistan to pronounce *talaq* in accordance with the minimal procedural requirements of the Pakistani Muslim Family Law Ordinance.

REFORM

In the light of the above analysis, we can now consider how the current law may be rationalized and how the hardship caused to members of ethnic minorities may be alleviated without sacrificing any substantial policy objectives.

Overseas divorces

The courts

The decision in *Berkovits v. Grinburg (Attorney-General Intervening)*[89] in relation to transnational *talaq*s should be overruled. It is submitted that there is ample basis on which to find that the wording of section 46(1) is ambiguous. In which case, such ambiguity should be resolved by looking at the mischief which the Act was meant to redress. The House of Lords in *Quazi*[90] found that the 1971 Act was designed to reduce the hardship caused by limping marriages. Whilst the 1986 Act was designed to resolve certain problems arising from the 1971 Act since none of them related to transnational divorces, in this context the limping marriage mischief is still the relevant one. Thus the ambiguity should be resolved in favour of recognizing the divorce and therefore preventing the limping marriage from arising.

Thus, with respect, it is not necessary, as Wall J suggests, to wait for Parliament to decide 'whether or not in an increasingly multi-racial and multi-ethnic society the refusal to recognize the transnational divorce can or should continue.'[91] The refusal to recognize such divorces has in fact emanated more from the courts than from parliament.

Statute

The restrictions on the recognition of informal foreign divorces should be removed by providing for application of the same jurisdictional requirements as for formal divorces. In parallel, the power to order financial provision after a foreign divorce in Part III of the Matrimonial and Family Proceedings Act 1984 should be extended to apply after informal divorces.

In relation to the former, the public policy defence is wide enough to allow the court to refuse recognition where the discriminatory nature of the divorce causes hardship to the wife. The latter ensures financial protection by allowing an award of financial provision where appropriate. The filter mechanism in the Matrimonial and Family Proceedings Act 1984 Part III allows the court to refuse leave in unmeritorious cases.

Extra-judicial divorces in the UK

The present absolute rule prohibiting recognition of extra-judicial divorces taking place in the UK should be removed. Two alternative proposals to replace the present regime may be suggested - the procedural and the radical proposals.

The procedural proposal

It has been suggested[92] that members of religious minorities should be allowed to have their marriages ended in accordance with the procedures required by their religious law after a court of law has directed that the civil law allows the marriage to be dissolved. The divorce could be recorded and confirmed by the civil authorities. The need to comply with all the civil law as well as the religious law requirements ensures that there is no evasion. The advantage to the members of ethnic minorities is that they can obtain a single divorce which is recognized by both civil and religious authorities. In this way, the opportunity for abuse, manipulation and blackmail is reduced.

The radical proposal

Religious divorces which do not, in practice, evade the safeguards of the civil law should be recognized. It is suggested that there are two elements in determining whether there is 'evasion':

1 *The nature of the religious divorce*: Only those religious divorces which incorporate the essential safeguards of the civil law would be recognized. The relevant authorities of each religious group would be able to apply for a licence allowing them to dissolve marriages. Such a licence would only be granted after close examination of the procedure and substance of the religious divorce law in question. Additional safeguards could be required as a condition for the grant of the licence. For example, if the Law Commission's proposals are enacted, the religious authorities could be required to agree not to grant or sanction a religious divorce until one year had elapsed from the time of the initiation of the religious divorce procedure.

2 *Who would be entitled to obtain a religious divorce*: As we saw above, at common law the crucial factor determining whether an extra-judicial divorce obtained within the jurisdiction would be recognized was the domicile of the parties. A return to that situation is undesirable, *inter alia*, because of the anomalies in the present rules of domicile,[93] together with the difficulties of applying them to marginal cases. Instead we should examine the marriage which is being terminated. If the parties celebrated the marriage in a particular religious form, whether or not they also contracted a civil marriage, it is logical that they should be allowed to terminate the marriage according to the rules of that religion, should one of them wish to do so. In such circumstances, it should be assumed that the parties are not obtaining a religious divorce in order to evade English domestic law but in order to meet the express or implied obligations into which they entered when contracting a religious marriage.[94]

Whilst the latter proposal seems administratively simpler, the former is preferred because it is less likely to prejudice good race relations. Approving some religious divorces and not others would seem to be invidious and divisive. Moreover, even if, in substance, religious divorce was no easier than civil divorce, the general population might perceive that particular religious groups were receiving favoured treatment, which could foster anti-racial feelings.

Religious bars to remarriage

Enactment of either of the two proposals advocated above would considerably ease the problem of the 'chained' wife provided that the civil courts refused to grant a civil dissolution of a religious marriage where one of the parties requested a religious divorce. It would thus become impossible for the husband to win his freedom to remarry without also granting the same to the wife or vice versa.

However, as the likelihood of either of these proposals being implemented in the current political climate seems slight[95] we need to consider more limited reforms which may find favour with the government. Models exist in New York and Ontario which, it has been suggested, could be adopted here.

The New York model[96]

In 1983 the New York '*get* law'[97] provided that a final decree of divorce would not be granted in respect of a marriage which has been solemnized by a clergyman or minister unless the plaintiff files a statement that he or she has 'taken all steps solely within his or her power to remove all barriers to the defendant's remarriage following the annulment of divorce'.

This model forms the basis of the clause[98] which was moved during the passage of the Matrimonial and Family Proceedings Act in 1984. Under this clause, the court would not grant a decree absolute in cases where one party had satisfied the court of the existence of a barrier to religious remarriage until the other party had removed the barrier or done everything in his or her power to do so. Whilst the Solicitor-General expressed sympathy with the purpose of the proposed clause, he was critical of the drafting, and the amendment was dismissed. However, his attitude does suggest that, given legislation properly drafted after appropriate consultation, the government would support a reform based on the New York model.[99]

The Ontario model

The Ontario Family Law Act 1986 tackles the problem[100] by penalizing the recalcitrant spouse in ancillary proceedings. Where one party has not removed all barriers to the other's religious remarriage, despite a request to do so, any application, pleadings or defence of the latter in ancillary proceedings may be struck out.

The principal advantage of this model over the New York model is that it may have an effect on the recalcitrant spouse who does not want a civil divorce at all. On the other hand, it is ineffective if there is no application for ancillary relief.[101] It has been suggested that the two models might be combined, thus providing two opportunities for the civil law to induce the recalcitrant spouse to remove the barriers to religious marriage.

The Law Commission's proposals

Under the new divorce regime recommended by the Law Commission and now adopted by the government, the hardship bar could potentially be raised in *all* cases by either party. Thus, there would seem to be scope to use the bar as a method of dealing with the recalcitrant spouse.[102] However, the language used in clause 4 of the draft bill is based on that in the current legislation,[103] under which there is some doubt as to whether refusal to grant or participate in a religious divorce would constitute grave hardship.[104] It is suggested that, in order to solve this problem, it should be specified expressly in the legislation that refusal to remove a religious barrier to remarriage is a basis for raising the hardship bar.[105]

The effect of such a provision would be similar to the New York model.[106] Since it would have the advantage of being situated within the general framework of the divorce law rather than requiring a separate procedure, it should be easier to secure acceptance of the reform as well as be simpler to implement.

However, two objections to the above proposal might be anticipated. First, it may be alleged that is it not right to single out one particular form of hardship. This objection is, however, misconceived, because the proposed provision would merely confirm that refusal to grant a religious divorce comes within the hardship bar. Confirmation is appropriate because of the uncertainty about the matter and because this particular form of hardship is not uncommon. As a result of this clarification, it is envisaged that a significant percentage of spouses, who would otherwise refuse to participate in a religious divorce, will agree to do so in order to avoid litigation. These considerations are not valid in respect of other possible types of hardship.

Second, opponents of the proposal may contend that it is inappropriate for the civil law to put pressure on people to comply with the requirement of their present or former religious faith. This argument misses the point that the recalcitrant spouse would only be 'pressurized' if he or she wishes to obtain the benefits of a civil divorce and, in particular, the right to remarry. On the contrary, it is argued that it is inappropriate for the court to grant the petitioner the ability to remarry, when he or she is denying this right to the respondent. The grant of the civil divorce in such circumstances is tantamount to condoning the petitioner's breach of an obligation, which has moral if not legal force, contained expressly or by implication in the marriage contract.

Finally, it should be emphasized that the proposed additions to the Law Commission's scheme are entirely consistent with the policy behind the reform. In particular, where one party refuses to remove a religious barrier to remarriage, it will not be possible to achieve the four principal objectives of divorce law stated by the Commission (that is, promoting maximum fairness; minimizing bitterness, distress and humiliation; enabling 'dead' marriages to be buried[107] and ensuring that the massive transition involved in divorce is as smooth as possible for the parties and their children).[108] First, as mentioned above, the civil law's insistence on the dissolution of Jewish marriages by civil divorce creates the unfair situation that one party can release himself from the marriage by civil decree but, in effect, denies his spouse the ability to remarry by not releasing her from the religious marriage into which they entered and to which the secular law gave full effect. Second, the unfairness of the legal system which allows this to happen will increase the bitterness and distress of the 'innocent' party. Third, the dead marriage has not been buried because it is still alive according to the system of law under which it was celebrated and one of the parties thereto is not free to remarry in accordance with the dictates of his or her conscience. Finally, the transition cannot be complete until the religious divorce is granted and, in the meantime, the parties' adjustment is hindered by the fact that they are in a state of limbo between the civil law, according to which they are divorced, and their religious law, under which they are still married.

CONCLUSION

We have seen that, whilst members of ethnic minorities will generally have no difficulty in obtaining civil divorces in this country, religious divorces obtained within the jurisdiction are of no validity and there are restrictions on the recognition of some religious divorces obtained abroad. Furthermore, the very fact that civil divorce is easily obtained provides opportunities for unscrupulous parties to blackmail their spouses by refusing to grant or participate in a religious divorce unless their demands are met.

Some may take the parochial view that these problems are caused by the religious law in question and that it is up to the religious authorities of the ethnic communities to solve them. However, it is submitted that, in a pluralistic society, the state cannot abdicate all responsibility for the problems caused by differences between the civil law and the religious law of its ethnic minorities.[109] Indeed, this principle seems to have been accepted in the express statutory recognition of Jewish and Quaker marriages. As mentioned earlier, the fact that religious marriages but not religious divorces are recognized exacerbates the problem of the 'chained' spouse.

It is suggested that the best method of solving the problems identified in this chapter is to provide for recognition to be accorded to the legal institutions of ethnic minorities[110] rather than to impose civil institutions on them, except in cases where the religious law causes hardship which can effectively be averted by the application of the civil law. For example, as we saw above, whilst restrictions on the recognition of certain religious divorces may have been well motivated, they do not in fact achieve their purpose. Prevention of hardship could be better achieved by recognizing the divorces and providing adequate financial remedies for the wife.

However, such reform proposals are unlikely to be considered seriously at government level until a policy of encouraging mutual tolerance and promoting religious and cultural pluralism[111] is officially adopted. Thus, those in government or seeking to govern in the future should be called upon to state their commitment to such a policy.

NOTES

1 Law Com. 190. These proposals are accepted by the government in *Looking to the Future: Mediation and the Ground for Divorce*, Lord Chancellor's Department (1995), Cmnd. 2799, London: HMSO.

2 See generally P.M. North (1975), 'Recognition of Extra-Judicial Divorce' *Law Quarterly Review, 91*, and P.M. North (1977), *The Private International Law of Matrimonial Causes in the British Isles and the Republic of Ireland*, Amsterdam: North-Holland, ch. 11 and S.M. Poulter (1986), *English Law and Ethnic Minority Customs*, London: Butterworth, ch. 5.

3 For a description of these, see D. Gordon (1988), *Foreign Divorces: English Law and Practice*, Aldershot: Gower, chs 1 to 3.

4 Under the Dissolution of Muslim Marriages Act 1939 and the Hindu Marriages Act 1955 respectively.

5 In particular, see the Pakistani Muslim Family Law Ordinance 1961. In Iraq, Syria and Tunisia, court proceedings are required before the *talaq* can take effect. See further, N. Anderson (1976), *Law Reform in the Muslim World.*

6 The recognition of Hindu extra-judicial divorces is now regulated by the Hindu Marriages Act 1955 s. 29. See Gordon, *op. cit.*, note 3 above, pp. 31–2.

7 For the text of an English orthodox *get* see S. Maidment (1974), 'The legal effect of religious divorce', *Modern Law Review*, **37**, (3), p. 611.

8 See Gordon, *op. cit.*, note 3 above, at p. 42.

9 *Varavand* v. *Varavand* (1964) 108 SJ 693.

10 See *D* v. *D* [1994] 1 FLR 38.

11 See S.M. Poulter (1989), 'Divorce reform in a multicultural society', *Family Law*, **19**, p. 99.

12 275 *Gets* were obtained under the auspices of the Rabbinical court in the UK in 1993 (Board of Deputies of British Jews: Annual Statistics).

13 See 316 H.L. Debs. col 213 *per* Lord Simon of Glaisdale.

14 Domicile and Matrimonial Proceedings Act 1973, s.5.

15 *Kapur* v. *Kapur* [1984] FLR 920 applying the words of Lord Scarman in *R.* v. *London Borough of Brent ex p. Shah* [1983] 2 AC 309. Settled purposes can include 'education, business or profession, employment, health, family or merely love of the place'.

16 *Onobrauche* v. *Onobrauche* (1978) *Family Law*, **8**, p. 107.

17 *Poon* v. *Tan* (1973) *Family Law*, **4**, p. 161.
18 For example, *Rukat* v. *Rukat* [1975] *Fam.* 63 and *Banik* v. *Banik* [1973] 1 WLR 860.
19 In the parliamentary debate on a proposed legislative solution in 1984, Peter Thurnham MP cited cases of hardship which had occurred in the Muslim community in which the husband had used his power to refuse to grant a religious divorce in order to make extortionate financial demands on the wife (see 161 HC Debs, cols 926 *et seq*).
20 See M.D.A. Freeman (1981), 'Jews and the law of divorce in England', *IV Jewish Law Annual*, 276, 280–3 and B. Berkovits (1989), 'Jewish Divorce', *Family Law*, **19**, 115.
21 This is the more common scenario. However, in a significant number of cases it is the wife who refuses to participate in the *get* procedure. See, for example, the Australian case of *Gwiazda* v. *Gwiazda*, Case no. M10631 of 1982 decided 23.2.1983 (discussed in A. Strum (1994), 'Jewish divorce: what can the civil courts do?', *Australian Journal of Family Law*, **225**, pp. 245–6.
22 See the discussion in Meiselman, *Jewish Women in Jewish Law*, at pp. 103 *et seq.*
23 This would overcome the problem that the present statement in the Ketubah that the marriage is in accordance with 'the laws of Moses and Israel' may well be insufficient to create an enforceable obligation to dissolve the marriage in accordance with civil law (see I. Breitowitz (1992), 'The plight of the Agunah: a study in Halacha, Contract and the First Amendment', *Maryland Law Review*, **51**, 312 at pp. 346–9.
24 It may have a morally persuasive effect. See discussion of the views of the English judiciary by Judge Myrella Cohen in 'The Tragedy of Divorce - The Ways Forward - The English Law' in *Justice* (Journal of the Association of Jewish Lawyers and Jurists), **4**, 32 (Winter 1995), at pp. 33–34.
25 In North America, where this issue has come before the courts on a number of occasions with varying results, there has been considerable discussion of the constitutional, contractual, public policy and Jewish law implications of 'compelling religious divorces', whether by means of enforcing the provisions of the marriage contract or of enforcing a clause in a separation agreement or consent order in which the husband undertakes to submit to, and comply with, the directions of a Rabbinical tribunal in order to obtain a *get*. (The fullest discussion is in Breitowitz, *op. cit.*, note 23 above, especially at pp. 338–75, but see also B. Meislin (1981), 'Pursuit of the wife's right to a *get* in United States and Canadian courts', *IV Jewish Law Annual*', p. 250 and H.P. Glenn (1980), 'Where heavens meet: the compelling of religious divorces', *Amer. J. Comp. Law*, **28**, 1. Whilst undertakings to cooperate in the *get* procedure are used in England (see Berkovits *op. cit.*, note 20 above at p. 117), there has been no case where enforcement of such an undertaking has been sought.
26 The objections based on separation of religion and state and of freedom of conscience are effectively refuted by Glenn, *op. cit.*, note 25 above, and Breitowitz, *op. cit.*, note 23 above. It is difficult to believe that the view that it is against public policy to make provision in relation to divorce at the time of the marriage would be upheld in the light of the modern policy of encouraging parties to agree on all matters arising from the breakdown of their marriage.
27 See Freeman, *op. cit.*, note 20 above, at pp. 282–3.
28 For a discussion of what type of compulsion is regarded as invalidating coercion see Breitowitz, *op. cit.*, note 23 above, at pp. 331–8. In general, threat of removal of privileges not recognized by Jewish law will not constitute inappropriate coercion. Thus, for example, a new Israeli statute allows courts to restrict recalcitrant parties *inter alia* from holding driving licences and bank accounts. However, the threat of payment of a fine or expropriation of property would be improper coercion.

29 B. Berkovits (1993), '*Get* and *Talaq* in English law: reflections on law and policy' in C. Mallat and J. Connors (eds), *Islamic Family Law*, London: Graham-Trotman.

30 Per Emery J in the Australian case of *In the Marriage of Gwiazda*, *op. cit.*, note 21 above. The judge granted a mandatory injunction ordering the recalcitrant spouse to appear before the Melbourne Rabbinical Court.

31 [1969] 1 All ER 1007.

32 Berkovits, *op. cit.*, note 20 above, p. 117, suggests that the refusal to grant a *get* would be conduct which it would be inequitable to take into account in assessing financial provision under s.25 Matrimonial Causes Act 1973 (as amended by Matrimonial and Property Proceedings Act 1984).

33 See note 28 and Berkovits, *op. cit.*, note 20 above, p. 117.

34 It is possible for marriages to be terminated by law without there being any divorce or annulment, in which case the common law rules would still apply. See, for example, *Viswallingham* v. *Viswallingham* [1980] 1 FLR 15, where according to the religious law, the marriage was terminated automatically by the conversion of one party to a different religion. The termination was not recognized on grounds of public policy.

35 See, for example, *Qureshi* v. *Qureshi* [1972] Fam. 173.

36 [1985] 3 All ER 1017 at 1031.

37 Gordon *op. cit.*, note 3 above at p. 115 provides a helpful table with a suggested classification of divorces.

38 *Quazi* v. *Quazi* [1980] AC 744.

39 See B. Berkovits (1988), 'Transnational Divorce: The *Fatima* Decision', *Law Quarterly Review*, **104**, p. 60.

40 *D* v *D* (*Recognition of Foreign Divorce*) [1994] 1 FLR 38.

41 *Chaudhary* v. *Chaudhary* [1984] 3 All ER 1017.

42 The requirements for recognition are contained in the Family Law Act 1986, s.46(2).

43 The requirements for recognition are contained in the Family Law Act 1986, s.46(1).

44 For *formal* divorces, it is sufficient if either party is habitually resident in, domiciled in or a national of the country where the divorce is obtained. For *informal* divorces, the divorce must be obtained in the country where at least one spouse is domiciled. In addition, an informal divorce will only be recognized if it is valid by the law of the domicile of the other party, whereas formal divorces are only tested in relation to one party. Domicile may be defined either according to English law or the law of the place where the party is alleged to be domiciled. Thus, in theory there are up to eight different countries where a formal divorce may be obtained and recognized (although it is most unlikely that each party has habitual residence, domicile in the English sense, domicile in the foreign sense and nationality in different countries); for informal divorces there are a maximum of four possibilities.

45 See the derogatory comments of Cumming-Bruce LJ about bare *talaqs* in *Chaudhary* v. *Chaudhary* [1984] 3 WLR 1017 at p. 1032.

46 [1986] AC 527.

47 Recognition of Divorces and Legal Separations Act 1971 s.2.

48 [1995] 2 All ER 683.

49 Also, with respect, construing the section as referring to 'one set of proceedings' (*ibid* at p. 692) seems to be a gloss on the statute and not the natural meaning. Furthermore, the argument (*ibid*) that because the phrases 'obtained by means of proceedings' and 'obtained in a country outside the British Island' appear in the same sentence they must mean 'obtained by means of proceedings in a country outside the British Islands' appears flawed. If that is what Parliament meant why was a superfluous

'obtained' added in. Surely, this might suggest that the two requirements are to be read separately!

50 *Ibid* at p. 695.

51 Previously the Domicile and Matrimonial Proceedings Act 1973 s.16(1).

52 See B. Berkovits (1988), *op. cit.*, note 39 above at pp. 75–78, *Law Quarterly Review*; M. Pilkington (1988), 'Transnational Divorces under the Family Law Act 1986', ICLQ, **37**, pp. 131, 137–141.

53 [1995] 2 All ER 683 at p. 696.

54 See, for example, *Lindo* v. *Belisario* (1795) 161 ER 531 in which the English court referred to the provisions of Jewish law to determine whether the marriage was valid.

55 *Moss* v. *Smith* (1840) 1 M & G 228 seems to be the earliest reported case dealing with a *get* obtained in England. It is suggested that Erskine J must have made the assumption that a valid Jewish divorce is possible. However, the case is not very helpful because the legal and evidential arguments are confused. Freeman (*op. cit.* note 20 above, at p. 277) claims that the legality of the practice of the Rabbinical Courts in exercising divorce jurisdiction, which they did prior to 1866, must 'be dubious to say the least'.

56 *Ganer* v. *Lady Lanesborugh* (1791) 1 Peake p. 17.

57 The rule in *Armitage* v. *A-G* [1906] P. 135.

58 As in *Har-Shefi* v. *Har Shefi* (No. 2) [1953] P. 2008 and *Qureshi* v. *Qureshi* [1972] Fam. 173..

59 In *Warrender* v. *Warrender* (1835) 2 Cl and F. 488, 534 the proposition that if a country allowed a marriage to be dissolved by consent of the parties without any judicial proceedings, such dissolution should be recognized in other countries was held to be 'so absurd' that 'it never could be for a moment entertained' (cited with approval by Swinfen Eady LJ in *R* v. *Superintendent Registrar of Marriages, Hammersmith ex p. Mir-Andwarrudin* [1917] 1 KB 634, 659–660 and 662.

60 Indeed there seems to have been more concern as to where the marriage took place than the divorce. Thus, in the *Hammersmith* case, it was the possibility of an *English* marriage being terminated by a *talaq* which most alarmed the court. In *Maher* v. *Maher* [1951] p. 342, Barnard J refused to recognize a *talaq* in Egypt, the husband's domicile, as dissolving an English registry office marriage because to do so would 'encourage and sanction the purely temporary union of English women and foreigners professing the Mohammedan religion during their limited residence in this country'.

61 As, for example, in India, Egypt and Israel.

62 The common law rules are still applicable in many Commonwealth countries. In some cases the common law rules have been expressly saved or even extended by statute. See, generally J.D. McClean (1983), *Recognition of Family Judgements in the Commonwealth*, London: Butterworth.

63 See, for example, 315 HL Debs (16.2.71) at cols 483–486 per Lord Hailsham; Law Com. 34; P. Bellet and B. Goldman's Explanatory Document, *Actes et Documents De La Haye*, vol. II (translation at (1971), *Family Law Quarterly*, **5**, p. 303, pp. 321–67) paras 9, 47 and 48 and A. Anton (1969), *ICLQ*, **18**, p. 620.

64 An amendment was moved in the House of Lords with the aim of overruling the decision in *Qureshi* v. *Qureshi* [1972] Fam. 173 316 H.L. Debs cols. 212 *et seq* (11.3.71). Although the amendment was withdrawn, the Lord Chancellor indicated that further consideration would be given to the issue (at cols 224–225).

65 *Ibid.*, cols 319–320.

66 That is, where the divorce was 'formal' and one party was domiciled in or a national of the country where the divorce was obtained.

67 Also, the restriction in s.16(2) of the 1973 Act was extended by providing that an informal divorce could not be recognized if either party was habitually resident in England and Wales for one year at the time the divorce was obtained. Further, an additional defence of lack of official certification (see. s.51(3) (b) (1)) was also added in respect of informal divorces.

68 Law Com No. 137, para. 6.11.

69 The only other example which has been found of different recognition rules for formal and informal divorces is in the Dutch International Divorce Act 1981. Under art. 2(1) all judicial and quasi-judicial divorces obtained 'after a proper process' are recognized. Under art. 2(2) other divorces will be recognized provided that it is evident that the non-initiating party has expressly or impliedly agreed to or thereafter acquiesced in the divorce. However, art. 3 provides further restrictions on the recognition of a dissolution by unilateral declaration of the husband *alone*. Such a divorce will only be recognized if divorce in this form is in conformity with his personal law and the dissolution is valid at the place where it was effected. (These requirements are in addition to the requirement of the wife's agreement or acquiescence.) The 'Explanatory Memorandum' Tweede Kamer (1979–1980) 16004 No. 3 p. 17 suggests that art. 3 would not apply to cases in which the cooperation or even the presence of a state or religious authority is also required.

70 473 HL Debs col. 1082 (22.4.86).

71 And where the parties are domiciled in different countries that the divorce is recognized by the country of the domicile of the other party.

72 See, for example, *Quazi* v. *Quazi* [1980] AC 744.

73 Matrimonial and Family Proceedings Act 1984, Part III, implementing the recommendations in Law Com. No. 117. It may be of interest that this solution was suggested as early as 1971 in the debates on the Recognition of Divorces and Legal Separations Bill 1971 (316 HL Deb at col. 224 (per Lord Chancellor) and at col. 226 per Lord Simon).

74 Provided that one of the jurisdictional links in s.15 exists. Leave must be obtained before making an application (s.13).

75 WP No. 77 para. 11.

76 [1986] 2 WLR 350.

77 Law Com. No. 137.

78 *Op. cit.*, note 3 above at pp. 170–173.

79 This situation is only likely to arise where there is want of jurisdiction, because the defences are discretionary.

80 See Anton's comment in relation to informal divorces in the Hague Conference Proceedings, *Actes et Documents De La Haye*, vol. II, p. 100. Cf. in the Dutch International Divorce Act art. 3 (note 67 above) where the consent of the wife is a relevant factor in determining whether the husband's repudiatory divorce should be recognized.

81 Law Com. No. 170. para. 3.18.

82 See the Law Society Family Law Sub-Committee's assertion that 'virtually any spouse can assemble a list of events, which, taken out of context, can be presented as unreasonable behaviour sufficient on which to found a divorce petition' in *A Better Way Out* (1979), London: The Law Society.

83 That is, empowering the courts to order financial provision although they did not grant the divorce. See p. 142 above.

84 For a comparative survey of attitudes to extra-judicial divorces taking place within the jurisdiction, see L. Palsson (1978), 'Marriage and Divorce in Comparative Conflict of Law', *International Encyclopedia of Comparative Law*, Tubingen: J.C.B. Mohr, vol. III Ch. 16 at paras 153–4. It should be mentioned that even countries not recognizing such divorces may recognize transnational divorces initiated in the forum provided that the divorce authority is seen as originating from outside the jurisdiction (see *Chaudry* v. *Chaudry* 159 NJ Super 556, 388 A.2d 1000 (1978)).

85 Marriage Act 1948 ss.26 and 47.

86 *Ibid.*, ss.41–44.

87 However, this may change if the Law Commission's one-year waiting period is introduced (see note 1 above).

88 See J. Young (1987), 'The Recognition of Extra-Judicial Divorces in the United Kingdom', *Legal Studies*, **7**, pp. 78, 86.

89 [1995] 2 All ER 683.

90 [1980] A.C. 744.

91 [1995] 2 All ER 683 at p. 696.

92 Berkovits, *op. cit.*, notes 20 and 29 above.

93 See Law Com. No. 168.

94 See comments in the New York case of *Stern* v. *Stern* (1979), *Family Law Reports*, **5**, (BNA) 2810; *NYLJ*, 8 August 1979, 13.

95 As evidenced by the rejection of the request by the Union of Muslim Organizations of UK and Eire for recognition of a separate system of Islamic Law. See S. Poulter 'The claim to a separate Islamic system of personal law for British Muslims' in C. Mallat and J. Connors (eds), *op. cit.*, note 29 above.

96 For detailed analysis of the law, and particularly its constitutionality, see Breitowitz, *op. cit.*, note 23 above, at pp. 375–97.

97 Domestic Relations Law, s.253.

98 See 161 HC Debs col 924 (13 June 1984).

99 See the draft bill proposed by Berkovits, *op. cit.*, note 29 above, at p. 143.

100 The New York approach was inappropriate in Ontario for constitutional reasons..

101 There is also a danger that if the husband grants a *get* because otherwise he will have his property taken from him this may constitute improper coercion (see note 28 above).

102 The Law Commission's proposals also provide for the court to postpone the granting of the divorce on certain specific grounds (see clause 6 of the draft bill appended to Law Com. Report No. 190). It is suggested that the fact that one party has refused to remove religious bars to remarriage should be added as a further ground for ordering a delay. This might deal with the situation where one party is deliberately 'dragging his/her feet' in dealing with the religious divorce rather than refusing to cooperate outright.

103 Matrimonial Causes Act 1973, s.5.

104 See page 135 above.

105 It would, of course, also be necessary to show that in the particular circumstances of the case, it would be wrong to dissolve the marriage until the barrier had been removed.

106 It would also be similar to the reform proposed by the Australian Law Reform Commission in Report No. 57, 'Multiculturalism. The Law' (1992) Sydney, at para. 5.42.

107 These objectives originate from the *Field of Choice*, Law Com. No. 6 (1966), but were reiterated by the Commission in Law Com. No. 170 and No. 190.

108 Law Com. No. 170 para. 3.50.

109 See, generally, Australian Law Reform Commission Report *op. cit.*, see note 106 above.

110 For full discussion of this issue see Poulter *op. cit.*, note 90 above.

111 In Australia, a government ministry has been set up to further this policy. In this connection, it may be of interest that Australia does not have a policy of restricting recognition of religious divorces (see Sykes and Pryles (1991), *Australian Private International Law*, 3rd edn, at p. 470) and that the Australian Courts have shown a willingness to help 'chained spouses' – see *In the Marriage of Gwiazda, op. cit.*, note 21 above.

8 Can Children Divorce their Parents?

*Michael Freeman**

INTRODUCTION

It was the Gregory Kingsley case[1] in the USA which first evoked the image of the child divorcing his parents, although it was by no means the first case of this kind.[2] However, in this context, the use of the concept of 'divorce' is both emotive and inaccurate, and it courts the misleading and sensational headline. Divorce is a licence to remarry and, as such, offers the opportunity to create a new relationship. The relationship of spouses is socially constructed: in comparison with the relationship between parent and child it is artificial in that it requires state intervention both to create it and to dissolve it.[3] By contrast, the parent–child relationship, being an incident of biology and genetics, is not subject to this control (at least outside the context of assisted reproduction[4] and adoption).[5] Parenthood is not licensed.[6] Nor does it come to an end upon divorce, either when this takes place in its true sense or when children 'divorce' parents.

When we talk of a child 'divorcing' his parents, we really raise the question of whether a child can choose where he or she lives and/or with whom. Not surprisingly, this raises controversy. To most, one of the characteristics of being a child is being deprived – and they would say rightly – of such choices. However, we are now witnessing a shift from children being seen as 'objects' to one where their subjectivity – their existence as individuals in their own right – is coming to be recognized. A generation ago children were accorded the right to be seen as patients in the context of medical practice.[7] Twenty years ago it was recognized that children who were victimized by abuse deserved the role of litigant.[8] In other areas, but not in education,[9] they have acquired the role of consumer. International

* Professor of English Law, University College London.

documents, in particular the UN Convention on the Rights of the Child, accord children the status of rights-bearer.[10] Article 12 of this Convention, recognizing the child's autonomy and granting participatory rights, is especially noteworthy.[11] And a significant strand[12] of the Children Act 1989 legitimates children as persons rather than objects of concern.[13] Yet, despite these advances, the metaphor of divorce evokes unease, possibly because, as a label – as a social construction – it comes with a ready-made package of associations.[14] And these, far from being associated with children, betray concerns with dysfunction and disintegration. The Lord Chancellor's White Paper *Looking To The Future* encapsulated some of these concerns[15] although, of course, it did not address the issue of the child who wishes to sever links with his or her own family.

Children were 'divorcing' their parents long before the problem was so designated. The accentuated concern is associated with the concept of divorce. When the phenomenon did not attract this particular label, it did not evoke the critical responses it does now.[16] A generation ago an Indian girl,[17] close to her eighteenth birthday, contested her parents' attempt to remove her from voluntary care.[18] Their goal was an arranged marriage which she wished to resist. The Court of Appeal held that there was no 'absolute' obligation on the local authority to return her to her parents.[19] There is little doubt that this strained interpretation would have been applauded by many of those who criticize today's 'divorce' cases. Yet, although no such label was used, the girl was, to all intents and purposes, 'divorcing' her parents. Similarly, in the USA, the *Polovchak* case[20] in the early 1980s was not characterized in terms of divorce, but the issues involved were little different from those in contemporary cases. A 12 year-old had emigrated with his parents from the USSR to the USA, but his father, not liking America, decided that he and his family should return to the Soviet Union. The 12 year-old, Walter, decided, however, that he did like his new country and wanted to stay. He accordingly ran away from home and refused to accompany his parents back to the Soviet Union. The case provoked enormous controversy, with the American Civil Liberties Union, which had campaigned for children's rights, supporting the father's case. 'We believe', it said, 'kids have rights, but not that a 12 year-old has the right to choose where his family should live.'[21] But Walter was not claiming any such right: he was claiming the right to decide where he would live.[22]

The issue, then, is not new. But the Children Act 1989 enables us to see it in a new light.

THE 1989 ACT AND EMPOWERMENT

The Children Act 1989 is not about empowerment.[23] Indeed, it may be said that its principal aim, however flawed in execution, is to address and improve children's welfare. The paramountcy which this is accorded in the very first subsection of the Act means that autonomy must often take a back seat. But the welfare checklist[24] nevertheless places the wishes and feelings of the child, considered in the light of age and understanding, first in the list of factors. To emphasize this, *Working Together*, in its post-Children Act form,[25] urges the involvement of children in child protection conferences 'whenever [they] have sufficient understanding and are able to express their wishes and feelings and to participate in the process of investigation, assessment, planning and review…'.[26] In a number of situations the Act provides that children may initiate court actions. For example, he or she may challenge an emergency protection order,[27] seek contact when in care,[28] ask for a care order to be discharged[29] and, as we shall see in detail, seek the court's leave to obtain an order (under s.8) making a decision as to where he or she is to live or with whom have contact.[30] It is usually a precondition that the child has sufficient understanding to make an application, but, surprisingly perhaps, this is not always so.[31] Since empowerment is often dependent upon representation, the more extensive use of guardians *ad litem* should also not be overlooked.[32] But nor should the disparity between such provision in the arena of public law and in private law disputes be ignored.[33]

The Children Act also recognizes the autonomy of the child in a number of provisions which give children, when 'of sufficient understanding to make an informed decision', the right to refuse to submit to medical and psychiatric examinations and other assessments.[34] The impact of the *Gillick* case,[35] and in particular of Lord Scarman's judgment,[36] is readily detectable in this language: indeed, it may be said to be one of the dominant influences on the Act.

COMPETENCE AND EMPOWERMENT

Lord Scarman, it will be recalled, linked empowerment to competence. A competent child is one who 'achieves a sufficient understanding and intelligence to enable him or her to understand fully what is proposed' and also has 'sufficient discretion to enable him or her to make a wise choice in his or her own interests'.[37] In these terms competence incorporates understanding and knowledge with wisdom. While there are dangers in conflating knowledge and wisdom, it is commonly done. Few adults are *Gillick*-competent, if competence hinges upon the ability to understand fully what is involved in a decision: many children who are well below the ages with which we tend to associate *Gillick*-competence are competent within the parameters of Lord Scarman's test if 'wise choice' is genuinely situated within the child's personal experiential knowledge of his or her 'own interests'. The courts, in a series of recent cases[38] which have held that a child's right to consent to medical treatment does not extend to a right to refuse such treatment, have failed to appreciate this. As Alderson and Goodwin have noted, 'professional, textbook knowledge is highly valued, personal experiential knowledge is discounted'.[39] This is what happened to the anorexic 17 year-old in *Re W*.[40] And, once such 'wisdom' is ignored, the child is assumed to be ignorant except insofar as he or she can recount medical or other professional information. It becomes easy then to discuss the contribution they can make to decision-making. Alderson and Goodwin argue that the non-competent child

> ...who figures in the legal imagination is treated as arational rather than irrational. When children are credited, at least, with a misguided rationality, the importance of explaining and correcting misunderstandings is accepted. If children are implicitly treated as arational, then enforced treatment without regard to the child's views is endorsed by the courts.[41]

This is what happened in *Re R*,[42] *Re W*[43] and other less publicized cases.[44] And it happens also outside the context of decisions about medical treatment.

Thus, for example, in *Re H*,[45] where in care proceedings it became clear that a 15 year-old and his guardian *ad litem* were giving conflicting instructions to a solicitor, the court had to interpret a Rule[46] which instructs solicitors to represent children in accordance with instructions received from the guardian *ad litem*

> ...unless the solicitor considers, having taken into account the views of the guardian ad litem and any direction of the court ... that the child wishes to give instructions which conflict with those of the guardian ad litem and that he is able, *having regard to his understanding*,[47] to give such instructions on his own behalf, in which case he shall conduct the proceedings in accordance with the instructions received from the child.

The boy concerned was described as of 'above-average ability'[48] (he was in the 'A' stream of a grammar school), but emotionally disturbed. A number of the court's conclusions repay examination. Thus, for example, Thorpe J held that

> ...the level of understanding that enables a child to make an informed decision whether to refuse to submit to a psychiatric examination is in all practical senses

> a much higher level than is required to enable him to give instructions to a solicitor on his own behalf.[49]

But why? Is the understanding and knowledge any greater or is it an underlying fear that the consequences of making an unwise decision in the former case are greater, more potentially deleterious to the child, than in the latter? Or is it once again a triumph of professional knowledge over personal, experiential insight?

It is also noteworthy that Thorpe J dismissed the argument of H's counsel that 'almost any child of 15 years and 8 months must be taken to have sufficient understanding to instruct a solicitor' with the riposte:

> Obviously a child suffering from a mental disability might not have such understanding. Obviously a child suffering from a psychiatric disorder might not have such a level of understanding.[50]

(But is it indeed 'obvious'?)

> But I cannot follow her to the conclusion that if a child is only suffering from some emotional disturbance then really there is little room to question his or her ability to instruct a solicitor. It seems to me that a child must have sufficient rationality within the understanding to instruct a solicitor. It may well be that the level of emotional disturbance is such as to remove the necessary degree of rationality that leads to coherent and consistent instruction.[51]

Yet, we do not question an emotionally disturbed adult's ability to instruct a solicitor. Are we right to do so in the case of a child? Have the consequences of this sort of reasoning and the decisions it leads to been thought through? The removal of autonomy can lead to the destruction of identity – a feeling of being out of control can exacerbate disturbance.[52] Despite his emotional problems, H probably[53] had the ability to make what Lord Scarman captured as a 'wise choice', even if he might have lacked the sort of professional knowledge that we associate with 'rationality'.[54]

CHILDREN AS PARTIES TO PROCEEDINGS

Re H was a public law case. Of greater relevance for the child who wishes to 'divorce' parents is the private law and the opportunities this presents for a child to participate in court proceedings.

Most media coverage of 'divorcing' cases has followed child-initiated actions. It is worth, however, first considering the status of the child in proceedings initiated by one of his parents. As Sir Thomas Bingham MR noted in *Re S*:

> ...the proposition that a boy of 11 should be accorded the full rights of a litigant to intervene in a dispute between his parents about the arrangements best suited to promote his welfare ... may be surprising to some.[55]

In *Re S* the boy's father applied for residence and contact orders. S was made a party to the proceedings and the Official Solicitor[56] was appointed to act as his guardian *ad litem*. The Official Solicitor recommended that S should continue to live with his mother (as he had done since age 5) and should see his father less frequently. However, it was the father's contention, supported by S, that S should live with him in North America. S contended from the outset of the proceedings that the Official Solicitor should not represent him and that he should be able to act independently through a solicitor. Under Rule 9.2A of the Family Proceedings Rules 1991 (as amended in 1992) a minor may 'begin, prosecute or defend' proceedings without a next friend or guardian *ad litem* with the leave of the court or where a solicitor considers the minor is able 'having regard to his understanding, to give instructions in relation to the proceedings' and has accepted instructions to act. The Rules also provide that a minor may apply to the court for the removal of a next friend or guardian *ad litem*.

The Court of Appeal held that it would not grant leave for a minor to take part in proceedings without a next friend or guardian *ad litem*; the minor intended to be legally represented, in which case the issue would be whether the minor had sufficient understanding to give coherent instructions. It stressed that it was 'understanding',[57] not age, that underpinned the test. At least with children, so the Master of the Rolls believed, understanding increased with the passage of time. He noted that

> ...different children have differing levels of understanding at the same age. And understanding is not an absolute. It has to be assessed relatively to the issues in the proceedings.[58]

He concluded that

> ...where any sound judgement on these issues calls for insight and imagination which only maturity and experience can bring, both the court and the solicitor will be slow to conclude that the child's understanding is sufficient.[59]

The Court concluded that it could not accede to S's request. Even were it to have done so, the Master of the Rolls believed, the continuing assistance of the Official Solicitor as *amicus curiae* would have been sought, 'so the gain to S might in any event have been small'.[60]

These last remarks were seized upon by Booth J in *Re H*.[61] Here, a 15 year-old boy was warded by his parents after the man with whom he was living was charged with sexual offences against other boys. He had been left in England when his parents moved to France. He now wished to stay in England and ran away each time he was taken to France. Like the previous case, *Re H* could be interpreted as one where a child wished to choose where he would live. The boy in *Re H* considered that the Official Solicitor who was representing him was not representing his views, and he applied to be allowed to continue to defend the proceedings without the Official Solicitor acting as his guardian *ad litem*, and for the removal of the Official Solicitor from that position. Booth J was of the opinion that H had sufficient understanding to participate as a party in the proceedings and so should be permitted to do so. It was 'not for [the] court ... to take into account what the court may or may not consider to be in the best interests of the child'.[62] As a result, the Official Solicitor's role as guardian *ad litem* ceased, but it was thought to be 'vital'[63] that he should continue in the capacity as *amicus*, 'an independent advisor to the court'.[64]

In *Re S* the Master of the Rolls had spoken of the need to strike a 'judicious balance' between recognizing the personality of children ('A child's wishes are not to be discounted or dismissed simply because he is a child. He should be free to express them and decision-makers should listen') and the fact that a child is, after all, a child ('children...are liable to be vulnerable and impressionable, lacking the maturity to weigh the longer-term against the shorter, lacking the insight to know how others will react and the imagination to know how they will react in certain situations, lacking the experience to measure the probable against the possible').[65] The solution hinted at in *Re S* and adopted in *Re H* reflects this balance: the child can dismiss the Official Solicitor, but the court retains him in a different, and, it has to be conceded, far from clear, capacity.

Neither in *Re S* (a residence application) nor in *Re H* (a wardship case) was the action initiated by the child. The Children Act, as indicated previously, does allow children in specified circumstances to initiate actions. It is the ability of children to seek residence orders which has given rise to the 'divorcing' parents phenomenon. To do so they must first obtain leave.

APPLYING FOR A RESIDENCE ORDER

A residence order settles the arrangements to be made as to the person with whom a child is to live.[66] It is governed by s.1 of the 1989 Act. Accordingly, the child's welfare is the paramount consideration,[67] and the court is not to make the order 'unless it considers that doing so would be better for the child than making no order at all'.[68] If an application is contested, regard must be had to the welfare checklist in s.1(3): a number of the factors including the ascertainable wishes and feelings of the child (which in 'divorcing parents' cases will be clear) and any harm the child is at risk of suffering[69] will be particularly pertinent.

A child cannot apply for a residence order as of right, as a parent or guardian can.[70] He or she must first apply for leave to make an application.[71] As a result of a Practice Direction, inspired no doubt by panic over a glut of well publicized applications by children wishing to 'divorce' their parents, the application must be made to the High Court.[72] The Court may only grant leave if it is satisfied that the child concerned has 'sufficient understanding' to make the proposed application.[73] Given that the child may well be eligible for legal aid in circumstances where the persons in whose favour the order is to vest are not, strategy may dictate that the child, rather than the adults concerned, make the application. However, there is no evidence that this factor is behind the number of cases brought by children, although it cannot be discounted.

Neither the Children Act nor the Rules, nor for that matter the Guidance, indicate what 'sufficient understanding' for the purpose of obtaining leave requires.[74] In one of the 'divorcing' parents cases (*Re CT*), Waite LJ[75] quoted with approval the remarks of Sir Thomas Bingham MR in *Re S* to the effect that:

> Where any sound judgement on these issues calls for insight and imagination which only maturity and experience can bring, both the court and the solicitor will be slow to conclude that the child's understanding is sufficient.[76]

That this approval is obiter needs to be stressed because, although Houghton-James perceives generosity[77] in the Court of Appeal's interpretation in *Re CT*, it would be difficult so to interpret the import of this language. On Sir Thomas Bingham MR's approved test who would have 'sufficient understanding'? Once again, we can see how knowledge and understanding have trumped wisdom.[78]

Re CT[79] is unusual in that the child concerned, a girl of 13 and a half, was in effect seeking to undo an adoption order.[80] She had re-established some contact with her biological father's relatives and wanted to live with an aunt and grandparents rather than with her adoptive parents. She consulted a solicitor who was satisfied that she was capable of giving instructions. She obtained leave from a county court[81] to apply for a residence order and then applied in her own right without the intervention of a next friend. The Court of Appeal disapproved of the High Court's attempt to require the girl to accept a guardian *ad litem* by means of wardship: wardship proceedings are family proceedings,[82] and Rule 9.2A(1) applies equally in wardship as in private law cases so that, once the conditions are satisfied, a child can bring and defend wardship proceedings without a next friend or guardian *ad litem*, and the court would have no power to impose one against his or her will. On the other hand, and despite what would appear to be clear language to the contrary,[83] the Court of Appeal ruled that it is the court itself, rather than the solicitor, which has the ultimate right to decide whether a child, who comes before it as a party without a next friend or guardian *ad litem*, has the necessary ability to instruct a solicitor. It followed that, if the court felt it necessary in order to protect the interests of the child, it could appoint a proper person to act as her next friend or guardian *ad litem*.

Seeking leave

The requirement to seek leave prior to making an application is intended to act as a filter process, as indeed it does. Unfortunately, we lack the statistical data which could enable us to gain an insight into the effectiveness of the leave procedure. Nevertheless, reported cases do help us to discover what some of the problems are and where the courts' concerns lie.

The courts are taking the applications seriously: certainly applications for leave to apply for a residence order are responded to with greater concern than similar applications by children for specific issue orders (if the contrasting approach of Johnson J in *Re C*[84] can be generalized). Both Johnson J in *Re C* and Booth J in *Re SC*[85] have stressed that children have statutory rights to initiate the process – rights that should not be 'impeded'.[86] The argument was put in *Re SC* that the person in whom parental responsibility would vest under the residence order should make the application, not the child. Booth J, rightly I would argue, dismissed this argument. She said:

> Although the court will undoubtedly consider why it is that the person in whose favour a proposed residence order would be made is not applying, it would in my opinion be wrong to import into the Act any requirement that only he or she should make the application[87] .... [The court] should not fetter the statutory ability of the child to seek any s.8 order ... if it is appropriate for such an application to be made.[88]

Children are not the only persons who require leave prior to seeking a residence order. It is therefore pertinent to examine whether leave applications by children are dealt with in a similar fashion to such applications by other persons, such as relatives or foster parents.[89] In *Re A. and W*,[90] the Court of Appeal held that an application by a foster mother for leave to apply for a residence order did not raise any question regarding the upbringing of a child,[91] with the consequence that the child's welfare was not the paramount consideration of the court in exercising its discretion.[92] Balcombe LJ said:

> In granting or refusing an application for leave to apply for a section 8 order, the court is not determining a question with respect to the upbringing of the child concerned. That question only arises when the court hears the substantive application.[93]

In this judgment he followed *F* v. *S*[94] which related to the question whether or not to grant leave for an adoption application to be made in respect of a ward of court.

This is not the only instance in which the courts have construed 'upbringing' narrowly.[95] The Lord Chancellor, in a debate on the Children Bill, did say that it was 'a word of general scope' which includes 'education and social life while being reared'.[96] It is therefore easy to see why an application by a foster mother for leave should not be one relating to a child's upbringing. But, even if this conclusion is right, is it also right that where the application for leave is made by a child it should be similarly so characterized? Booth J, who was referred to *Re A and W* and *F* v. *S*, refused to distinguish between the situations. She held that 'no distinction can be drawn between an application for leave made by a child and an application made by any other person. In neither case does the initial application fall within s.1(1) of the Act'.[97] She also appeared to hold that the checklist in s.1(3) was also irrelevant,[98] but, even if she is right as regards the upbringing/paramountcy point, this would not follow and cannot be right.[99]

Nonetheless I doubt whether she *is* right to refuse to distinguish an application by a child for leave from one by some other interested party. These applications are not made by happy children, but by troubled ones who are seeking help. To distinguish leave and the substantive application in such a way as to withdraw welfare paramountcy concerns from the former is not only artificial but, I believe, fails those children who need these concerns to be addressed. If a parent confronted by a child about to apply for a residence order were to ward the child,[100] the child's welfare would be the 'golden thread' running through the parent's application.[101] There is some support for my view in Johnson J's judgement in *Re C*.[102] His judgement was delivered two days before that of Booth J, and both are *ex-tempore*. Having decided that the considerations in s.10(9) of the Children Act 1989 were inapplicable to applications by children (a question to which I will return), he deduced:

> ...therefore, the principle that must guide my consideration ... is that laid down by Parliament in s.1(1) of the 1989 Act, namely that the child's welfare shall be my paramount consideration'.[103]

He does not seem to have been referred to *Re A and W* or to *F* v. *S* (certainly neither is quoted in his judgment), and it is consequently difficult accordingly to vest his judgment on this point with much authority. Further, his reason for coming to this conclusion – the inapplicability of the s.10(9) considerations – does not have any force. And yet his conclusion does *seem* right. However, it is likely that the judgement of Booth J, being the better reasoned one, will be followed with the consequence that welfare will not determine whether the application proceeds or not.

In one important respect, the refusal to accept that an application for leave relates to upbringing means that applications by children are treated similarly to applications by others. But there are other differences, and the Act itself is clear about two of these. S.10(9) states:

> Where the person applying for leave to make an application ... is not the child concerned, the court shall, in deciding whether or not to grant leave, have particular regard to –
>
> (a) the nature of the proposed application...;
> (b) the applicant's connection with the child;
> (c) any risk there might be of that proposed application disrupting the child's life to such an extent that he would be harmed by it; and
> (d) where the child is being looked after by a local authority –
> (i) the authority's plans for the child's future; and
> (ii) the wishes and feelings of the child's parents.

This checklist of factors obviously does not apply where the application for leave is by a child, although it is not obvious why (a) and (c) (and (b) suitably adapted) should have been excluded. It was the exclusion of the guidelines for children's applications that led Johnson J to conclude that he must instead seek guidance in s.1(1).[104] This was a fallacy no doubt, but understandable in the circumstance. By listing factors as in s.10(9), the court is guided in the exercise of its discretion. If neither s.10(9) nor the paramountcy principle applies, how is the court to exercise its discretion? Is it required to do more than be satisfied that the child has 'sufficient understanding'? Booth J thinks so. She says: 'It does not ... follow that the court is bound to grant leave once the test of s.10(8) is satisfied. The court still has a discretion whether or not to do so'.[105] But where does this discretion come from and how is it to be judicially exercised? If a child has satisfied the judge that he or she has sufficient understanding – as did the 14 year-old in

Re SC – what other hurdles can he or she be expected to surmount? If leave is refused, it may be impossible for any court to decide matters relating to the child's welfare (this applies also, of course, if it is decided the child lacks sufficient understanding), for no one else may be prepared to bring the child's problems to the attention of a court (or to social services). It therefore seems wrong to refuse leave for reasons outside the statutory framework.

The second difference is that only a child needs to establish he or she has sufficient understanding to make a s.8 application. A child who fails to establish this is left with no recourse to the courts: he or she may well be in the kind of distress that calls for an investigation of his or her circumstances and, if the court is concerned, it could order a s.37 investigation.[106] However, if it does not do this, or if the local authority thus appraised of the court's concern, does not pursue the matter any further,[107] the child can do no more. There is some irony in the fact that a child's cry for help may go unnoticed or be ignored because he or she does not meet a threshold of competence. And if, as is distinctly possible, the distressed and incompetent are also those in whom no one else is showing an interest, the problem is even greater.

Sufficient understanding

What is meant by 'sufficient understanding'? The case law offers some guidance. The judgement of Sir Thomas Bingham MR in *Re S* has already been cited: the court recognized that children had 'individual minds and wills, views and emotions',[108] although they were nevertheless children and, as such, needed to be protected, for example, against their inability to distinguish short- and long-term interests. Since the test is of understanding, too much weight should not be accorded to the child's age.[109] In two unreported cases in 1992 children of 11 years of age succeeded in their applications.[110] And in the unreported case of *Re H*,[111] Butler-Sloss LJ said that 'rule 9.2A[112] would be extremely valuable for the older teenager and is most unlikely to be used in regard to younger children' (in this case they were aged 7 and 10). This does not take us very far.

An increasing amount of research is taking place in relation to a child's competence to participate in legal proceedings, and further guidance on a child's understanding may be sought in this.[113] One of the most enlightening of studies is that by Weithorn and Campbell[114] who compared the response of 9, 14, 18 and 21 year-old participants to hypothetical decision-making problems concerning medical and psychological treatment. The 14 year-olds did not differ from the adult groups on any of the major standards of competency to consent: evidence of a choice; understanding of the facts; reasonable decision-making process; reasonable outcome of choice. Even the 9 year-olds were as competent as the average adult, according to the standards of evidence of a choice and reasonableness of choice. This is consistent with Lewis's finding that, when elementary schoolchildren were given essentially unlimited access to the school nurse for routine medical care, their health-care behaviour was very similar to adults with similar demographic characteristics.[115] These findings, Melton observes, present 'a conservative estimate of children's capacities'.[116] The reason for this is that where children have experience with, and overt permission for, participation in decision-making, their competence in reasoning increases: the more autonomy children are given, the better they are able to exercise autonomy.[117]

Research by Peterson-Badali and Abramovitch is also helpful, although both of their studies[118] are concerned with the criminal justice process. The first of these reports throws light on children's understanding of the role of lawyers. They found that 'a majority of even the youngest subjects [those between 9 and a half and 11 and a quarter] demonstrated an adequate understanding of the concept of defense counsel as an advocate in the criminal process'.[119] By contrast, even much older children – those of 14 and 15 – showed substantial ignorance of the principle of lawyer–client confidentiality when probed regarding the lawyer's ability to reveal information to specific parties – but then so did young adults. The results of the second study revealed that 'a majority of even the 10-year-old subjects used legal rather than moral criteria in making their plea decisions'.[120] The authors commented:

> The actions of these children clearly indicate their ability to distinguish a legal domain, with its own set of rules and principles, from the domain of morality.[121]

They advocate extending research to include even younger children to explore the origins of children's legal reasoning ability.

Research has also been carried out on children's competence to participate in divorce custody decision-making[122] It was found that 14 year-olds performed as well as 18 year-olds in stating a custodial preference. This finding is consistent with earlier work and comes as no surprise. But it was also found that 9 and 10 year-olds were as competent as the 14 and 18 year-olds according to the reasonableness of preference or the rationality of reasons standard – a conclusion which finds support in the Weithorn and Campbell research previously referred to. Work by Garrison in particular is suggestive for the 'divorcing parents' context. But, as she warns, her study 'assessed competence rather than actual performance in custody decision-making'.[123] Real-life factors, such as stress, may adversely affect children's decision-making abilities. Melton also makes the following point:

> ...that children have the *capacity* to perform competently and responsibly does not mean that they will exercise such maturity of judgment, particularly when the decision is made under circumstances of great stress or when social norms elicit undesirable behavior.[124]

It is increasingly obvious also that, when sufficient understanding is tested, the way questions are asked of the subjects will have an impact on the answers. For an adult, poorly worded questions may simply be a nuisance: for a child, they may be a potentially serious source of miscommunication. In an important recent study Anne Graffam Walker indicates three sources of communicative mischief:

1 age-inappropriate vocabulary;
2 complex syntax; and
3 general ambiguity.[125]

She is surely right to observe that:

> ...the real question of children's linguistic competence in evidentiary settings belongs not to the children, but to the adults. It is our adult legal system that the children are caught up in, it is our adult language in which proceedings are conducted, it is our adult assumptions about both law and language upon which communication in the courts is based.[126]

It is her view, which recent English practice indubitably endorses, that 'we are not doing as well as we might in integrating children linguistically into a system not built for them'.[127] Those who construct our judicial process do not know enough about children's cognitive and linguistic capabilities. Yet there is now research evidence into these cognitive and psychological issues if our judges, lawyers, guardians *ad litem* and others involved in eliciting evidence from children were prepared to examine it.[128]

In whose favour?

In *Re SC* it was made clear that a residence order cannot be made in favour of the child him or herself.[129] This is obvious from the language of s.8(1) of the Act which lays down that a residence order means 'an order settling the arrangements to be made as to the person with whom the child is to live'. It would be straining language to interpret 'person' to include the child him or herself. Further, as Booth J notes in *Re SC*, a residence order vests parental responsibility in the persons in whose favour the order is made if that person is not the parent or guardian of the child.[130]

This is a legitimate interpretation of the statutory provision, but it has to be re-emphasized that the legislature was not addressing the central issue of this chapter. The question therefore must be raised, as a matter of policy, whether children should be able, in effect, to emancipate themselves. Clearly, the vesting of parental rights in themselves is a logical absurdity. But is there scope for children to 'divorce' parents without 'marrying' themselves to other adults? If children can, as is usually supposed, leave home at age 16, is there a case for allowing them to ask a court to remove decision-making powers away from parents and to vest these same powers in the children? A child, after all, can marry at age 16 with the permission of a court if parental consent is refused. The case for an emancipation statute is a strong one but I doubt whether there would be any support for one in a society more concerned to control children than to recognize their individuality or integrity. The spectre of the single-parent family and of juvenile crime would presumably dominate the debate. Nevertheless, the drafting of a statute to allow self-emancipation through a court order at age 16 should be seriously considered.

CONCLUSION – AND REFORM

The explosion of cases and news stories in 1992 and 1993 created an unnecessary moral panic. There is unlikely to be a large number of applications by children who wish – in the colourful language of our times – to 'divorce' their parents. The structure is, however, in place, although it may be doubted whether those who designed it ever thought that it would be used in this way. An emancipation statute lies in the future. It will, I think, come, but not yet.

For the present it is worth pondering on the experience of the litigation discussed in this chapter, and on the lessons which we may learn from it. It has raised problems and suggested reforms.

First, there is the leave requirement. This operates as a filter but duplicates work unnecessarily. Is there any reason why a child should not be able to apply as of right for a s.8 order? I can see none and would recommend the removal of the leave requirement.

Second, if the leave requirement is to be retained, there should be clarification as to the factors governing the exercise of the court's discretion. It is difficult to see how such an application cannot relate to the upbringing of a child. The parallel drawn in *Re SC* with an application for leave by a foster mother is illusory. The paramountcy test should apply, and the welfare checklist in s.1(3) would also be relevant.

Third, if leave is to continue to remain a first hurdle and neither the paramountcy test nor the welfare checklist is to be relevant, then it must follow that, once the court has determined that the child has 'sufficient understanding', it must grant leave for the application to be made. There are no other possible criteria for the exercise of discretion.

Fourth, more sustained attention must be given to appreciating what is meant by 'sufficient understanding'. It must be realized that competence involves experiental knowledge as well as 'book work' learning: indeed, the former is more relevant in this context than the latter. Courts should be made aware of the growth of empirical evidence on the development of children's capacities. If, in other areas of law, the courts are encouraging references to legal academic literature, let them have the courage to refer to, and cite, the research data of psychologists which offer greater insight into children's competence than the intuitive arguments the judges currently use and which were presented in the cases discussed in this chapter.

But, if 'sufficient understanding' is to remain the linchpin, do we need a judicial determination of this at all? Would it not be better for specially qualified guardians *ad litem* to determine this? The courts would still have to rule upon whether a residence order vesting parental responsibility in adults other than parents was in the child's best interests.

NOTES

1 See *Kingsley* v. *Kingsley* 623 So. 2d 780 (Fla. Dist. Ct. App. 1993). Gregory Kingsley's case is different from the English cases discussed in this chapter. He was a foster child 'in limbo' in the Florida foster care system. He wanted to terminate relations with his biological parents and facilitate adoption by his foster parents. He was assisted in this by the fact that his wished-for adoptive father was a lawyer. The adoptive father has written on the case: see George H. Russ (1993), 'Through the eyes of a child, "Gregory K.": a child's right to be heard', *Family Law Quarterly* **27**, p. 365. Rather as with the English cases the 'media miscontrued a relatively ordinary case … as a pathbreaking legal event' (per Barbara B. Woodhouse (1993), 'Hatching the egg: a child-centred perspective on parents' rights', *Cardozo Law Review*, **14**, p. 1836, 1836–7). Andrew Shapiro (1993) hailed Gregory Kingsley as the 'Rosa Parks of the movement to expand the rights of children against the traditional prerogatives of biological parents' ('Children in court – the new crusade', *The Nation*, 27 September, p. 301). A good note on the case is supplied by Christina Dugger Sommer (1994), 'Empowering children: granting foster children the right to initiate parental rights termination proceedings', *Cornell Law Review*, **79**, p. 1200. This article does not address the separate question of parents divorcing their children, in particular the concept of emancipation, found in a large number of US states. On this see Carol

Sanger and Eleanor Willemsen (1992), 'Minor changes: emancipating children in modern times', *University of Michigan Journal of Law Reform*, **25**, p. 239.

2 *Polovchak* v. *Meese* 774 F. 2d 731 (1985) is a celebrated earlier instance. Walter Polovchak is quoted eight years later (when 20) to say 'As every day goes by I'm happier and happier I made the decision' (*International Herald Tribune*, 11 April 1988, p. 3).

3 Ironically the trend is towards making the former more regulated than the latter. Books on family law will soon have to devote more space to the mechanics of marriage than the process of divorce.

4 A striking instance of which is *R* v. *Ethical Committee of St Mary's Hospital, Manchester ex p. Harriott* [1988] 1 FLR 512. This was discussed by Catherine Steven (1987), 'The unnatural selection of suitable parents', *The Independent*, 23 October.

5 The principle established in *A* v. *Liverpool C.C.* [1982] AC 363 applies to decisions taken by adoption agencies. See *Re W* [1990] 2 FLR 470. But see also *Re T* [1994] 1 FLR 632, particularly the remarks of Balcombe LJ at p. 644.

6 But see Hugh La Follette (1980), 'Licensing parents' *Philosophy and Public Affairs*, **9**, p. 182 (there is a reply by Lawrence E. Frisch (1982), *Philosophy and Public Affairs*, **1**, p. 173 and a response to this by La Follette at p. 181). Also of value is John Harris (1989), 'The right to found a family' in Geoffrey Scarre (ed.), *Children, Parents and Politics*, Cambridge: Cambridge University Press, p. 133.

7 Family Law Reform Act 1969 s.8(1) (consent at 16). See also s.8(3) (interpreted by many – though not now the Court of Appeal – to mean that consent below the age of 16 is not precluded). For the different attitude of the courts see *Gillick* v. *West Norfolk and Wisbech A.H.A.* [1986] AC 112 and *Re R* [1992] 1 FLR 190 and *Re W* [1993] 1 FLR 1.

8 The Maria Colwell case of 1973–74 catapulted this problem to public attention and was a catalyst for the Children Act 1975.

9 See Michael Freeman, 'Children's rights as protection and autonomy: education as a test-case' in R. Davie (ed.), *Children's Rights and Children's Education*, London: Fulton Press (forthcoming).

10 On which see Lawrence J. Le Blanc (1995), *The Convention on the Rights of the Child*, Lincoln, Nebraska: University of Nebraska Press. More generally see Cynthia Price Cohen (1993), 'The developing jurisprudence of the rights of the child', *St Thomas Law Review*, **6**, p. 1.

11 Said by Marta Santos Pais (1992) to make a child a 'principal' in the Convention (see 'The United Nations Convention on the Rights of the Child', *Bulletin of Human Rights*, **91/2**, pp. 75, 76.

12 But only a strand. See Lorraine Fox-Harding (1991), 'The Children Act 1989 in context: four perspectives in child care law and policy', *Journal of Social Welfare and Family Law*, pp.. 179 and 285.

13 The phrase may be traced to the Cleveland Report, Cm. 412, London: HMSO, 1988.

14 As 'mugging' did a generation ago. See Stuart Hall (1978), *Policing The Crisis*, London: Macmillan.

15 Cd. 2424, London: HMSO, 1993.

16 Thus, cases in which girls (often from the Indian sub-continent) warded themselves to leave, or stay away from, home were treated in a more subdued fashion.

17 *Krishnan* v. *L.B. of Sutton* [1970] Ch. 181.

18 What we would now call 'accommodation' (s.20 of Children Act 1989).

19 But cf. *Bawden* v. *Bawden* [1979] QB 419.

20 *Polovchak* v. *Meese* 774 F. 2d 731. See also *Schleiffer* v. *Meyers* 644 F. 2d 656.

21 *The Sunday Times*, 3 August 1980.
22 An earlier case is *Re Snyder* 532 P. 2d 278 (1975). The court found 'the parent–child relationship had dissipated to the point where parental control [was] lost' (p.281).
23 David Hodgson is one to suggest it is.
24 See Children Act 1989, s.1(3).
25 In contrast to the first edition in 1988. Dept. of Health, *Working Together*, London: HMSO.
26 *Ibid.*, para. 6. 13.
27 Children Act 1989, s.45(8).
28 *Ibid.*, s.34(2).
29 *Ibid.*, s.39(1).
30 *Ibid.*, s.10(2), (8).
31 See *ibid.*, s.34(2).
32 See *ibid.*, s.41.
33 See J. Roche (1991), 'Once a parent always a parent', *Journal of Social Welfare and Family Law*, p. 345.
34 For example in section 38(6).
35 *Gillick* v. *West Norfolk and Wisbech A.H.A.* [1986] AC 112.
36 This has emerged as the *ratio*, although at the time Lord Fraser's judgement, which had more support, was thought to contain this. And he merely transferred authority to make decisions from parents to professionals.
37 *Gillick*, *op. cit.*, note 35 above, p. 167.
38 *Re R* [1992] 1 FLR 190; *Re W* [1993] 1 FLR 1; *Re S* [1994] 2 FLR 1065.
39 P. Alderson and A. Goodwin (1993), 'Contradictions within concepts of children's competence', *International Journal of Children's Rights*, **1**, pp. 303, 305.
40 [1993] 1 FLR 1.
41 Alderson and Goodwin, *op. cit.*, note 39 above, p. 305.
42 [1992] 1 FLR 190.
43 [1993] 1 FLR 1.
44 *Re K, W and H* [1993] 1 FLR 240; *South Glamorgan C.C.* v. *W and B* [1993] 1 FLR 574.
45 [1993] 1 FLR 440.
46 Family Proceedings Courts (Children Act 1989) Rules 1991 r. 12(1)(a).
47 My emphasis.
48 *Re H*, *op. cit.*, note 45 above, p. 443.
49 *Ibid.*, p. 449.
50 *Ibid.*
51 *Ibid.*
52 See M.D.A. Freeman (1993), 'Removing rights from adolescents', *Adoption and Fostering*, **17**,(1), p. 14; see also S. Melzac (1992), 'Secrecy, privacy, survival, repressive regimes and growing up', *Journal of the Anna Freud Centre*, **15**, p. 205–24; W. Yule (1992), 'Post-traumatic stress disorders in children', *Current Opinion in Paediatrics*, **4**, p. 4.
53 It is impossible to come to a categorical conclusion on the facts available.
54 On which see Judith Hughes's comment: 'If rational is what nineteenth-century gentlemen are, then children no less than women will come to grief in the rationality stakes' 'Thinking about children' (in Geoffrey Scarre (ed.), *Children, Parents and Politics*, Cambridge: Cambridge University Press, 1989, pp. 36–51, at p. 38).
55 [1993] 2 FLR 437, 439.
56 On the role of whom see David Venables (1990), 'The Official Solicitor', *Family Law*,

20, p. 53 and M. Hinchcliffe (1989), 'The role of the Official Solicitor in child abuse cases' in Allan Levy (ed.), *Focus on Child Abuse*, London: Hawksmere, p. 86.

57 *Re S*, op. cit., note 55 above, p. 444.

58 *Ibid.*

59 *Ibid.*

60 *Ibid.*, p. 449.

61 [1993] 2 FLR 552.

62 *Ibid.*, p. 557.

63 *Ibid.*

64 *Ibid.*, p. 578.

65 *Re S, op. cit.*, note 55 above, p. 448. See also *Re CT* [1993] 2 FLR 278, 280 per Waite LJ.

66 Children Act 1989, s.8(1).

67 *Ibid.*, s.1(1).

68 *Ibid.*, s.1(5).

69 A good illustration of which is *Re H* [1993] 2 FLR 552, where the possible alternative arrangement involved a suspected sex abuser.

70 See Children Act, s.10(4). Parent includes an unmarried father.

71 See *ibid.*, s.10(8). This subsection (the 'sufficient understanding' provision) is the only mention of the child requiring leave.

72 [1993] 1 FLR 668 and see *Re AD* [1993] 1 FCR 573.

73 See Children Act 1989, s.10(8).

74 See 'The Children Act 1989 Guidance and Regulations', Volume 1, *Court Orders*, London: HMSO, 1991, para. 2.43 which merely paraphrases s.10(8). Masson's annotation in *Current Law Statutes Annotated* notes that the test of understanding may be different according to the type of application (p. 29) but, other than quoting from Lord Scarman's judgement in *Gillick* v. *West Norfolk and Wisbech A.H.A.* [1986] AC 112, does not take the definition any further. Waite LJ in *Re CT* [1993] 1 FLR 278, 281 also notes that the Act and the Rules do not further define 'sufficient understanding'.

75 [1993] 2 FLR 278, 281–282.

76 [1993] 2 FLR 437, 444.

77 Hazel Houghton-James (1994), 'Children divorcing their parents', *Journal of Social Welfare and Family Law*, pp. 185, 197.

78 Cf. *ante*, 164. On the 'trumping' metaphor see R. Dworkin (1977), *Taking Rights Seriously*, London: Duckworth.

79 [1993] 2 FLR 278.

80 That this cannot be done can be seen from the case of *Re B* [1995] 1 FLR 1.

81 The case antedates *Re AD* and the *Practice Direction.* A similar case today would have to be transferred upwards to the High Court.

82 See Children Act 1989, s.8(3)(a).

83 *Re CT, op. cit.*, note 79 above, pp. 288–9.

84 [1994] 1 FLR 26.

85 [1994] 1 FLR 96.

86 *Re C, op. cit.*, note 84 above, p. 27.

87 *Re SC, op. cit.*, note 85 above, p. 100.

88 *Ibid.*

89 Foster parents with whom a child has lived for three years do not need leave (see s.10(5)(b)), but local authority foster parents may need the consent of the local authority to apply unless they are relatives or the child has lived with them for at least three years preceding the application (s.9(3)).

90 [1992] Fam. 182.
91 See Children Act, s.1(1).
92 So that the child's welfare did not determine the course to be followed (see Lord MacDermott in *J* v. *C* [1970] AC 668).
93 *Re A and W*, *op. cit.*, note 90 above, p. 191.
94 [1973] Fam. 203. But it has been held that the grant of leave by the courts in applications for the removal of a child under Part III of the Adoption Act 1976 is governed by the welfare test in s.6 of that Act. See *Re C* [1994] 2 FLR 513.
95 Another (in my opinion) is *Richards* v. *Richards* [1984] AC 174 (ouster application by mother). And see, for confirmation that the Children Act has not altered this, *Gibson* v. *Austin* [1992] 2 FLR 437.
96 Hansard HL vol. 502, col. 1168.
97 *Re SC, op. cit.*, note 85 above, p. 99.
98 The two arguments are seen as inextricably linked, so that if one is dismissed, so is the other (see *ibid.*).
99 The court must have regard to the checklist in any contested s.8 application: where the court is hearing an application for leave to apply for a s.8 order it is surely 'considering whether to make … a section 8 order' (s.1(4)(a)).
100 Cf. the facts of *Re AD* [1993] 1 FCR 573.
101 Per Dunn J in *Re D* [1977] Fam. 158.
102 *Re C*, *op. cit.*, note 84 above.
103 *Ibid.*, p. 28.
104 [1994] 1 FLR 26, 28.
105 [1994] 1 FLR 96, 98.
106 In *Re CE (Section 37 Direction)* [1995] 1 FLR 26, there was such a direction in a case where parents sought a residence order after a 14 year-old left home to live with her boyfriend's parents.
107 This impotence is striking in *Nottinghamshire County Council* v. *P* [1994] Fam. 18.
108 [1993] 2 FLR 437, 448.
109 Note Sir Thomas Bingham MR's comment that 'different children have differing levels of understanding at the same age' ([1993] 2 FLR 437, 444).
110 See *The Independent*, 11 November 1992 and *The Independent*, 12 November 1992.
111 Court of Appeal (Civil Division) Transcript No. 769, cited in *Re S* at p. 447.
112 Inserted into the Rules by amendment in 1992.
113 A good survey article is Elizabeth S. Scott (1992), 'Judgment and reasoning in adolescent decisionmaking', *Villanova Law Review*, **37**, p. 1607.
114 L. Weithorn and S. Campbell (1982), 'The competency of children and adolescents to make informed treatment decisions', *Child Development*, **53**, p. 1589.
115 S. Lewis (1983), 'Decision making related to health: when could/should children behave responsibly?' in G. Melton, G. Koocher and M. Saks (eds), *Children's Competence To Consent*, New York: Plenum Press.
116 G. Melton (1983–84), 'Developmental psychology and the law: the state of the Art', *Journal of Family Law*, **22**, pp. 445, 464.
117 See R.W. Belter and T. Grisso (1984), 'Children's recognition of rights violations in counselling', *Professional Psychology: Research and Practice*, **15**, p. 899; J. Tapp and G. Melton (1983), 'Preparing children for decision making: implications of legal socialization research' in Melton *et al.*, *op. cit.*, note 115 above at p. 215.
118 M. Peterson-Badali and M. Abramovitch (1992), 'Children's knowledge of the legal system: are they competent to instruct legal counsel?', *Canadian Journal of Crimi-*

nology, **34**, p. 139 and idem (1993), 'Grade related changes in young people's reasoning about plea decisions', *Law and Human Behavior*, **17**, p. 537.

119 Peterson-Badali and Abramovitch (1992), *op. cit.*, note 118 above, pp. 139, 156.

120 *Idem* (1993), *op. cit.*, note 118 above, pp. 537, 549.

121 *Ibid.* And see, for a consistent conclusion, E. Turiel (1983), *The Development of Social Knowledge: Morality and Convention*, Cambridge: Cambridge University Press.

122 Ellen Greenberg Garrison (1991), 'Children's competence to participate in divorce custody decisionmaking', *Journal of Clinical Child Psychology*, **20**, p. 78.

123 *Ibid.*, p. 85.

124 Melton, *op. cit.*, note 116 above, pp. 465–6.

125 A.G. Walker (1993), 'Questioning young children in court', *Law and Human Behavior*, **17**, p. 59.

126 *Ibid.*, p. 78.

127 *Ibid.*

128 In addition to work already cited, I would recommend S.J. Ceci, M. Toglia and D.F. Ross (1987), *Children's Eyewitness Testimony*, New York: Springer-Verlag; S.J. Ceci, D.F. Ross and M. Toglia (1989), *Perspectives on Children's Testimony*, New York: Springer-Verlag; A.G. Walker (1990), 'Language at work in the law: the customs, conventions and appellate consequences of court reporting' in J.N. Levi and A.G. Walker (eds), *Language in the Judicial Process*, New York: Plenum, pp. 203–44. Also useful as an overview is Gary B. Melton (1987), *Reforming The Law: Impact of Child Development Research*, New York: Guilford Press.

129 *Re SC*, *op. cit.*, note 85 above, p. 100.

130 *Ibid.* See Children Act 1989, s.12(2).

9 Feminism, Gender and the Consequences of Divorce*

June Carbone

INTRODUCTION

Despite its critics, feminism involves no more – and no less – than what Kate Bartlett calls 'asking the woman question'.[1] As a subject of inquiry, feminism claims as its focus women's interests and experiences, varied as they may be. As a theoretical endeavour, feminism examines the forces underlying those experiences in terms of the construction of gender – that is, the attributes society accords men and women by virtue of gender, and the consequences that follow. In examining divorce,[2] the influence of gender is pervasive, and feminism attempts to provide a systematic account of that influence in order to explain women's divorce experiences, and ensure that women's interests are fully taken into account in the determination of public policy.[3]

As a descriptive undertaking, there is near unanimity, both within feminist circles and without, as to the role of gender in accounting for the economic consequences of divorce. Women generally, for reasons attributable to gender, earn less than men. Marriage increases the gap as married women, who bear the overwhelming responsibility for child-rearing, earn less than single women, while married men increase their earnings over single men. At divorce, mothers overwhelmingly retain physical custody of their children, and the pressures of single parenthood interfere with labour force participation. David Chambers calculates that it would take 75–80 per cent of a married family's total income for a mother with two children to maintain the same standard of living on her own.[4] Few women are in a position to increase their income that dramatically, and no divorce system

* This chapter has been adapted from 'A Feminist Perspective on Divorce' in (1994), *The Future of Children*, **4**, pp. 183–209, a publication of the Center for the Future of Children, the David and Lucille Packard Foundation.

provides that level of support. Accordingly, divorce almost inevitably lowers the standard of living of the custodial family and, for systemic reasons related to gender, leaves the vast majority of divorced women in a financially more precarious position than their former husbands.

Despite the near unanimous embrace of this picture of divorce, there is considerable disagreement, both within feminist circles and without, as to the implications. The disagreement starts with the central feature of the gendered division of family responsibilities: what Mary Becker describes as mothers' greater, and qualitatively different, attachment to their children.[5] Economist Victor Fuchs goes so far as to conclude that, in women's quest for economic equality, it is not the fact that women raise children that places them at a disadvantage, but 'that, on average, women have a stronger demand for children than men do, and have more concern for children after they are born'.[6]

Nonetheless, feminists have been slow to call attention to this central difference in men and women's approach to family. When feminist scholarship does acknowledge it, it is without agreement on cause and effect. And although the source of women's greater attachment to children may well be irrelevant to the determination of public policy, feminists are no closer to agreement on possible solutions.[7] 'Liberal' feminists[8] believe that it is the gendered division of labour itself that ensures women's subordination to men and that, unless there is genuinely shared responsibility for childbearing, equality is impossible.[9] 'Cultural feminists' or 'feminists of difference' believe that the principal problem is not that women disproportionately care for children, but that society so undervalues child-rearing.[10] In between are many feminists who believe that equality requires both greater sharing of the responsibility for child-rearing *and* greater support for the child-rearing role.[11]

Given these differences, there is no 'feminist analysis' of divorce. Nonetheless, there is a feminist account of the ways in which the gendered division of labour during marriage leads to the effective impoverishment of many women and children, and in which women's greater involvement with their children increases their vulnerability at divorce. There is also feminist agreement that the existing system fails to provide adequately either for child-rearing or for greater equality between men and women. Feminist reform proposals, which cover a broad spectrum of approaches, share a commitment to alleviating the vulnerability that accompanies devotion to children.

THE GENDERED DIVISION OF FAMILY RESPONSIBILITIES

Mothers' attachment to their children: the ideological divide

In approaching the central difference between men and women's approach to family responsibilities – mothers' greater, and qualitatively different, attachment to their children – feminists have been uncharacteristically silent. Mary Becker explains this silence toward maternal feelings in terms of 'myth and taboo'.[12] The myth is that all women find their greatest emotional fulfilment in children, especially infants, while all fathers are emotionally distant from their children, especially infants. The taboo is one 'against realistically exploring either the intense pleasures or the difficulties and the pains of women's relationships with their children'.[13]

Until Mary Becker's article, the taboo was particularly strong among feminists, and particularly strong also within the legal establishment. Because the initial wave of modern feminism focused on the workplace, feminists feared that, by acknowledging the special role of motherhood for many women, all women would be defined exclusively in motherhood's most restrictive terms. Carol Sanger writes that:

> Motherhood is a central but confusing icon within our social structure. It is at once dominating and dominated, much as mothers are both revered and regulated. The reverence and regulations are not so much in conflict as in league. The rules remind women of how to behave in order to stay revered. This reverence is something more than a fan club for mothers. It matters in such practical and concrete ways as keeping one's children, having credibility in court, getting promoted at work, and so on.[15]

In the face of such perils, many feminists concluded that silence was the safer course.

As Becker documents, however, there is a growing literature that suggests substantial differences in the way mothers and fathers relate to their children with important implications for divorce policy. Although this literature necessarily relies on subjective assessments, the empirical data that exists supports Becker's assertions. She notes two studies in particular. Louis Genevie and Eva Margolies, who interviewed a representative sample of mothers, report that more than 90 per cent feel that a mother's love is different from other forms of love.[16] They describe it as more intense, involving a greater feeling of identity, 'a feeling that one's child is part of oneself'.[17] The mothers surveyed overwhelmingly believed that fathers are less emotionally involved with their children than mothers are, and a 'shocking 50 percent ...

did not think much of their husbands as fathers, describing them, in varying degrees, as uninvolved and overly critical'.[18]

While the Genevie and Margolies study interviewed only mothers, a study of what the researchers term 'dual-mother' families – families in which both father and mother 'mother'[19] – reports similar results. In this non-randomly selected sample, both parents identified themselves as the 'primary caretaker'[20] and performed at least 35 per cent of the child care. Nevertheless, both the mothering mothers and mothering fathers in this study report that the mothers were more emotionally involved in their children's lives and felt the connection between self and child as sharper and more unconscious, more 'primary'. The study found that: 'Both mothers and fathers agreed that it would be the mothers who would actually be more devastated by the actual loss of a child'.[21]

The studies that Becker cites are inherently limited. In the first one, the researchers interviewed only mothers; in the second, a non-random sample of mothers and fathers was used. Both studies relied on self-reports, and both are inevitably influenced by cultural reinforcement of existing gender stereotypes. Nonetheless, the study results correspond to literary attempts to capture the experience of mothering,[22] and to much observed behaviour. At divorce, mothers are much more likely to seek physical custody of their children than are fathers, and non-custodial mothers are more likely to remain in contact with their children than are non-custodial fathers.[23]

Although few question that gender differences exist in parents' relationships with their children, there is considerable controversy over both cause and 'cure'.[24] First, with respect to the source of observed gender differences, there is a disagreement as to which discipline holds the most promise. Nancy Chodorow's work uses the insights of Freudian psychology (however unlikely a source of feminist scholarship) to argue that the fact that women are more likely to be caregivers than men reproduces the traits associated with mothering as girls identify with their caregivers and boys do not. Sociobiologists, in contrast, insist that natural selection encourages women to invest more heavily in each of their inherently limited number of offspring while encouraging men to father more profligately. Biochemists attempt to explain gender differences in terms of chemicals and hormones. No resolution among these competing theories is in sight. Nor is any final answer likely because of the inevitable interactions among such factors. Even, for instance, if chemical differences were found to be influential determinants of behaviour, it would still be difficult, with respect to any complex behaviour, to resolve the role of genes versus experience in determining the precise chemical mix.

In the face of scientific uncertainty, ideology acquires that much greater significance. Radical feminists emphatically reject the attribution of observed gender differences to women's 'true' preferences; they maintain that it is impossible to know what women would prefer in the absence of the patriarchal system that now exists.[25] Liberal feminists fear that any emphasis on the way in which women 'mother' differently from fathers will resurrect an ideal of motherhood that precludes women's access to status, power and independence;[26] they therefore prefer, as a matter of strategy, not to call attention to such differences. Only cultural feminists or feminists of difference have been willing to address the issue directly.

Martha Fineman, whose work marks the emergence of the feminism of difference within US family law, stresses the importance of defining feminist methodology, not in terms of grand theory, but in terms of the concrete impact on the lives of women.[27] Central to that impact, Fineman maintains, are the material and emotional circumstances that arise from women's greater connection to their children, culturally determined or not.[28] Fineman concludes that taking women's concern for children into account is essential to effective divorce reform, and that

> ...[c]ontemporary custody discourse trivializes women's emotional investment in their primary caretaking relationship with their children. It is perhaps on this level that reformist discourse has been least sensitive to women's reality.[29]

Consensus on consequences

Whatever the causes of the gendered division of family responsibilities, there is little disagreement about consequences. The expectation that women will bear primary responsibility for child-rearing (and men will not) exerts a powerful influence not just on the respective roles of marital partners, but on the lives of many men and women who never enter marriage. Despite recent changes, gendered differences in earning capacity are commonplace and they owe much of their origin and longevity to the gendered division of responsibility within the family.

In examining wage differentials, it is important to emphasize that recent changes in women's labour force participation have been overwhelmingly characterized by the large-scale movement of married middle-class mothers into the labour market,[30] but *not* by a corresponding increase in fathers' participation in homemaking. Barbara Bergmann estimates that working women average 28.1 hours of 'unpaid' family work per week to their husband's 9.2 hours and that

> ...husbands of wives with full-time jobs averaged about two minutes more housework per day than did husbands in housewife-maintaining families, hardly enough additional time to prepare a soft-boiled egg.[31]

Combining paid and unpaid labour, Victor Fuchs concluded that between 1960 and 1986 women increased their total hours by almost 7 per cent while men's fell by the same proportion.[32] Wives, whatever their workforce participation, still assume an overwhelmingly greater share of the responsibility for the family's domestic needs than do their husbands.[33] Women's increasing participation in the market has been characterized to a far larger degree by greater specialization among women, as working mothers hire other women to help care for their children, than by any lesser specialization between men and women.

This gendered division of labour within the family has consequences for women's earning capacity. Economists attribute the 'wage gap'[34] to a combination of discrimination (including channelling women into low positions segregated by gender),[35] differences in human resources,[36] and family responsibilities. While economists differ considerably in the relative importance they attribute to each factor,[37] they agree that each contributes to the wage gap and that each factor reinforces the other.[38] Joshi and Newell, for example, observe that:

> The expectation of a domestic division of labour between men and women encourages a sex-stereotyping in education and the labour market which puts all women, whether or not they ever become mothers, at a disadvantage relative to men.[39]

Mavis Maclean argues further that divorced women face not just discrimination against all women, but negative employer attitudes toward those women who shoulder sole responsibility for their children.[40]

Apart from the earnings gap between men and women generally, there is substantial evidence that married women, because of family responsibilities, experience a drop in earning capacity with lifelong consequences. First, human resource theorists posit that interruptions in labour force participation have a significant effect on earnings. Soloman Polachek finds that, while levels of educational attainment are comparable for men and women, women experience more labour market interruptions than do men, and that approximately half of the wage gap between all male and female workers can be explained on the basis of those interruptions.[41] Second, studies show that income varies with family status. Blau and Kahn note that in the USA during the late 1980s the gender gap for single workers was only 5 per cent while the gender gap for married workers was a far more substantial 41 per cent.[42] By the age of 40, married women earn only 85 per cent of the wages per hour earned by unmarried women, while married men earn more than unmarried men at every age.[43] In the UK, this gap may be magnified further by the greater tendency of married women to take part-time employment.

According to the 1987 Census of Employment, part-timers constituted 41.6 per cent of all female employees compared to only 5.9 per cent of male employees and 27 per cent of working mothers in the US.[44] Finally, a comparison of age and earning profiles for men and women demonstrates that, while women's earnings lag only slightly behind men's during women's early years in the labour force, women miss out on the rapid increase in earnings men experience in their late twenties and thirties – the peak child-bearing years for women.[45] Joshi estimates the lost earnings directly attributable to child-bearing at £135 000 per family.[46]

The differences between men and women, and between single and married workers, magnify the disparity between husbands' and wives' financial prospects at divorce. Maccoby and Mnookin's study of Californian divorce found that, where both spouses worked during the marriage, the women, on average, earned only half as much as the men.[47] Victor Fuchs' 1985 data show that, where both spouses worked outside the home, three out of four husbands had hourly earnings greater than their wives, and for half the couples the wife's wage was less than two-thirds of her husband's.[48] Adding the fact that married women work fewer hours outside the home, Sylvia Hewlett emphasizes that 'On average, *married women earn less than half the earnings of married men*'.[49] Women's greater participation in the labour force has not equated to participation on the same terms as men.

THE FAILURE OF EXISTING DIVORCE POLICY TO ACCOUNT FOR CHILD-REARING

Existing divorce law largely reflects the reforms adopted in the wake of recognizing no-fault grounds for divorce, and much of the controversy that attends modern divorce centres on two issues:

1. Is the movement from fault to no-fault responsible for the inadequate provision for women and children in modern divorce law?
2. Do the existing grounds for such provisions provide an adequate basis for future decisions?

The short answer is that modern divorce law makes no systematic provision for child-rearing in an era of widespread marital dissolution.

The adoption of no-fault grounds for divorce

The primary societal provision for child-rearing has long been the insistence that child-rearing occur within lifelong unions in which husbands and wives were assigned highly differentiated roles, and the wife's position was legally and practically dependent on the husband's.[50] Traditional marriages emphasized the husband's role as head of household and his obligation to provide support.[51] Wives were expected to subordinate their own opportunities to the needs of their families. Family law enforced the exchange by making divorce difficult and potentially expensive for the responsible party. In the USA, reformers justified the move away from fault as a way to remove the hypocrisy and deceit inherent in a system that made divorce available only if one party – and only one party – were at fault.[52] In England, the Law Commission declared in 1966 that the objectives of a good divorce law should include 'the decent burial with the minimum of embarrassment, humiliation and bitterness of those that are indubitably dead'.[53] Yet, no-fault did more than simply eliminate abandonment, adultery and extreme cruelty as prerequisites for divorce; it fundamentally undercut legal recognition of marriage as a set of lifelong obligations. 'Fault', in its primary sense, rested on the premise that there was no right to leave a marriage in the absence of conduct by the other spouse – adultery, desertion, extreme cruelty – that could be said to have already ended the relationship. Fault, as the assignment of responsibility for the break-up, influenced custody and, in many jurisdictions, determined alimony and property divisions. Support was intended to place the 'innocent' wife in the position she would have enjoyed had she remained her husband's 'lawful wife'. Alimony could be denied altogether to the guilty.[54] Although, in practice, support awards were rarely as generous as such a standard implied for the 'innocent', and not always so draconian for the 'guilty',[55] the principle served the law's primary objective: reinforcing the societal sanctions against divorce.[56]

No-fault eliminated the fault system's principal justification for post-divorce adjustments – the guilty spouse's continuing responsibility for the well-being of the family left behind – although the effect was not immediately apparent. England's initial reform legislation, like that of a number of US states, simply added irretrievable breakdown to the traditional fault grounds for divorce and required continued adherence to the principle that the courts should seek, if practicable and just, to

> ...place the parties in the financial position in which they would have been if the marriage had not broken down and each had properly discharged his or her financial obligations and responsibilities towards the other.[57]

Nonetheless, by 1973, the Court of Appeal had instructed the lower courts that matrimonial misconduct is to be considered relevant only in the most extreme cases, and the Law Commission found in 1980 that many courts openly rejected the principle of 'persisting obligation', or termed it impracticable.[58] Eekelaar and Maclean conclude that:

> ...when the legislature made a definite, if not totally successful, move away from fault-based divorce in 1971, the only rationale for these principles collapsed. For if divorce is viewed as an entitlement on the establishment of irretrievable breakdown, and such breakdown is not necessarily linked to fault, there can be no basis for using financial provisions as penalties or consolations. The retention of the fiction of the marital support obligation was no longer tenable.[59]

Support grew, in England, the USA and elsewhere, for a 'clean break' between the former spouses. With the 'irretrievable breakdown' of the relationship, all marital obligations came to an end, and, with women's growing workforce participation and insistence that they were self-sufficient equals, the very concept of 'support' seemed archaic. In the USA the Uniform Marriage and Divorce Act of 1970 adopted the 'clean break' as its primary objective. Following divorce, there would be no continuing obligation from one spouse to another. The only surviving relationship would be with the children. To the extent that one spouse needed assistance, an adjustment in the property division, rather than a support award, was preferred because the property division could be finalized with the divorce.[60]

The English Law Commission reached similar conclusions in 1981. It advocated replacing the principle of 'persisting obligation' in favour of legislation that would 'embody the principle that the interests of the children should be seen as a matter of overriding importance'. Within this context, the Commission emphasized placing greater weight on the 'importance of each party doing everything possible to become self-sufficient', and achieving, wherever possible, a once-and-for-all settlement.[61] The Matrimonial and Family Proceedings Act of 1984 incorporated these principles. To promote self-sufficiency, the legislation required courts to consider any 'increase in that [earning] capacity which it would in the opinion of the court be reasonable to expect a party to the marriage to take steps to acquire'. Like the US legislation, the English Act encouraged courts to favour orders that would sever the financial obligations between the parties as soon as possible and to limit any continuing obligation

> ...only for such term as would in the opinion of the court be sufficient to enable the party in whose favour the order is made to adjust without undue hardship to the termination of his or her financial dependence on the other party.[62]

With the declining importance of fault and the movement away from the 'separate spheres' ideology that defined women's roles in exclusively domestic terms, custody law also changed – although more dramatically in the USA than elsewhere. Martha Fineman describes a transformation in the USA from a system of 'old, tested, gendered rules that permitted predictable, inexpensive decisions' explicitly favouring women to a complex legal determination 'in which a man who pursues a custody case[63] has a better than equal chance of gaining custody'.[64] The changes resulted from two factors. First, the traditional rules which recognized an explicit presumption favouring mothers in determining the custody of children 'of tender years' were eliminated in favour of gender neutral standards.[65] Second, with the refusal to consider fault came a refusal to consider any aspect of the parties' relationship. Many US states, for example, enacted statutes favouring joint physical and legal custody without regard for whether the parents could cooperate sufficiently to make it work in practice;[66] in other states, courts consider the 'best interests of the child' prospectively only. In such determinations, the father's greater financial resources, even if the product of his lack of involvement with the children during the marriage, might outweigh the mother's greater contact and emotional commitment.[67] While mothers still overwhelmingly retained physical custody under the new rules, they did so partly because few fathers pursued custody.[68]

The combination of the changes in the grounds for divorce, support and custody amounted to a wholesale withdrawal of legal recognition and financial support for the child-rearing role. Mothers consequently are asked to meet 'greater responsibilities with fewer resources' than their former husbands.[69] In England, Eekelaar and Maclean reported that only 11 per cent of divorced single mothers enjoyed incomes above the poverty line compared with 71 per cent of the general population, and that maintenance payments do little to improve their financial position.[70] Lenore Weitzman concluded, in her examination of Californian divorce,[71] that: "Just one year after legal divorce, men experience a 42 percent improvement in their postdivorce standard of living, while women experience a 73 percent decline.'[72] Although the actual figures vary, every study of divorce since Weitzman's has confirmed her picture of financial hardship for women and children.[73] To the extent that these studies are controversial, the controversy focuses on two issues: the size of the disparity between men and women, and the suggestion that no-fault is responsible.

Weitzman's figures have provoked the greatest controversy. Duncan and Hoffman,[74] without contesting Weitzman's underlying data, dispute her calculation that women experience a 73 per cent drop in their standards of living. Weitzman arrived at the 73 per cent figure by taking the per capita income figures and applying them to a needs standard calculated in accordance with the Bureau of Labor Standards Lower Standard Budget for an urban family adjusted for family size and composition.[75] Attempting to perform the same calculations, Duncan and Hoffman find Weitzman's figure of 73 per cent 'suspiciously large'; they recalculate the drop in living standards at 33 per cent. Annemette Soreson reviews a variety of divorce studies, including those of Weitzman and Duncan and Hoffman, and concludes that much of the variation depends on the studies' assumptions as to the measure of economic status (for example, per capita income versus standard of living) and the economies of scale that come with presence of children. She concludes that there is no single correct measure.[76] In addition, as Weitzman herself notes, both Weitzman's and Duncan and Hoffman's calculations overstate the increase in men's standards of living to the extent that they lose out on or need to purchase substitutes for the services their wives performed without pay, but understate the drop in women's income to the extent that there is less than full compliance with support orders – a common occurrence in the families studied.[77] All of the writers acknowledge, however, that these methodological issues go to the magnitude of the decline women and children experience, not to the existence of serious gender-based inequality.[78]

The second issue is the suggestion that no-fault is responsible for the dire economic circumstances women and children face at divorce. In both England and the USA, adoption of no-fault grounds for divorce raised concern that the new divorce law would function as a 'wife stuffing bill' that would allow husbands to trade their wives at will,[79] and the English reforms permitted the courts to refuse to grant a divorce based on five-years' separation without consent if 'the dissolution of the marriage will result in grave financial or other hardship to the respondent'.[80] In the USA economists have argued that no-fault divorce California-style, which bars any consideration of fault, eliminated the bargaining power of the 'innocent spouse' who could trade her consent to the divorce for financial protection. Weitzman's 1985 book, *The Divorce Revolution*, which documented the economic consequences of divorce for women and children, fuelled the sense that no-fault had contributed to the problem.

The empirical support for any claim that the change in the grounds for divorce is by itself – or even primarily – responsible for the economic plight of divorced women and children, however, is thin. First, the claim assumes that men are more likely than women to be held responsible for the divorce. At first glance this appears to be true. In England and Wales, for example, women initiate 71.4 per cent of divorces, and in 73.3 per cent of the cases, the stated grounds for the dissolution are adultery or behaviour incompatible with the continuation of the marriage.[81] However, 99 per cent of the cases are uncontested, and English and Welsh law permits a divorce more easily in cases based on adultery or unreasonable behaviour. Accordingly, there is no way of telling whether these figures reflect an accurate assessment of responsibility. In California, which does not permit any consideration of fault, a recent study showed that women, in the small sample studied, also initiated the majority of divorces, but the 70 per cent figure for couples under the age of 45 became a 50/50 split between men and women over the age of 45. Moreover, while 30 years ago the principal causes of divorce were alcoholism, mental illness, and desertion (and, as in England today, the stated causes were likely to be adultery or mental cruelty), the single biggest issue cited by younger women in a recent California study was the failure of the marriage to satisfy their emotional needs.[82] A major factor in the move to no-fault in the first place was the lack of societal consensus as to what constitutes good cause to end a marriage, and in the absence of such a consensus, there is no way to determine whether a return to fault would necessarily benefit the mothers of small children who are frequently portrayed as the casualties of divorce.[83]

Second, the data examining correlations between the existence of fault grounds for divorce and divorce awards is inconclusive. In the study about bargaining that has received the most attention in the USA, Elizabeth Peters compared the alimony and child support awarded in 'fault' states with that awarded in 'no-fault' states, and found the amounts in 'fault' states to be more generous. Her research, however, like Weitzman's, has been criticized on the grounds that it does not separate changes in the grounds for divorce from contemporaneous changes in the legal standard for alimony, child support or property awards,[84] and, as Herma Hill Kay emphasizes, the broad social changes that accompanied divorce reform.[85]

Finally, a number of studies show that fault-based awards, whether or not higher than no-fault awards, have never been sufficient to prevent financial hardship. Jana Singer uses Weitzman's own data to emphasize that the financial awards made under fault-based divorce never lived up to the law's promise to protect the standard of living enjoyed during the marriage, and may not have been much more frequent than no-fault awards.[86] William Goode's 1956 study of divorced women in Detroit concluded that

> ...the divorced wife receives relatively little property from the split of joint possessions, is given very little child support, and in two-fifths of the cases does not receive this support regularly.[87]

English studies similarly show that maintenance awards during the period in which fault was the sole grounds for divorce typically amounted to only a fraction of the maximum sums then applicable for magistrates' court orders, and that modern English awards, as part of a system in which 70 per cent of divorces are based on fault grounds, do not appear to be any more successful than US awards in preventing financial hardship.[88]

Even if the empirical data were less equivocal, however, there would be little feminist support for a return to fault. Jana Singer, invoking a liberal feminist perspective, emphasizes the ways in which the fault system constituted a 'double-edged sword' that reinforced the value of a woman's domestic activities in ways that restricted 'women's options outside the home and risk hurting women in the long run by suggesting that the causes and cures for inequality lie solely in the domestic sphere'.[89] Martha Fineman, while otherwise rejecting much of the liberal feminist concern that family law reform will hurt women's position in the workplace, rejects altogether the emphasis on the traditional family that is central to the fault system.[90] Weitzman herself does not advocate reintroducing fault principles,[91] and Herma Hill Kay emphasizes the importance of taking the 'blackmail' out of divorce that prompted no-fault reforms in the first place.[92] Given the myriad difficulties with the fault system, the larger issue is not whether no-fault grounds for divorce are an improvement over fault grounds, but whether the property, support and custody provisions adopted in the wake of no-fault reform provide an adequate basis for the future.

The adequacy of existing divorce doctrine

The true 'divorce revolution' concerns not the generosity of divorce awards, but the permanence of marriage. Fault principles, which arose during the era in which marital bonds were treated as sacred obligations that no 'man' could put asunder, were never intended to treat marital dissolution as anything other than a rare – and tragic – exception to the general order. Nonetheless, in Western nations generally, divorce rates have risen steadily since 1900, and they accelerated dramatically after the 1960s.[93] Greater popular acceptance of divorce both preceded and followed the legal changes, and, as the reforms made marital dissolution easier, divorce rates skyrocketed.[94] No-fault swept the 50 US states within 16 years of the original Californian legislation,[95] and by 1979, the divorce rate had doubled.[96] In Western Europe, Goode documents similar patterns, noting that, of currently marrying couples, only 40–50 per cent (from about 35 per cent in Sweden to about 55 per cent in the UK) will still be married after they have reached the age of 50.[97] Between 50–60 per cent of the children born in the USA in the early 1980s are likely to experience the break-up of their parents' marriage by age 18, and one in five British children can already expect to spend some time as part of a single-parent family.[98] These single-parent families are overwhelmingly headed by women, and the deprivation and disadvantage experienced by female-headed households after divorce has been documented worldwide.[99] Under the fault system, marriage, not divorce awards, served as the principal source of provision for children. Marriage is no longer so dependable.

In this context, the critical issue becomes not whether no-fault is better or worse than the fault system it replaced, but whether current law adequately provides for child-rearing in an era of divorce. Weitzman's book identified the elements that prevent the existing system from responding more adequately, and Eekelaar and Maclean demonstrated that many of the same factors are at work in England. First, divorce could effect a clean break between the spouses *and* adequately provide for both resulting households only to the extent that the property settlement constituted an appropriate resolution of the couple's combined affairs. Few marriages, however, end with significant accumulations of property, and, in those marriages with some property, it consists overwhelmingly of the family home.[100] Therefore, even if all available property were awarded to the custodial parent, it is unlikely to be enough to meet the family's post-divorce needs.

Nonetheless, there is substantial variation from jurisdiction to jurisdiction in the role the property settlement plays. Under no-fault, California mandates a 50/50 division of community property.[101] Many common law (as opposed to community property) states, in contrast, give the courts discretion to use the property division, rather than maintenance awards, to address need. Suzanne Reynolds observes, however, that, even in these states, divisions in which a custodial mother receives more than 50 per cent – that is, more than the share to which she is entitled without taking need into account – are rare.[102] In England, by contrast a recent study found that:

> ... we are a property country, rather than a maintenance country. What *really* matters, at least for couples who own their home, is the disposition of that home. The importance of the home as the repository of virtually the whole of the couples' transferable wealth has been exaggerated by rapid house-price inflation, particularly in the 1980's. As house prices have outstripped wages, many divorces are characterized by the transfer of large capital sums *and* by the woman's continued dependence on Family Credit or (more commonly) Income Support. She may own the roof, but she continues to live in near poverty.

The study concluded that, because of state support for home ownership, which is more generous than other forms of state support, the disposition of the family home can have a major impact on the relative financial status of husband and wife following divorce. Nonetheless, the allocation of the home to the custodial parent is usually combined with little to no maintenance, and the structure of state support, which terminates at low levels of employment, makes it difficult to become independent.[103] At best, therefore, the property division, particularly when coupled with significant state subsidies, can effect a more equitable division of the parties' assets; there is little evidence, however, that the property division alone could, in any but the wealthiest families, provide a basis for equalizing post-divorce standards of living.

Second, existing law provides no coherent legal basis for thinking about spousal support, and the courts do not fully implement the legal bases that exist. The provisions in the Uniform Marriage and Divorce Act that limit spousal support to cases in which a spouse is incapable of self-support or employment outside the home are minimal at best. Long-term homemakers who earn a fraction of their former husband's salaries are, in the language of the Uniform Marriage and Divorce Act, 'able to support [themselves] through appropriate employment', and the custodial mothers of small children limited to low-paying jobs with flexible hours do not have children 'whose conditions or circumstances make it appropriate that the custodian not be required to seek employment outside the home'.[104] In England, the adoption of the Matrimonial and Family Proceedings Act of 1984 also enshrined a clean-break policy. A recent study of solicitors emphasized their support for independence between the adults as a sensible goal, and concluded that the solicitors regarded income transfers 'as short term bridging assistance while the custodial parent adjusted to her new circumstances'.[105]

In the USA, a growing number of states have begun to recognize lost earning potential as a basis for spousal support, and there have been a number of recent appellate decisions reversing lower court failures to award support to long-term homemakers.[106] Full recognition of the loss in earning capacity associated with child-rearing, however, would require lifetime support and, even where states recognize the principle, few decisions fully implement it.[107] Moreover, provisions of this sort primarily benefit older homemakers, rather than the far more numerous younger mothers bearing responsibility for dependent children.[108]

Third, although the law recognizes a clear continuing obligation to children, fathers bear relatively little of the post-divorce responsibility for child-rearing, child support awards do not begin to make up the differences, and compliance is poor at the levels awarded. Unlike the provisions for spousal support, US child support guidelines permit consideration of the 'financial resources of the custodial parent', and often of the impact of custody on the custodial parent's employment prospects.[109] English law also clearly recognizes the primacy of the children's interests at divorce. Nonetheless, child support awards have never accounted for more than a small fraction of child-care costs. The single biggest reason is that the custodial parent assumes the overall responsibility for the child's well-being,[110] while the other parent contributes a fixed sum in which the impact on the new household has been a larger factor in both the amount set and individual compliance than the hardship imposed on the family left behind.[111]

Compounding the paucity of the awards has been a wholesale lack of compliance.[112] The most frequently cited US figures come from a 1981 study that found no payment in 25 per cent of all cases and partial payment in another 25 per cent.[113] Eekelaar and Maclean reported in England that maintenance was ordered, or paid voluntarily in 68 per cent of the divorces involving children but that, at the time of the interview, money was changing hands in only 36 per cent of the cases involving children.[114] A recent White Paper, *Children Come First*, reiterated the finding that compliance was low and enforcement ineffective.[115]

The level of child support has been so egregiously low that the US Congress has amended federal child support laws five times since 1980.[116] State law now requires employers to withhold child support payments from delinquent parents, and starting in 1994, from all parents, whether delinquent or not.[117] The 1984 legislation required states to adopt discretionary guidelines and the 1988 legislation made the guidelines mandatory.[118]

The low levels of child support in the UK also prompted action, culminating in the adoption of the 1991 Child Support Act.[119] The Act created a new agency – the Child Support Agency – to handle child support assessment and collection, and set a more mechanistic formula for the determination of child support awards.[120] Maclean notes that 'British policy had traditionally accepted the status quo in an ad hoc way, permitting the man to devote his income to his present family while the first family was supported by the state though social security', and that the new law marks a shift toward greater emphasis on parental obligation.[121]

While feminists have hailed the new laws, on both sides of the Atlantic, these efforts have yet to bear fruit. The early indications in the USA are that recent changes have increased the amount of child support collected only marginally, and that deviations from the 'mandatory' guidelines are common, with downward deviations more likely for high earning parents and upward deviations more frequent for low earners.[122] These results suggest that courts are more influenced by the non-custodial parent's obligation to assist in meeting the child's basic needs than by any obligation to provide a standard of living commensurate with that of the non-custodial parent.[123]

In the UK, the Child Support Agency has been enormously controversial and widely branded a 'failure' or worse. Critics charge that the new laws impose draconian obligations on those voluntarily paying support, largely for the benefit of the Treasury, while doing little to increase collection from parents engaged in wholesale avoidance. The most criticized provisions have been 1) the disregard of previous settlements, including lump sum property awards intended to substitute for child support; 2) the pound for pound substitute of child support for state benefits; 3) the failure to consider individual circumstances that make some awards confiscatory; and 4) the inefficient processing of cases.[124] Early this year, the government announced changes that would cap the amounts assessed at a percentage of income, and introduce greater flexibility. It also proposed procedural changes, and a maintenance credit that would soften the diminution in state benefits.[125]

In both countries, there appears to be a willingness to embrace the principle that all parents ought to contribute to the support of their children without full recognition that to do so would, without substantial state support, preclude a comfortable standard of living for many second families.

* * *

The overall picture of the relationship between the gendered division of labour and the financial consequences of divorce is remarkably similar in both the UK and the USA. Nonetheless, there are at least two sharp differences. The first involves the relationship between state benefits and private divorce payments. In the US, public assistance is less widely available and more stigmatized than in the UK. Partly as a result, divorce debates overwhelmingly concern the division of resources between separating couples with sufficient income to be worth fighting over; public assistance is invisible. Welfare policy, in contrast, and the corresponding conservative efforts to reduce welfare budgets, focus far more on never-married parents with less political clout. The result is two systems of child support enforcement: for the middle class, a private adversarial system that transfers support from the non-custodial parent to the other household, and for the poor, a state-administered system that collects support to offset state benefits.

In the UK, public assistance and private divorce payments have long been seen as part of a single system.[126] State support has been an important factor in custodial parents' well-being following divorce, and a justification for relatively low private awards. Increased government collection efforts cut across class lines, and the efforts to reduce state assistance budgets involve more divorced than never-married parents.

These differences have important political and ideological consequences. In the US, feminists who have lobbied strongly for increased collection of divorce awards are ambivalent about state collection used to offset public benefits, while fathers' groups who contest divorce administration are less likely to oppose governmental enforcement efforts.[127] In the UK, in contrast, implementation of the Child Support Agency ignited a firestorm of protest that united fathers' groups of all social classes, women who identify with second rather than first families, and those who distrust government intervention more generally. The one constant in both countries is the limited record of compliance.

The other difference involves custody. The United States has gone well beyond most other countries, including the UK, in embracing gender-neutral custody standards, and an ideal of shared parenting. Although most children still reside with their mothers, joint legal custody is becoming the norm and, in California, more than 20 per cent of divorces result in joint physical, as well as legal, custody. These developments correspond with two heated, if largely inconclusive debates. First, are children better off if both parents remain involved in their upbringing following divorce, or are they more likely to thrive if clear authority is given to one parent? One set of studies claims to show that children do better when their fathers remain involved.[128] These studies typically compare the children of highly motivated fathers with the general population, or alternatively, the children of divorced parents with those of married parents. Either way, there is no true control group, and therefore no way to be sure that it is fathers' contact *per se* that produces the results.[129] A second set of studies documents the harmful effects of parental conflict on children.[130] These studies suggest that forcing continued contact, for example, imposing joint physical custody on parents who both want sole custody, may have harmful effects on children. Again, however, there is no way to determine whether it is the conflict associated with joint physical custody, as opposed to conflict that preceded the end of the marriage or conflict that might occur with sole custody and visitation, that produces the harmful effects.

Second, game theorists predict that joint custody preferences, in a system in which mothers are more likely than fathers to place the children's interests ahead of their own, may contribute to children's relative impoverishment in divorce bargaining.[131] Interview studies demonstrate that, in the USA, many men threaten to seek custody as a ploy in negotiations to reduce the amount of child support.[132] Others seek joint physical custody in an effort to substitute greater parenting for reduced financial obligation.[133] The impact of this type of strategic bargaining is difficult to test empirically.[134] Maccoby and Mnookin found that mothers who obtained sole physical custody in high-conflict cases did not appear to receive less support at a statistically significant level. At the same time, for the smaller group of mothers whose divorce decrees provided for joint physical custody, but residence with the mother (a group of cases generally settled later in the bargaining process), 'a higher degree of legal conflict does appear to be associated with *lower* child support awards'.[135] Custody standards may therefore indirectly affect the financial picture, particularly in cases settled through negotiation, mediation or arbitration.[136]

FEMINIST PROPOSALS FOR REFORM

The overriding factor underlying the feminist critique of existing divorce policy is that child-rearing is important and expensive, and that it is an expense borne disproportionately by women. The egalitarian model of husbands and wives holding comparable jobs and sharing domestic responsibilities largely does not exist. The pretence that men and women are equally capable of self-support at divorce effectively assigns custodial mothers primary responsibility both for caring for and supporting their children. When high rates of mother custody are combined with high rates of divorce and low levels of support, an overall shift in the responsibility for child-rearing from parents to mothers emerges.[137]

The consequence of this shift is not just more work for women. Middle-class women – that is, well educated women with good employment prospects – face a clear choice between family and career. In both the USA and the UK, many have delayed or foregone marriage and had fewer children once married.[138] Although the most recent US data shows that more of these women are now choosing to become single parents rather than forego parenthood altogether, the net result is a smaller cohort of middle-class children as a percentage of the total.[139] Moreover, of those children born to middle-class parents, many end up being raised in conditions of relative poverty because of divorce. Finally, children born in working-class or poor families are more likely than middle-class children to experience divorce, and their mothers are less likely to be awarded private support at all.[140] The hardships divorce imposes on middle-class women and children constitute a disaster for the poor. Taken together, these changes amount to a systematic disinvestment in the next generation. In the USA, the proportion of children living in poverty in 1986 was almost double that of adults while in 1960 and 1970 the poverty rate of children was only one-third the adult rate.[141] Although divorce is not the only cause, it is a major contributing factor to a wholesale decline in the well-being of children.[142]

While there is little dissent from this picture, there is less agreement about why it occurred or about how to fix it. The cultural feminist critique places principal responsibility on what Martha Fineman terms 'the illusion of equality'. In her 1983 account of divorce reform in Wisconsin, Fineman blames the poverty of existing divorce discourse, and the refusal to acknowledge the value of maternal nurturing.[143] She claims that divorce reform and, indeed, discussions of the role of women in society generally, focus on two images: women as victims, dependent on men, and handicapped by their inability to participate in the labour market on male terms, and women as equals, fully capable of succeeding on the same terms as men. Missing, Fineman believes, is a recognition of the needs of children, of the importance of nurturing for their well-being, and of the fact that mothers, upon divorce, are asked to meet greater demands with fewer resources than their former husbands. Fineman terms the concept of equality as an 'illusion' that devalues women's connections with their children and prevents recognition of the support needed for the child-rearing role.[144] She echoes Weitzman's conclusion that:

> As long as women are more likely than men to subordinate their careers in marriage, and as long as the structure of economic opportunity favors men, and as long as women contribute to their husband's earning capacities, and as long as women are likely to assume the major responsibilities of child rearing, and as long as we want to encourage the care and rearing of children, we cannot treat men and women as equals in the divorce settlement. We must find ways to safeguard and protect women, not only to achieve fairness and equity, but also to encourage and reward those who invest in and care for our children and, ultimately, to foster true equality for succeeding generations.[145]

Herma Hill Kay, in her review of no-fault divorce and its aftermath, agrees that the unequal position of men and women at divorce results from the unequal division of labour during the marriage and that, at least in the short run, there must be legal recognition of the financial consequences of those roles.[146] Kay nonetheless expresses the concern shared by many liberal feminists that:

> In the long run, however, I do not believe that we should encourage future couples entering marriage to make choices that will be economically disabling for women, thereby perpetuating their traditional financial dependence upon men and contributing to their inequality with men at divorce....
>
> Episodic analysis[147] offers a theoretical structure within which men and women can view their responsibilities to each other and to their children in a different light. By emphasizing the bright line that separates the unique female tasks of pregnancy and childbirth from the common male and female responsibility for childrearing, episodic analysis suggests that, when both parents are available, neither should become the primary nurturing parent.
>
> ...[M]en, like women, should be able to draw an important aspect of their self-esteem and identity from their parental roles. Women, like men, should be able to lead productive, independent lives outside the family. Female dependency should no longer be the necessary result of motherhood.[148]

To implement this view of family life, Kay notes that

> ...since ... Anglo-American family law has traditionally reflected the social division of function by sex within marriage, it will be necessary to withdraw existing legal supports for that arrangement as a cultural norm.[149]

While the liberal feminist embrace of shared parenting and the cultural feminist dismissal of the 'illusion of equality' seem diametrically opposed, much of the theoretical conflict disappears in practice. Kay's embrace of shared parenting is aspirational; she sees joint custody, for example, as drawing 'strength from shared parenting during the marriage' without addressing whether it is appropriate in a marriage in which one parent bore the entire responsibility for child-rearing. Fineman, in contrast, focuses on the ways in which the concept of equality imposes a straitjacket on divorce decisions made in the context of existing marriages in which there are neither equal employment opportunities nor equal assumption of domestic responsibilities. Karen Czapanskiy bridges much of the gap between the two positions by using the military distinction between volunteers and draftees to explain the ways in which the existing system reinforces the traditional division of household labour. Czapanskiy observes that:

> Fathers are given support and reinforcement for being volunteer parents, people whose duties toward their children are limited, but whose autonomy about parenting is broadly protected. Mothers are defined as draftees, people whose duties toward their children are extensive, but whose autonomy about parenting receives little protection.[150]

She argues that the key to achieving Kay's goal of shared parenting in a world characterized by the inequalities that Fineman describes is to emphasize the relationship between rights and responsibilities. She is critical of the emphasis of fathers' rights groups on equal division of family assets (as though the children did not exist) and equal authority over the children's future (as though differences in parental contribution did not exist), but not equal responsibility for the children's well-being. Czapanskiy concludes that equal rights should follow from, not precede, and certainly not be independent of, shared responsibilities.

IMPLEMENTATION

Most feminists, whatever their differences in emphasis, would embrace both greater sharing of parental responsibilities and greater support for child-rearing as important objectives. In considering the best ways to accomplish these ends, there are both broad areas of agreement and some differences on particular proposals. But there is no dissent from the connection between the gendered division of responsibility for child-rearing and the disadvantages women experience in the workplace and at divorce. Most feminist scholars would advocate broad-based reform that includes examination of the workplace as well as the family, and public as well as private support for child-rearing.

Workplace reform

In considering alternatives, proposals for reform extrinsic to divorce are essential and may well command the broadest support. Virtually all feminist writing about the workplace emphasizes the need to make employment more compatible with child-rearing. For fathers to be able to participate more effectively in their children's upbringing and for mothers to avoid the marginalization that presently accompanies their child-care responsibilities requires reform of the workplace. Adequate and affordable day care, more flexible hours and leave, and greater protection for interrupted and part-time employment would all contribute to greater recognition and support for the caregiving role. Liberal feminists, such as Kay and Okin, who emphasize the importance of shared parenting, view these reforms as essential.[151] Feminists of difference, such as Fineman and O'Connell, who place greater emphasis on the special qualities associated with maternal caregiving, also embrace the reforms as important for women's protection.[152] In 1986 the Committee on Women's Rights of the European Parliament proposed that

> ...a comprehensive solution to the problems of single women with children could be provided by a policy guaranteeing all women equal opportunities whatever their family status and founded on access to paid employment.[153]

Public support

Virtually all scholars of the family similarly conclude that adequate provision for children requires public support. While divorce reform may improve the quality of life for middle-class children, in many poor families, the parents' combined post-divorce resources cannot adequately provide for the children. Moreover, the primary private solutions, expanded support obligations and more effective enforcement, work particular hardship on the fathers and mothers least able to pay.[154] Drawing on an extensive body of feminist literature challenging the traditional distinctions between public and private, Deborah Rhode and Martha Minow emphasize that

> ...marriage has presented a promise – between the members of the couple and also between the couple and society – that the costs of traditional gender roles will not be borne by women alone but will be spread throughout society.[155]

There are two primary forces opposing the feminist call for greater public support. The first is ideological. Conservatives have sought to decrease collective provision and discourage the 'dependency culture'.[156] They seek to encourage families to take responsibility for their own members and prefer greater efforts to make absent parents pay to expanded public support. Feminists have been critical of much of this analysis because it overlooks the fact that dependency inevitably accompanies child-rearing. The custodial parent cannot both devote herself to her children and assume the type of labour force role that ensures financial self-sufficiency. Accordingly, feminists are wary of the notion that dependency is *created* by either divorce or public support.

The second issue is the disincentive effects that public support may create. Support adequate for child-rearing, it has been said, encourages more children, more divorces and less workforce participation. The relationship between the availability of public support and workforce participation is direct. The higher the level of public support, the larger the number of people who can receive more from the state than they can earn on their own and the more attractive it becomes to elect state aid. This effect is aggravated by the so-called 'poverty trap', under which, as Davis and Cretney explain, 'those who manage to lift themselves a little above the state poverty line may lose associated means-tested benefits such as free school meals, or rent and rate rebates'.[157] In the USA, the lost benefits also include medical care.[158] Moreover, the new income may be taxed, and the taxes, together with the extra expenses of working such as child care costs, may bring net income down towards, or even below, the income support level provided by the state. A single parent would have to earn substantially more than the amount of state support to break even.

In the divorce context, however, the larger issue underlying the discussion of incentives to encourage employment concerns the question of whether single parents should have to work. In 1979 the Supplementary Benefits Commission emphasized that:

> ...our support for better working opportunities for lone parents is not based on the view that they ought to be supporting themselves. Many lone parents believe it is better to concentrate their efforts exclusively on the difficult and important task of bringing up children single handed, and they are entitled to do that. Freedom of choice should be the aim.[159]

Maclean concludes that, while divorced women in the UK are unlikely to have a higher standard of living than in the USA, they do have a wider range of choices.[160]

For feminists, this issue is a difficult one. The ideology underlying the Supplementary Benefit's Commission approach is one that places primary responsibility for child-rearing on women, and continues to lock women into a dependent role because of it.[161] Liberal feminists are accordingly wary. The principal alternative, however, is an approach like that in the USA of decreasing the amount or duration of public support to a level where most single parents have little choice but to work full-time. This approach constitutes a clear denial of the costs and benefits of child-rearing – the many single parents who cannot afford adequate child care are often forced to rely on poor substitutes in order to be able to feed their children – and imposes a particularly heavy burden on women and children. Liberal feminists and cultural feminists would both prefer an approach that combined greater direct support for children (medical care and Head Start pre-school programmes, for example) with greater support for working parents such as subsidized child care.

The second incentive issue concerns the relationship between public support and divorce. An extensive body of literature tracks the relationship between expanded economic opportunities for women and higher divorce rates.[162] The greater the ability of women to make it on their own, whether through employment or with public assistance, the greater their ability and willingness to end unhappy marriages. Conservatives object that the availability of public support therefore contributes to the breakdown of the family,[163] but feminists are united on this issue. A significant factor in women's inequality has been their inability to leave unsatisfactory relationships.[164] The greater the number of choices women enjoy outside of marriage, the greater the prospects for independence and equality within relationships.

The third issue is the relationship between state support and the decision to bear children. This issue focuses more on non-marital births than on divorce, and it is a major factor in the current US debate on welfare reform. The issue is a complex one in that it combines teenage decisions to proceed with an unplanned pregnancy rather than elect abortion, adoption or a shotgun marriage with those of older women who choose to have babies on their own. To address this issue fully requires an examination of sexual mores, reproduction choice and the idea of financial responsibility. A full discussion of these issues is beyond the scope of this chapter except to note that a feminist response would encourage teenagers to postpone childbearing, not in order to 'save themselves' for marriage but to encourage young girls to take a more active role in developing their own lives.

The allocation of resources at divorce

Addressing divorce itself, feminists emphasize the need for a more equitable allocation of resources and burdens. The single most consistent theme is the need to reexamine the allocation of resources following divorce. Lenore Weitzman charges that '[t]he omission of the career assets from the pool of marital property makes a mockery of the equal division rule'.[165] Susan Moller Okin is convinced that it is judges' tendency 'to regard the husband's postdivorce income as first and foremost *his*' that best explains judicial reluctance to order adequate levels of support under discretionary standards, and she joins Weitzman in embracing the principle that '[b]oth postdivorce households should enjoy the same standard of living'.[166] Martha Fineman and Herma Hill Kay, in the midst of their disagreement on virtually everything else, share enthusiasm for proposals, commonly referred to as 'income sharing', that would equalize the post-divorce living standards of the two resulting households.[167] Eekelaar and Maclean, following their comprehensive review of the justifications for maintenance after divorce, embraced an equalization principle – at least for families with children.[168]

There are three principal justifications for income sharing. First, as Jana Singer notes, post-divorce income particularly in families with children in which the higher-earning spouse is not also the primary caretaker, inevitably reflects the division of labour within the marriage. Wage-earners can devote themselves fully to their work and still enjoy children largely because of the contributions of the other spouse. Caretakers who cut back on their own employment do so, at least in part, relying on the income of the other spouse. Given the difficulties of calculating the impact of marriage on post-divorce earning capacity, and the fact that adjustments are inherently limited by the higher-earning spouse's ability to pay, equalization of post-divorce standards of living offers a certain, easily administered solution that underscores the concept of marriage as a shared enterprise. Singer accordingly proposes that post-divorce income be equalized for a period proportionate to the length of the marriage, with separate provision for child support.[169] Because such a provision is a reflection of the arrangements within the marriage, it is independent of, and should not be adjusted in accordance with, either party's remarriage or the birth of additional children.

There are two primary criticisms of this model of income sharing. The principal feminist criticism is that an exclusive emphasis on husband and wife does not go far enough in providing for children, particularly if the children are still young and the marriage was a short one. These feminists therefore emphasize a second rationale: the continuing responsibility of both parents for the well-being of the custodial family. Jane Rutherford suggests a per capita income division for a period that may exceed the length of the marriage.[170] Most other proposals, like Susan Moller Okin's, advocate comparable standards of living (rather than equal income) for the two resulting households, either for a period proportionate to the length of the marriage or until the children reach the age of majority, whichever is the longer.[171] To the extent that these proposals are based on obligation to the children rather than spousal obligations, however, they should take into account remarriage and the birth of new children.

The other major criticism centres on the fact that, while a portion of post-divorce income may be jointly determined, another, potentially larger, portion is individually determined, particularly after short marriages or marriages without children. Ira Ellman argues vigorously that the husband is neither responsible for societal discrimination generally nor for the choices his wife makes before the marriage, and that any adjustment of post-divorce income should therefore be tied to the effects of the marriage.[172] Eekelaar and Maclean observe that in the absence of agreement, 'we are not sure that the fact of joint parenthood in itself establishes a claim to an equal sharing in all assets, however substantial, should the marriage terminate'.[173] Mary Ann Glendon has long maintained that 'childless and child-rearing marriages involve different social, political and moral issues and should therefore be analyzed separately',[174] suggesting that an income-sharing approach justified for one type of marriage might not be appropriate for all.

Feminist writers such as Jane Rutherford, however, respond to both types of criticism with a third rationale for income sharing. Noting that all men benefit from the societal discrimination against women and that, even in childless marriages, women assume a much greater share of the domestic responsibilities, she concludes that income sharing ought to redress the general inequality in men and women's prospects even if the income disparity in a particular marriage does not reflect the marital division of labour. Jana Singer, while also advocating that income sharing be independent of the presence of children, bases her conclusion on an investment theory of marriage that treats marriage as an economic partnership in which the spouses exchange implied promises to share post-divorce income.[175] For Singer, income sharing depends on the same partnership principles that underlie the equal division of marital property, not on the particular arrangements of a given relationship.[176]

Income sharing, at least in its broadest forms, represents the clearest feminist response to the financial issues now addressed by both spousal support and child support provisions. Virtually all feminists emphasize the need to replace discretionary standards with firm and easily administered rules to overcome judicial bias. Most feminists, like Susan Moller Okin and Joan Williams, emphasize the importance, in both symbolic and practical terms, of securing recognition of post-divorce income as jointly rather than individually owned. Many feminists, particularly the feminists of difference, insist on treating the mother–child relationship as a unit rather than addressing the needs of women separately from the provision for children.[177] Finally, many feminists agree with Jana Singer that only income-sharing proposals adequately recognize differences among women and adequately provide both for those women performing traditional and non-traditional roles.[178]

Child custody

Feminists are united on the need for greater support for child-rearing without agreement on who the caregivers should be. The broad consensus on the need to address the financial consequences of divorce does not carry over to the issue of custody. Feminists who place the greatest priority on dismantling traditional gender roles have the greatest enthusiasm for joint custody. Bartlett and Stack present a classic liberal feminist defence of joint physical and legal custody in arguing that:

> Feminist critics have focused on the concrete and immediate effects of joint custody laws. These critics have ignored another critical feature of the law: its expressive or symbolic power to alter social expectations and norms….
>
> From the point of view of ideology, rules favoring joint custody seem clearly preferable. Joint custody stakes out ground for an alternative norm of parenting. Unlike the 'neutral' best interests test or a primary caretaker presumption, these rules promote the affirmative assumption that both parents should, and will take important roles in the care and nurturing of their children. This assumption is essential to any realistic reshaping of gender roles within parenthood. Only when it is expected that men as well as women will take a serious role in childrearing will traditional patterns in the division of childrearing responsibilities begin to be eliminated in practice as well as in theory.[179]

Bartlett and Stack argue that many of the criticisms of joint custody result from judicial bias and that better implementation, rather than an alternative standard, offers the best way to promote women's interests.

In contrast, Mary Becker presents the feminist case for a maternal deference standard in which courts defer to a fit mother's custody preferences, whether she prefers sole maternal custody, sole paternal custody, joint legal and physical custody or something in between. Becker starts by arguing that

> …mothering and fathering continue to be different activities; mothers tend to be more intensely involved in their children's lives and tend to have greater empathy for their children.[180]

She continues:

> ...regardless of whether we **should** make equal parenting our primary goal, it is not occurring. Women continue to be the primary caretakers physically and emotionally even in dual-wage families. Women continue to invest more emotionally in children than men. We continue to socialize our daughters to do so. We should not, therefore, ignore their pain when they lose custody at divorce. Rather, we must judge custody standards in light of the emotional needs of women and children.[181]

In concluding that even a primary caretaker standard does not adequately address the needs of women and children, Becker reviews implementation of such a standard in West Virginia. She demonstrates a systematic bias against women, especially at the trial court level and especially where:

1 the fathers did more than the average father;
2 the mother 'voluntarily' separated from the child at some time for some reason; and
3 the mother was sexually active outside marriage.[182]

Becker emphasizes that, in considering these issues, judges applied a less favourable standard to women than to men even when operating under a standard thought to favour women. After a review of the alternatives, she concludes that only explicit deference to maternal preferences (a 'maternal deference' standard) can overcome pervasive male bias in the application of otherwise neutral standards, and provide adequate recognition and protection for women on an issue so central to their well-being.

While few other feminists have embraced an explicitly gender-based standard, there is strong support for a primary caretaker preference. Martha Fineman, like Mary Becker, emphasizes the 'qualitative differences between the contributions of primary caretakers (typically mothers) and primary earners (typically fathers) to the upbringing of children'.[183] She is particularly critical of joint custody statutes 'which formally grant fathers equal control over their children, regardless of who provides the day-to-day care and nurturing'.[184] To reward 'demonstrated care and concern for children', Fineman advocates a primary caretaker standard that she believes will 'ensure a good future for children in our culture' by encouraging 'nurturing and concern for children in a concrete way'. Such a standard, Fineman acknowledges, 'may currently operate to the advantage of mothers, but if we value nurturing behavior, then rewarding those who nurture seems only fair'.[185]

Elizabeth Scott, who supports Fineman's effort to reward demonstrated care and concern for children, is nonetheless critical of a winner-take-all custody system that ignores the reality of the many modern marriages in which caretaking is shared, albeit in a variety of different ways. She proposes a proportional custody system in which parents are awarded joint legal and physical custody in accordance with the level of responsibilities they assumed during the marriage.[186]

The dispute over the nature of the maternal role is central to the divisions in modern feminism. The differences between those who favour dismantling the gendered division of responsibility for children and those who celebrate mothers' special connections to their children are largely unbridgeable. Nonetheless, there are at least four aspects of custody that command broad feminist agreement: systematic discrimination against women in litigation and mediation; inadequate response to domestic violence; inappropriate resolution of high conflict disputes; and inequitable distribution of rights and responsibilities following divorce.

Bartlett and Stack, in their defence of joint custody, mention judicial bias against women as an important factor undermining effective implementation; they place particular emphasis on the tendency of judges to take more seriously the demands of men's jobs than women's and the failure to restrain male efforts to coerce, antagonize and manipulate their former spouses.[187] Becker and Fineman base at least part of their appeal for maternal deference and primary caretaker standards, respectively, on distrust of judicial discretion. The fact that outcomes in litigated cases in the USA (men win over 50 per cent of the cases studied) diverge so radically from settled cases (sole maternal physical custody in 80–90 per cent of cases nationally) and so frequently employ gender-stereotyped assumptions persuades virtually all feminists to favour restricted judicial discretion.

Similarly, however much many feminists agree that fathers should remain involved in their children's upbringing, they also share a broad concern about requiring such contact in inappropriate cases. The legal system has historically downplayed the incidence and importance of domestic violence and has responded ineffectually where its existence is indisputable.[188] Many courts do not recognize spousal abuse as grounds for denying custody or access despite the evidence linking parents' conduct to subsequent abusive behaviour by children who grow up with such role models, and despite the need for continued cooperation between the mother and father to make joint physical or legal custody or access effective.[189]

More complex is the resolution of high-conflict disputes. A number of studies emphasize the role of conflict as a destructive factor in children's adjustment to divorce. Fineman fears that joint custody creates an incentive for husbands to seek shared physical or legal custody as a form of retaliation against their wives, and for courts to impose joint legal or physical custody in order to literally split the child between the parents thereby avoiding a decision in difficult cases.[190] Proponents of joint custody, such as Bartlett and Stack, similarly acknowledge the potential for abuse and argue that strict guidelines are necessary to preclude joint physical or legal custody in inappropriate cases, such as those involving domestic violence, and to guard against the use of shared custody as an extension of marital manipulation and discord.[191]

Finally, virtually all feminists agree that the current allocation of rights, responsibilities and resources is inequitable. Karen Czapanskiy effectively summarizes the criticisms of many feminists when she concludes that

> ...what is wrong with joint custody is that it adds rights rather than responsibilities. And what many parents and children need are responsibilities rather than rights.[192]

Like Bartlett and Stack, Czapanskiy starts with the proposition that the expressive goal of the new ideal ought to be a 50–50 division of parental responsibilities, and that both parents' relationship and responsibilities to the child should continue after divorce. Like Becker and Fineman, however, she also believes that the care which women provide is undervalued. To remedy this, Czapanskiy advocates proportionality in the assignment of parental responsibilities with far greater recognition given to the 'nonparallel allocation of nonfinancial responsibilities' – that is, the fact that mothers assume a much greater proportion of day-to-day care. Rather than describe the resulting arrangement in terms of either primary caretaker or joint custody preferences, Czapanskiy advocates a 'parenting plan', in which parents discharge their respective obligations through a combination of custodial and financial contributions to the child that bring into better balance the full range of children's needs (from buttered toast for breakfast to college financing) and the variety of parental contributions.

CONCLUSION

Despite their divisions, feminists agree that the large-scale movement of married mothers into the labour market has not been accompanied by a corresponding increase in men's assumption of domestic responsibilities and that, in an era of high rates of divorce, women bear a disproportionate share of the burden of child-rearing without access to a commensurate share of the family's resources. While feminists may disagree as to whether genuinely shared child-rearing, independent of gender roles, is possible or desirable, they embrace Susan Moller Okin's conclusion that justice requires protection for those whose assumption of domestic responsibilities renders them vulnerable.

NOTES

1 K.T. Bartlett (1990), 'Feminist legal methods', Harvard Law Review **103**, pp. 829–88. See also C. Sanger (1993), 'Feminism and disciplinarity: The curl of the petals', *Loyola of Los Angeles Law Review*, **27**, pp. 225–68.

2 A thorough feminist critique might well start with questioning the focus of this article on divorce. The importance of divorce stems from reliance on the nuclear family as the primary mechanism for ensuring the financial well-being of children. There are many feminist critiques of the traditional family, and of the workforce structure that makes access to a man's higher earning capacity central to the financial well-being of women and children. For a review of the relationship between family and workplace, see J. Williams (1993), 'Woman and property' in R.H. Chused, (ed.) *A Property Anthology*, Cincinnati: Anderson Publishing Co. For a critique of the traditional family, see H. Eisenstein (1983), 'The public/domestic dichotomy and the universal oppression of women', in *Contemporary Feminist Thought*, Boston: G.K. Hall. See also Z. Eisenstein (1983), 'The state, the patriarchal family, and working mothers' in I. Diamond, (ed.), *Families, Politics and Public Policy: A Feminist Dialogue on Women and the State*, New York & London: Longman.

Moreover, the emphasis on divorce often focuses on those families with enough money to be worth fighting over. In poor families, financial awards are less important, and custody is less likely to be an issue than in wealthier families. See, for example, L. Weitzman (1985), *The Divorce Revolution: The Unexpected Social and Economic Consequences for Women in America*, New York: The Free Press, p. 233. A broader discussion would therefore examine provision for the family outside of the divorce system. See, for example, S.P. Erie, M. Rein and B. Wiget (1983), 'Women and the Reagan revolution: thermidor for the social welfare economy' in Diamond, (ed.), *op. cit.*, note 2 above.

3 Among the divisions among feminists is disagreement over the importance of children. Some feminists, particularly 'cultural feminists' or 'feminists of difference' (see discussion below), believe that one of the important differences between men and women is that women care about children more than men do, are more willing to sacrifice their own interests for those of their children, and are at a disadvantage in negotiations with men as a result. These feminists believe that increasing the importance society attaches to children will benefit women, and that emphasizing the importance of children should be a central part of feminist strategy. Other feminists, particularly 'liberal feminists' or 'sameness feminists', have attacked the identification of women's interests with children's interests and insisted that women's interests be considered in their own right. For a discussion of the differences between the two groups, see generally J. Williams (1989), 'Deconstructing gender', *Michigan Law Review* **87**, pp. 797–845. For a discussion of how these differences affect divorce and other social policy issues, see C. Joffee (1983), 'Why the United States has no child care policy' in Diamond (ed.) *op. cit.*, note 2 above; also J. Carbone and M.B. Brinig (1991), 'Rethinking marriage: feminist ideology, economic change, and divorce reform'. *Tulane Law Review*. **65**, pp. 953–1010, 1005–9; V. Fuchs (1988), *Women's Quest for Economic Equality*, Cambridge, Mass.: Harvard University Press, pp. 67–72.

4 D. Chambers (1991), *Making Fathers Pay: The Enforcement of Child Support*, Chicago: University of Chicago Press, cited in M. Maclean (1991), *Surviving Divorce*, New York: New York University Press, p. 16.
5 M. Becker (1992), 'Maternal feelings: myth, taboo, and child custody', *Review of Law and Women's Studies*, **1**, pp. 133–224.
6 Fuchs, *op. cit.*, note 3 above, p. 68. See also M. Fineman (1991), *The Illusion of Equality: The Rhetoric and the Reality of Divorce Reform*, Chicago: University of Chicago Press, p. 174.
7 M.A. Mason (1988), *The Equality Trap*, New York: Simon and Schuster.
8 The terminology is Robin West's. See R. West (1988), 'Jurisprudence and gender', *Chicago Law Review*, **55**, p. 1–72.
9 See, in particular, H.H. Kay (1987), 'Equality and difference: a perspective on no-fault divorce and its aftermath', *Cincinnati Law Review*, **56**, pp. 1–90 and K.T. Bartlett and C.B. Stack (1986), 'Joint custody, feminism and the dependency dilemma', *Berkeley Women's Law Journal*, **2**, pp. 9–41, and the discussion of their work below.
10 See, for example, notes 3 and 4 above. Cultural feminists agree with those who favour traditional family values in their emphasis on the importance of motherhood and childrearing. They disagree in that they believe women should be able to devote themselves to children without becoming dependent on or subordinate to men in so doing.
11 See, for example, K. Czapanskiy (1991), 'Volunteers and draftees: the struggle for parental equality', *UCLA Law Review*, **38**, pp. 1415–81. In addition, there is a radical feminist perspective that rejects both accounts. Carol MacKinnon (1987) ('Feminism, marxism, method and the state: toward feminist jurisprudence', *Signs*, **8**, p. 635–658, 635–36) argues that there is no reason to believe that women's existing preferences reflect women's true preferences – that is, the preferences women would choose in a society free from patriarchal oppression. See also C. Littleton (1983), 'Restructuring sexual equality', *California Law Review*, **75**, pp. 1279–1337, 1333 and G. Lerner (1986), *The Creation of Patriarchy*, New York and Oxford: Oxford University Press, p. 229. Radical feminists, however, tend to concentrate their critique on marriage and the traditional family rather than on divorce. See note 2 above.
12 Becker, *op. cit.*, note 5 above.
13 *Ibid.*, p. 136.
14 Becker cites Martha Fineman as one of the first family law scholars to acknowledge the different positions of mothers and fathers: Fineman, *op. cit.*, note 6 above. See C. Sanger (1992), 'M is for the many things', *Review of Law and Women's Studies*, **1**, pp. 15–67, for a review of the literature on motherhood. Outside of family law, there has been greater discussion of these issues. See, in particular, N.J. Chodorow (1990), 'What is the relation between psychoanalytic feminism and the psychoanalytic psychology of women?' in D.L. Rhode (ed.), *Theoretical Perspectives on Sexual Difference*, New Haven and London: Yale University Press.
15 Sanger, *op. cit.*, note 14 above, p. 18.
16 L. Genevie and E. Margolies (1987), *The Motherhood Report: How Women Feel About Being Mothers*, New York: MacMillan.
17 *Ibid.*, p. 84.
18 *Ibid.*, p. 319.
19 Nancy Chodorow describes 'mothering' as socializing and nurturing a child: N. Chodorow (1978), *The Reproduction of Mothering: Psychoanalysis and the Sociology of Gender*, Berkeley: University of California Press, p. 11.

20 'Primary caretaker' is a term of art in US family law used to describe the parent who assumes the major responsibility for 'the performance of the following caring and nurturing duties of a parent: (1) preparing and planning of meals; (2) bathing, grooming and dressing; (3) purchasing, cleaning, and care of clothes; (4) medical care, including nursing and trips to physicians; (5) arranging for social interaction among peers after school, i.e., transporting to friends' houses or, for example, to girl or boy scout meetings; (6) arranging alternative care, i.e., babysitting, day-care, etc.; (7) putting child to bed at night, attending to child in the middle of the night, waking child in the morning; (8) disciplining, i.e., teaching general manners and toilet training; (9) educating, i.e., religious, cultural, social, etc.; and (10) teaching elementary skills, i.e., reading, writing and arithmetic': *Garsky* v. *McCoy*, 278 SE 2d 357, 363 (W. Va. 1981).

21 D. Ehrensaft (1987), *Parenting Together: Men and Women Sharing the Care of their Children*, New York: Free Press, p. 114.

22 See generally Sanger, *op. cit.*, note 14 above; A. Rich (1986), *Of Woman Born: Motherhood as Experience and Institution*, New York: Norton; M. French (1987), *Her Mother's Daughter*, New York: Ballantine; J. Swigart (1991), *The Myth of the Bad Mother: The Emotional Realities of Mothering*, New York: Doubleday.

23 For a systematic review of the data suggesting that women have a greater demand for children than men, see Fuchs, *op. cit.*, note 3 above, pp. 67–73. Fuchs concludes that the 'evidence concerning a gender difference with respect to children is not air-tight, but its appearance in so many different contexts makes this explanation more credible than any other that has been proposed', p. 68.

24 There is not necessarily a 'feminist' position as to whether gender differences in nurturing exist just as there is no necessary feminist position on the existence of earning disparities between divorcing spouses. Rather, there is a feminist critique of the studies employing economic or other social science methodologies to the extent those studies exclude women's perspectives or otherwise reflect systematic bias. See, for example, Fineman, *op. cit.*, note 6 above, pp. 127–43.

25 See, in particular, MacKinnon, *op. cit.*, note 11 above.

26 See J. Williams (1991), 'Domesticity as the dangerous supplement of liberalism', *Journal of Women's History*, **2**, pp. 69–88. Williams, for example, says of Carol Gilligan's work on gender differences in moral reasoning that 'Gilligan identified, not differences in women's actual *behavior*, as she assumed, but instead women's "voice" in a much more literal sense: she gave a status report on female gender ideology in the late twentieth century' (emphasis in original) p. 69. Williams' critique would apply with similar force to the studies on which Becker relies.

27 Fineman, *op. cit.*, note 6 above, p. 8.

28 Fineman quotes Victor Fuchs, who (*op. cit.*, note 3 above) observes:

> Suppose women were better than men at producing and caring for children but had no particular desire to do so, while it was the men who wanted the children and cared more about their welfare. We would probably still see the same division of labor we see now, but men would have to pay dearly for women's services. The present hierarchy of power would be reversed.

29 Fineman, *op. cit.*, note 6 above, p. 174.

30 The labour force participation of women generally increased from 35 per cent to 51 per cent in the period from 1960 to 1986 and for mothers of young children, the percentage rose from 20 to 50 per cent: Fuchs, *op. cit.*, note 3 above, p. 13. Working-class mothers have never had the luxury of staying out of the labour force. See W.

Chafe (1977), *Women and Equality: Changing Patterns in American Culture*, New York: Oxford University Press, p. 23.

31 B. Bergmann (1986), *The Economic Emergence of Women*, New York: Basic Books, p. 263. Robinson reports a generational change, however, finding that between 1965 and 1985, women's time spent on housework declined from 27 to 20 hours per week while the time spent by men increased from 5 to 10 hours per week. J.P. Robinson (1988), 'Who's doing the housework?', *American Demographics*, December, p. 24; Hochschild's findings, however, are closer to Bergmann's. A. Hochschild, with A. Machung (1989), *The Second Shift: Working Parents and the Revolution at Home*, New York: Viking.

32 Fuchs, *op. cit.*, note 3 above, p. 78.

33 For a review of the sociological and economic literature attempting to explain the failure of men to assume greater responsibility for housework, see P. England and G. Farkas (1986), *Households, Employment and Gender*, New York: Aldine Publishing Co. , pp. 94–9.

34 Mason (*op. cit.*, note 7 above, pp. 123–4) observes that the wage gap remained relatively constant with women earning about 60 cents for every dollar earned by men for more than half of century. For a comprehensive examination of the differences between men and women's earnings, see C. Goldin (1990), *Understanding the Gender Gap: An Economic History of American Women*, New York and Oxford: Oxford University Press. By the late 1980s, however, the wage gap finally began to narrow. See Fuchs *op. cit.*, note 3, p. 49. Susan Moller Okin notes that, in 1987, women who worked year-round at full-time jobs earned 71 per cent of the amount earned by full-time working men and that the increase to 71 per cent was due as much to a drop in men's income as a gain in women's. *Justice, Gender and the Family*, New York: Basic Books, p. 144. By 1991, however, the hourly gap, as opposed to Okin's earning gap, had narrowed to 78 per cent. J. Younger (1992), 'Light thoughts and night thoughts on the American family', *Minnesota Law Review*, **75**, pp. 891–915 at p. 896, n. 38. Economists attribute some of the change to an increase in women's human capital. See Goldin, p. 73.

35 Economists differ significantly in the importance they attribute to discrimination at least in part because they disagree on how to define and measure it. Victor Fuchs (*op. cit.*, note 3 above, p. 56), explains that some economists attempt to measure the extent of the wage gap due to differences in human capital (typically about half of the gender differential), and then assume that the rest is due to discrimination. He finds these studies flawed, partly because the characteristics controlled for, such as experience, may themselves reflect discrimination and partly because these studies fail to account for other gender based differences such as those in mortality. England and Farkas (op. cit., note 33 above, pp. 159–63) note that statistical measures of discrimination are difficult because 'we seldom have data containing information on the qualifications of applicants and employees, their preferences for job placement and promotion, and the resulting occupational distribution' and because of the feedback problems that Fuchs emphasizes. They rely therefore on studies of managerial attitudes that reveal consistent prejudices favouring male applicants over female applicants for higher-paying jobs to demonstrate the existence of discrimination, although the studies on which they rely fail to indicate the degree to which such discrimination has changed over time.

Fuchs and England and Farkas agree with other economists, however, that a major factor in the wage gap is the tracking of women into lower-paying jobs. Economists attribute between 6 and 39 per cent of the wage gap to such occupational segregation depending on the methodology and number of positions used. For a review of these studies, see S.A. Hewlett (1986), *A Lesser Life: The Myth of Women's Liberation in America*, New York: Warner Books, p. 430, n. 33. Hewlett sets the overall figure at about 15 per cent. Economists argue that discrimination excluding women from higher-paying 'male' jobs 'crowds' women into the lower-paying occupations open to them, depressing wages further as supply increases. England and Farkas (pp. 166–72) observe, though, that this thesis does not correspond sufficiently well with empirical data to provide a full explanation, and they argue that other factors, including employer discrimination against *positions* identified with women, and the interaction of discrimination with family responsibilities, are necessary to provide a complete picture. For a comprehensive review of these issues, see Goldin, *op. cit.*, note 34 above.

36 In what England and Farkas (*op. cit.*, note 33 above) termed in 1986, 'the most exhaustive analysis to date', Corcoran and Duncan attributed 44 per cent of the earnings gap between white men and women to experience – that is, years out of the labour force since completing school, years of work experience prior to one's current job, years with present employer, the proportion of working years that were full-time, absences due to illness of oneself or others, limits placed on hours or location, and so on. M. Corcoran and G.J. Duncan (1979), 'Work history, labor force attachment, and earning differences between the sexes', *Journal of Human Resources*, **14**, pp. 3–20. The relationship between the earnings of African–American men and women is more complex, given the interaction of race and gender. For a summary of the statistics showing the gap between African–American men and women to be narrower than that between white men and women, see C.J. Bruch, and N.J. Wikler (1985), 'Economic consequences', *Juvenile and Family Court Journal*, Fall, pp. 5–26, 9–10.

37 Conservative economists attribute a higher percentage of the wage gap to differences in human capital and family responsibilities; liberal economists attribute a higher percentage to discrimination: see Hewlett, *op. cit.*, note 35 above, p. 74 and n. 23.

38 Fuchs (*op. cit.*, note 3 above, pp. 60–4) emphasizes that '[w]omen's homemaking responsibilities reduce their earnings, and, in a feedback loop, the lower earnings induce behavior that further depresses women's labor market opportunities'. See also England and Farkas, *op. cit.*, note 33 above, for an explanation of the feedback effects that they find pervasive between the employment and household aspects of sexism. For a discussion of the differences among economists on the relative importance of discrimination see B. Bergman (1983), 'Feminism and economics', *Academe*, September – October, pp. 22–5.

39 H. Joshi and M.L. Newell (1986), *Family Responsibilities and Pay Differentials: Evidence for Men and Women Born in 1946*, Discussion paper no. 157 (March), London: Centre for Economic Policy Research. See also Blau and Ferber who characterize the interaction from a different starting point, observing that 'even a relatively small amount of initial labor market discrimination can have greatly magnified effects if it discourages women from making human capital investments, weakens their attachments to the labor force, and provides economic incentives for the family to place priority on the husband's career': F.D. Blau and M.A. Ferber (1986), *The Economics of Women, Men and Work*, Englewood Cliffs, NJ: Prentice Hall.

40 Maclean, *op. cit.*, note 4 above, pp. 95–112.

41 S.W. Polachek (1984), '*Women in the Economy: Perspectives on Gender Inequality*, Paper presented at the US Commission on Civil Rights Conference on Comparable Worth, 6–7 June. See also S.W. Polachek (1987), 'Occupational segregation and the gender wage gap', *Population and Research Review*, **6**, pp. 47–67. Other studies attribute between 25 to 44 per cent of the wage gap to work tenure. See, for example,

Corcoran and Duncan, *op. cit.*, note 36 (44 per cent), and N.F. Rytina (1982), 'Tenure as a factor in the male–female earnings gap', *Monthly Labor Review*, April, pp. 32–4 (25 per cent).

42 F.D. Blau and L.M. Kahn (1992), 'The gender earnings gap: learning from international comparisons', *AEA Papers and Proceedings*, **82** (2), pp. 533–8.

43 Fuchs, *op. cit.*, note 3 above, pp. 59–60.

44 Maclean, *op. cit.*, note 4 above, pp. 50–1.

45 Hewlett, *op. cit.*, note 35 above, pp. 83–4. Hewlett also notes that the number and spacing of children affects the wage differential as well (p. 82).

46 Maclean, *op. cit.*, note 4 above, p. 54.

47 E.E. Maccoby and R.H. Mnookin (1992), *Dividing the Child: Social and Legal Dilemmas of Custody*, Cambridge and London: Harvard University Press, p. 59. 53 per cent of the divorcing women, however, had not worked full-time during the marriage, with 31 per cent not working outside the home at all, and the others employed less than 30 hours per week.

48 Fuchs, *op. cit.*, note 3 above, p. 52.

49 Hewlett, *op. cit.*, note 35 above, p. 82. (emphasis in original). See also S.M. Bianchi and D. Spain (1986), *American Women in Transition*, New York: Russell Sage, p. 202. Bianchi and Spain observe that, in the USA, the 26 per cent of all wives who work full-time earn 63 per cent as much as the average full-time working husband while the average wife who works for pay earns only 42 per cent as much as the average husband. In the UK, women generally are less likely to work full-time than in the USA, and Eekelaar and Maclean found that, at divorce, 55 per cent of mothers with dependent children were likely to be in the labour market, but only one-third were working full-time. J. Eekelaar and M. Maclean (1986), *Maintenance After Divorce*, Oxford: Clarendon Press, p. 91.

50 See, for example, M. Maclean (1994), 'Child Support in the U.K.: making the move from court to agency', *Houston Law Review*, **31**, pp. 515, 516–518; S. Cretney (1992), 'Divorce – a smooth transition?' *Family Law*, **22**, pp. 472–4, at p. 472.

51 Kay, *op. cit.*, note 9 above, p. 78.

52 *Ibid.*, p. 62.

53 See Eekelaar and Maclean, *op. cit.*, note 49 above, p. vix.

54 Eekelaar and Maclean (*ibid.*, pp. 10–12) trace the origin of the principle that the wife was to be put in the same position as she would have been in had she remained his 'lawful wife' to the 1917 case of *Hulton* v. *Hulton*, 33 TLR 137 (1917). The English ecclesiastical courts and early US cases had tended to follow a one-third rule influenced by dower concepts, awarding the wife one-third of her husband's income, often in lieu of a property settlement. Eekelaar and Maclean note, however, that both of these principles were discretionary and that alimony awards rarely were so generous in practice.

55 Whatever the law, alimony awards of any kind never occurred in more than a small percentage of all divorces, and 'guilt' barred alimony only in some, not all jurisdictions. See, in particular, J. Singer (1989), 'Divorce reform and gender justice', *North Carolina Law Review*, **67**, pp. 1103–21; M. Melli (1986), 'Constructing a social problem; The post-divorce plight of women and children', *American Bar Foundation Research Journal*, pp. 759–72, at p. 759, n. 2; Eekelaar and Maclean, *op. cit.*, note 49 above, pp. 9, 11.

56 See Eekelaar and Maclean, *op. cit.*, note 49 above, pp. 14–15. For a more extensive discussion of the relationship between fault and the rationales for post-divorce support, see M. Brinig and J. Carbone (1988), 'The reliance interest in marriage and divorce', *Tulane Law Review*, **62**, pp. 855–905, and J. Carbone (1990), 'Economics,

feminism and the reinvention of alimony: a reply to Ira Ellman', *Vanderbilt Law Review*, **43**, pp. 1463–1501.

57 Matrimonial Proceedings and Property Act 1970, s.5(1); subsequently reenacted as Matrimonial Causes Act 1973, s. 25, cited in Eekelaar and Maclean, *op. cit.*, note 49, p. 12. The bulk of US commentary tends to focus on California, which in 1969 abolished consideration of fault for any purpose in the divorce proceedings. New York, in contrast, adopted legislation more like England's. In the mid -1960s, it added no-fault grounds to existing fault grounds, and continues even now to permit some consideration of marital misconduct. In addition, New York is closer to the English scenario in that it rewrote the legislation governing the financial consequences of divorce several years after adopting no-fault grounds, while California changed both provisions simultaneously. For an account of the changes in New York, see M. Garrison (1990), 'The economics of divorce: changing rules, changing results', in S.D. Sugarman and H.H. Kay (eds), *Divorce Reform at the Crossroads*, New Haven, CT: Yale University Press. For a review of the English changes and more recent proposals to change the grounds for divorce, see Cretney, *op. cit.*, note 50 above.

58 *Wachtel* v. *Wachtel* [1973] Fam. 72, cited in Eekelaar and Maclean, *op. cit.*, note 49 above, p. 36.

59 *Ibid.*, p. 15.

60 The 1970 Uniform Marriage and Divorce Act, for example, authorized a court to award maintenance only if the spouse seeking the award '(1) lacks sufficient property, including marital property apportioned to him, to provide for his reasonable needs, and (2) is unable to support himself through appropriate employment or is the custodian of a child whose conditions or circumstances make it appropriate that the custodian not be required to seek employment outside the home': UMDA, 308(a) (1), (2) (1970). This language was retained in the 1973 version. The UMDA did allow, however, the custodial parent's resources to be considered in determining child support. See UMDA 309 (2) (1970).

61 Law Com. no. 112, para. 24, cited in Eekelaar and Maclean, *op. cit.*, note 49 above, pp. 49–50. The Commission also left open the possibility that the courts could continue to take marital conduct into account.

62 Matrimonial Causes Act, ss. 25 (2) (a), 25A (2), 31 (7) (a) as inserted by the Matrimonial and Family Proceedings Act 1984, ss. 3, 6 as cited in Eekelaar and Maclean, *op. cit.*, note 49 above, pp. 50–1.

63 Fineman (*op. cit.*, note 6 above, p. 221, n. 35) does not distinguish between physical and legal custody in this passage, and the studies she cites refer to both forms of custody.

64 *Ibid.*, pp. 79–80, 90. Fineman cites two studies: N. Polikoff (1982), 'Why mothers are losing: A brief analysis of criteria used in child custody determinations', *Women's Rights Law Reporter*, **7**, pp. 235–43 and Weitzman, *op. cit.*, note 2 above, pp. 231–5. Weitzman's figures show that, in 1977 in Los Angeles, 63 per cent of the small number of fathers who requested either physical or legal custody received it, a figure that includes both contested and uncontested cases. Polikoff (pp. 236–7) cites Weitzman and four other studies of court records. Three of the studies show men winning about half the time; the other 38 per cent of the time. Becker (*op. cit.*, note 5 above, pp. 182–3 and 192–201) further reports two studies, one in a North Carolina county under a best interests standard and her own study of West Virginia appellate cases applying a primary caretaker standard, in which fathers received sole physical custody in over 60 per cent of litigated cases at the trial level. Maccoby and Mnookin (*op. cit.*, note 47 above, p. 273) similarly find that where custodial conflicts are

resolved after a court-appointed evaluation, through negotiations on the courthouse steps or through adjudication, there is a 50-50 division between mothers and fathers. Becker and Polikoff also review individual cases to demonstrate the bias toward women in the decisions. Maccoby and Mnookin suggest selection bias to the extent that only the fathers with the strongest claims pursue them through the conclusion of litigation.

Fineman's point is not so much that mothers are losing custody, but that the legal system trivializes mothers' emotional connection with their children by failing to grant express legal recognition of the importance of those connections, and increases the likelihood of biased decision-making in the process (p. 174).

65 The express maternal presumption common earlier in the century has disappeared and is widely believed to be unconstitutional. Virtually all states decide custody in accordance with a 'best interests of the child standard'. Thirty-seven states authorize joint legal and physical custody awards, with a few states requiring the agreement of both parents and a few states recognizing a rebuttable presumption that joint custody is in the child's best interests. One state, West Virginia, has adopted a primary caretaker standard in which sole legal and physical custody is awarded to the parent who assumed the greater responsibility for the child's care during the marriage. See C.S. Bruch (1988), 'And how are the children?', *International Journal of Law and the Family*, **2**; pp. 106–26. In England, the maternal presumption 'is now said to be nothing more than an assumption of human nature and certainly not a principle of law': M.D.A. Freeman (1991–92), 'England: rethinking family rights and responsibilities', *Journal of Family Law*, **30**, pp. 295–317 at p. 312.

66 Maccoby and Mnookin, *op. cit.*, note 47 above, pp. 273–4: 'Our most disturbing finding ... concerns the frequency with which joint physical custody decrees are being used by high-conflict families to resolve disputes.' See also Bruch, *op. cit.*, note 65 above, pp. 109 and 122 for a review of the studies assessing joint custody. In England, in contrast, the courts have continued to be wary of joint custody. M.D.A. Freeman (1987–88) 'England: New response to old problems', *Journal of Family Law*, **26**, pp. 69–96, 81–2.

67 Becker, *op. cit.*, note 5 above, p. 178 and nn. 173 and 174, Fineman, *op. cit.*, note 6 above, p. 132, and Bruch *op. cit.*, note 65 above, p. 113.

68 See Mason, op. cit., note 7 above, p. 87. In England, as well, 90 per cent of mothers tend to retain custody: Maclean, *op. cit.*, note 4 above, p. 115.

69 Fineman, *op. cit.*, note 6 above, p. 76.

70 Eekelaar and Maclean, *op. cit.*, note 49 above, pp. 68, 90–9.

71 Weitzman, *op. cit.*, note 2 above.

72 *Ibid.*, p. 339 (emphasis in original deleted).

73 See, for example, T. Arendell (1986), *Mothers and Divorce: Legal, Economic and Social Dilemmas*, Berkeley: University of California Press (90 per cent of the women in the small sample studied found themselves at or near the poverty line; four years later only nine of sixty were able to halt the economic fall prompted by divorce, p. 37); G. Duncan and S. Hoffman (1988), 'What are the economic consequences of divorce?', *Demography*, **25**, pp. 641–5 (reporting 30 per cent drop for women); J. Wallerstein and J. Kelly (1980), *Surviving the Breakup: How Children and Parents Cope with Divorce*, New York, Basic Books (three-quarters of the divorced women studied in an affluent county experienced a significant decline in their standard of living); H.R. Wishik (1986), 'Economics of divorce: an exploratory study', *Family Law Quarterly*, **20**, 79 (120 per cent gain for men; 25 per cent drop for children, 33 per cent drop for women, assuming all support paid); J. McLindon (1987), 'Separate but, unequal: the economic disaster of divorce for women and children', *Family Law*

Quarterly, **21**, pp. 351–78; R.B. Bell (1988), 'Alimony and the financially dependent spouse in Montgomery County, Maryland', *Family Law Quarterly*, **22**, pp. 225–84; B.R. Rowe and A.M. Morrow (1988), 'The economic consequences of divorce in Oregon after ten or more years of marriage', *Williamette Law Review*, **24**; pp. 463–84; see Garrison, *op. cit.*, note 57 above.

74 Duncan and Hoffman, *op. cit.*, note 73 above.

75 Weitzman, *op. cit.*, note 2 above, pp. 337–8.

76 A. Sorenson (1992), 'Estimating the economic consequences of separation and divorce: A cautionary tale from the United States' in L. Weitzman and M. Maclean (eds), *Economic Consequences of Divorce: The International Perspective*, Oxford: Clarendon Press.

77 Weitzman, *op. cit.*, note 2 above, pp. 324 and 341.

78 Joan Krauskopf observes: 'Even those who criticize Weitzman's figures differ on amount, not on significant disparity in standard of living between ex-husbands and ex-wives': J. Krauskopf (1989), 'Theories of property division/spousal support: searching for solutions to the mystery', *Family Law Quarterly*, **23**, pp. 253–78, at p. 271, n. 65.

79 Fineman, *op. cit.*, note 6 above, p. 64.

80 Eekelaar and Maclean, *op. cit.*, note 49 above, p. 35.

81 The Law Commission (1990), *Family Law: The Ground for Divorce*, London: HMSO, p. 3.

82 *Healthpoint: Mills-Peninsula Hospital*, January–February 1992 (reporting on a study by Joan Kelly, Director of the Northern California mediation center). Maclean (*op. cit.*, note 4 above, p. 12) observes that in the UK and in France women outnumber men by three to one in seeking divorce.

83 Indeed, there is a significant difference between younger and older women in another respect. The major factor in predicting rates of remarriage for women is age. Younger women, even with children, enjoy rates of remarriage largely comparable to those for men. Older women, with or without children, remarry at much lower rates. Accordingly, for older women, the biggest loss with the end of the marriage may be the opportunity to be married at all. For younger women, the bigger issue is the father's contribution to childrearing. For a discussion of these issues, see Brinig and Carbone, *op. cit.*, note 56 above.

84 For a summary of these studies, see A. Parkman (1992), *No-fault Divorce: What Went Wrong*? Boulder, CO: Westview Press, pp. 79–87.

85 Kay, *op. cit.*, note 9 above, p. 67.

86 Singer, *op. cit.*, note 55 above, pp. 1106–10.

87 W.J. Goode (1956), *After Divorce*, New York: The Free Press. Republished in 1965 as *Women in Divorce*.

88 Eekelaar and Maclean, *op. cit.*, note 49 above, pp. 34–5. This study, however, focused only on divorced women drawing national assistance. See also H. Jacob (1986), 'Faulting no-fault', *American Foundation Research Journal*, pp. 773–80.

89 Singer, *op. cit.*, note 55 above, p. 1113.

90 Fineman, *op. cit.*, note 6 above, pp. 11–12.

91 Weitzman, *op. cit.*, note 2 above, pp. 366, 382–3.

92 Kay, *op. cit.*, note 9 above, p. 62.

93 W.J. Goode (1992), 'World changes in divorce patterns', in Maclean and Weitzman (eds), *op. cit.*, note 76 above, p. 16.

94 For a review of the economic and empirical literature on the relationship between the divorce rate and the adoption of no-fault, see Parkman, *op. cit.*, note 84 above, pp.

71–9. Parkman argues that '[i]t appears that no-fault divorce was a response to rather than a cause of the forces that caused an increase in the divorce rate' and that following adoption of no-fault there was an increase in the divorce rate for a short period that reflected, at least in part, pent-up demand. For a review of the historical and sociological forces underlying no-fault, see Kay, *op. cit.*, note 9 above, pp. 66–7. In a comparative analysis, Goode, (*op. cit.*, note 93 above, p. 18) emphasizes that: 'Coupled with this major increase [in divorce rates] has been a general liberalization of divorce laws during this period, but it is worth noting that some countries had made that step *before* the sharp upwards movement of the divorce rate, while others took that step while it was occurring.'

95 Parkman, *op. cit.*, note 84 above, pp. 71–9.

96 See *ibid.*, pp. 72–3. Using somewhat comparable figures, the English divorce rate has also doubled since the 1969 enactment of divorce reform: Freeman, *op. cit.*, note 65 above, p. 296. Goode (*op. cit.*, note 93 above, p. 17) notes, further, that in examining the number of divorced women as the percentage of all women, the rates increased sixfold between 1960 and the late 1980s.

97 *Ibid.*, p. 16.

98 S.M. Okin (1989), *Justice, Gender and the Family*, New York: Basic Books, p. 160. Maclean *op. cit.*, note 4 above, p. 15. Okin also notes that divorce rates are dramatically higher for African–Americans. In 1983, there were 126 divorced white women for every 1000 married women; for black women, the ratio was 297 to 1000 (p. 160). In 1985, 28 per cent of ever-married white women and 49 per cent of ever-married black women were separated, divorced or widowed.

99 Maclean, *op. cit.*, note 4 above, p. 128. In both the USA and the UK, for example, approximately half of single-parent families fall below the poverty line, and Maclean describes two-thirds of single-parent families, but only one-third of all families, as living close to poverty (p. 16 – citations omitted). See also D. Rhode and M. Minow (1990), 'Reforming the Questions, Questioning the Reforms: Feminist Perspectives on Divorce Law' in Sugarman and Kay, *op. cit.*, note 57 above.

100 Eekelaar and Maclean, *op. cit.*, note 49 above, pp. 46–7, 86.

101 Kay, *op. cit.*, no. 9 above, n. 196.

102 S. Reynolds (1988), 'The relationship of property division and alimony: the division of property to address need', *Fordham Law Review*, **56**, pp. 827–916.

103 G. Davis, S. Cretney, K. Bader and J. Collins (1992), 'The relationship between public and private financial support following divorce in England and Wales' in McLean and Weitzman, *op. cit.*, note 76 above, p. 310–41, 320–26.

104 UMDA, s. 308 (a) (1), (2) (1970), note 60 above.

105 E. Jackson and F. Wasoff with M. Maclean and R. Dobash (1993), 'Financial support on divorce', *International Journal of Law and the Family*, **7**, pp. 230–54, at p. 251. Eekelaar and Maclean (*op. cit.*, note 49 above, p. 90), report that courts ordered maintenance in only 11 per cent of childless marriages, and 10 per cent of the divorces involving independent children.

106 A. Estin (1993), 'Maintenance, alimony and the rehabilitation of family care', *North Carolina Law Review*, **71**, pp. 721–803.

107 Weitzman, *op. cit.*, note 2 above, pp. 32–6. Weitzman (*op. cit.*, note 47 above, pp. 129–30), for example, found alimony awarded at all in only 17 per cent of the divorces she examined; Maccoby and Mnookin claim that the current California rate in the two relatively wealthy counties they studied is closer to 30 per cent, but put the national total at only 8.1 per cent. They also note that the level of the California awards is slightly lower than the US average and compliance is also lower. They

suggest that in other states only fathers with relatively high incomes are ordered to pay spousal support, and that these men have greater ability and propensity to pay.

108 Ann Estin (*op. cit.*, note 106 above), provides a systematic examination of the lack of support in existing legal provisions for family caregivers. She argues that recognition of lost earning capacity is most commonly invoked to justify support for older women divorced after a long marriage, and is rarely awarded to younger women capable of self-support.

109 Kay, *op. cit.*, note 9 above, p. 49.

110 Czapanskiy, *op. cit.*, note 11 above.

111 N.D. Hunter (1983), 'Women and child support' in I. Diamond (ed.), *Families, Politics and Public Policy*, New York & London: Longman, p. 206. It is also rare for combined spousal and child support payments to exceed a third of a man's income: see Parkman, *op. cit.*, note 84 above, p. 82; Eekelaar and Maclean, *op. cit.*, note 49, pp. 93–9. The English White Paper, *Children Come First*, found that maintenance awards represent only about 11 per cent of the total net income of absent parents on above average incomes: *Children Come First*, Cm. 1264, 2 vols, London: HMSO, 1990.

112 Weitzman, *op. cit.*, see note 2 above, pp. 278–81.

113 Okin, *op. cit.*, note 98 above, p. 165.

114 Eekelaar and Maclean, *op. cit.*, note 49 above, p. 90–6.

115 *Op. cit.*, note 111 above. See also J. Eekelaar (1991), 'A child support scheme for the United Kingdom: an analysis of the White Paper', *Family Law*, **21**, pp. 15–21. See also D. Chatterton, 'The cost of the single parent', *Family Law*, **24**, pp. 23–5. Chatterton, summarizing the finding of the White Paper, reported that only 30 per cent of lone mothers [this includes never-married as well as divorced mothers] and 3 per cent of lone fathers receive support in any form from the other parent, compared to the 70 per cent who receive state support. The average amount of maintenance awarded was £16 per child, dropping to £12 per week in families with three or more children. Two in five lone parents experienced one or more periods where the absent parent did not pay anything, and 80 per cent of the arrears in DSS cases were never recovered. The amount the DSS did recover amounted to no more than 5 per cent of the total value of the arrears.

Maccoby and Mnookin's mid-1980s study (*op. cit.*, note 47 above, pp. 250–1) in two Californian counties found that more than half (57 per cent) of the fathers fully complied; 23 per cent paid nothing, and 19 per cent made partial payments. On average, fathers paid between two-thirds and three-quarters of the child support awarded and compliance diminished over time.

116 'Note: Title i of the Family Support Act of 1988 – The quest for effective national child support enforcement continues', *Family Law Quarterly*, **29**, 1990–91, pp. 149–70, 149.

117 H.D. Krause (1990), 'Child support reassessed: limits of private responsibility and the public interest' in Sugarman and Kay, *op. cit.*, note 57 above, p. 170.

118 Hunter, *op. cit.*, note 111 above, p. 207. See also *Children Come First*, *op. cit.*, note 111 above, on the extreme role of discretion in English awards. Moreover, in England, the feminist critique of the male-dominated exercise of discretion extends to the solicitors who negotiate settlements as well as the judiciary. See G. Davis (1994), 'The day before yesterday', *Family Law*, **24**, pp. 323–5.

119 Child Support Act, 1991, ch. 48 (UK).

120 Maclean, *op. cit.*, note 50 above.

121 *Ibid.*, pp. 528–30.

122 See, for example, Marily L. Ray and Center for Human Services Research and

Evaluation, *Evaluation Project Report, 1993*, Ithaca, N.Y.: The Finger Lakes Law and Social Policy Center.

123 See Weitzman, *op. cit.*, note 2 above, pp. 270–4. Maccoby and Mnookin (*op. cit.*, note 103 above, p. 130) report that child support payments constitute no more than a fraction of mothers' post-divorce family income. See, for example, Davis, Cretney, *et al.*, *op. cit.*, note 103 above, pp. 319–20; Eekelaar and Maclean, *op. cit.*, note 49 above, pp. 93–9.

124 Maggie Rae (3 February, 1995) 'A lifeline for the agency,' *New Law Journal* **145**: 140. See also Patricia Hewitt, (5 April, 1994) 'Oz and the art of maintenance', *The Independent*, p. 16.

125 *Ibid.* And see now the Child Support Act 1995.

126 Compare, for example, Eekelaar and Maclean's study of English divorce, *op. cit.*, note 49, with Weitzman's examination of California divorce, *op. cit.* note no. 2. Eekelaar and Maclean systematically incorporate state benefits as a major factor in evaluating the economic position of women following divorce, while Weitzman pays much less attention to public assistance.

127 Harry Krause (*op. cit.*, note 117) argues that child support enforcement laws in the USA have now gone about as far as they can without imposing unfair hardships on men, and he joins David Chambers in maintaining that such laws are already being enforced in counterproductive and unduly harsh ways on teenage fathers, particularly those from poor and minority backgrounds. Many feminists who otherwise favour strict child support enforcement are concerned about the possible disproportionate effect on poorer men, and believe that the only possible satisfactory solution is a greater assumption of public responsibility, which has never been as generous in the USA as it has been in England. See, in particular, Hunter, *op. cit.*, note 111, pp. 207–14. But see Maccoby and Mnookin (*op. cit.*, note 47 above, p. 265), who conclude that: 'In sum, not only could most fathers in our sample afford to pay the full amount of support awarded; they could afford to pay more.'

128 For a feminist critique of these studies, see Fineman, *op. cit.*, note 6.

129 See, for example, Sara McLanahan's evaluation of these studies, concluding that lack of income, rather than fathers' absence, shows the strongest effects. In Weitzman and Maclean, *op. cit.*, note 76, at 302. See also Paul R. D'Amato (1994), 'Life Span Adjustment of Children to Their Parents' Divorce', in *Children and Divorce, The Future of Children*, **4**: pp. 143–164.

130 See, in particular, Janet R. Johnston (1994), 'High-Conflict Divorce', in *Children and Divorce, The Future of Children*, **4**: pp. 165–182.

131 Fuchs, *op. cit.*, note 3 above, pp. 67–73 and Parkman, *op. cit.*, note 84 above, pp. 81–82. Game theory is defined as 'a theoretical approach to interactive decision making, used in economics to analyze situations where prices and quantities are the outcome of bargaining by individual participants, rather than the automatic result of a competitive market' (Fuchs, *op. cit.*, note 3 above, p. 71).

132 Weitzman (*op. cit.*, note 2 above, p. 310) puts the figure at one-third. See also Mason, *op. cit.*, note 7 above, p. 83 and Arendall, *op. cit.*, note 73 above, pp. 23–4. Maccoby and Mnookin (*op. cit.*, note 47 above, p. 102) found that 20% of the fathers in their study who told the researchers that they wanted maternal custody in fact requested joint physical custody or father custody.

133 Hunter, *op. cit.*, note 111 above, p. 208.

134 See Weitzman, *op. cit.*, note 2 above, p. 310, sources cited in note 127 and R.H. Mnookin and L. Kornhauser (1979), 'Bargaining in the shadow of the law: the case of divorce', *Yale Law Journal*, **88**, pp. 950–997.

135 Maccoby and Mnookin, *op. cit.*, note 47 above, p. 158 (emphasis in original). In the group of mothers who obtained sole physical custody, high conflict was a negative factor in predicting support awards but the results were not statistically significant. Maccoby and Mnookin also note the possibility that the custody threats, on average, were not that credible. One wonders if the difference between the two populations, mothers who received sole custody as opposed to mothers who received joint physical custody, but mother residence, may not have been that the fathers in the latter sample had more credible threats. See Table 7.6, p. 151, indicating that 40 per cent of the cases settled after evaluation resulted in joint physical custody compared to 25 per cent of the case settled after mediation and 19 per cent of the cases settled earlier. *Ibid.*, p. 157.

136 See F. Kaganas and C. Piper (1994), 'The divorce consultation paper and domestic violence', *Family Law*, **24**, pp. 143–45. See also T. Grillo (1991), 'The mediation alternative: process dangers for women', *Yale Law Journal*, **100**, pp. 1545–1610.

137 The other part of this picture is an increase in births to never-married mothers. In the UK, 33 per cent of lone parents are divorced women, 31 per cent are single women, 18 per cent are separated women and 6 per cent are widows. All lone fathers taken together equal 11 per cent: Chatterton, *op. cit.*, note 115 above, p. 23.

138 See Fuchs, *op. cit.*, note 3 above, pp. 96–104. Sue Shipman, 'Female refuseniks withdrew from gender wars; the opportunity costs of being a mother are too high for many modern women', *The Independent*, 11 April, 1995, p. 13; Polly Toynbee, 'Till death, dispute or boredom do us part: Divorce is to be made a little easier, but also a little harder. Will it make any difference to our behaviour?' *The Independent*, 28 April, 1995, p. 17.

139 For higher-earning women in the USA, the increase is a small, but sharp one: from 3 to 6.4 per cent for college-educated women and 3 to 8.3 per cent for professional women in the period from 1982 to the present: 'Daughters of Murphy Brown', *Newsweek*, 2 August 1993, p. 58 citing US Bureau of the Census Figures released in July 1993. 62.5 per cent of all US children were considered middle class in 1989 compared with 74.6 per cent in 1969. During the same period, the percentage of low-income children rose from 19.4 to 29.1 per cent and the percentage of high-income children grew slightly, from 6.0 to 8.4 per cent: US Bureau of the Census (1992), 'Current Population Reports', *Households, Families, and Children: A 30 Year Perspective*, Washington, DC: US Government Printing Office, pp. 23–181.

140 See Fuchs, *op. cit.*, note 3 above, p. 89; Okin, *op. cit.*, note 98 above, p. 160; Weitzman, *op. cit.*, note 2 above, pp. 178–82; Eekelaar and Maclean, *op. cit.*, note 49 above, p. 69. In England, the courts sometimes view the availability of social security benefits as a cause for reducing maintenance liability (Eekelaar, *op. cit.*, note 115 above, p. 15).

141 Fuchs, *op. cit.*, note 3 above, p. 107. In England, the proportion of single-parent families receiving income support has also risen from under 20 per cent in 1961 to 40 per cent in 1979 to 66 per cent by 1990 (Eekelaar, *op. cit.*, note 115 above, p. 15). Eekelaar and Maclean noted in their earlier study (*op. cit.*, note 49 above, p. 71) that, for women living alone with children following divorce, only 18 per cent earned 140 per cent of the supplementary benefit entitlement compared with 71 per cent of the general population. More generally, accounts indicate that, in the UK, three times more children are poor than in 1979, and at least part of the increase is attributable to the growing number of single parent families. Trevor Mason, *Press Association* Newsfile, 20 March, 1995.

142 Fuchs, *op. cit.*, note 3 above, pp. 104–10. McLanahan surveys the existing literature on the well-being of children and concludes that low income, often a consequence of

divorce, rather than divorce itself corresponds most closely with a decline in the well-being of children. S. McLanahan (1992), 'Intergenerational consequences of divorce: the United States perspective' in Maclean and Weitzman , *op. cit.*, note 93 above, pp. 305–6. See also Eekelaar and Maclean, *op. cit.*, note 49 above, pp. 80–4, discussing the lower educational attainment of children whose parents divorce.

143 Fineman, *op. cit.*, note 6 above.

144 *Ibid.*, p. 175.

145 Weitzman, *op. cit.*, note 2 above, pp. 365–6.

146 Kay, note 9 above, p. 79.

147 Kay (ibid., p. 80, n. 388) defines 'episodic analysis' as 'an analysis that accords legal significance to biological reproductive sex differences only during the specific episodes when those differences are being used for reproductive purposes'.

148 *Ibid.*, pp. 80–81 and 85.

149 *Op. cit.*, see note 8 above, p. 85.

150 *Op. cit.*, note no. 96 above, p. 1416.

151 See also Joan Williams, note 26 above.

152 M.E. O'Connell (1988), 'Alimony After No-Fault: A Practice in Search of a Theory', *New England Law Review*, **23**, pp. 437–513. For an extensive critique of the concept of dependency, see Martha Fineman (1995), *The neutered mother, the sexual family, and other twentieth century tragedies*, New York: Routledge.

153 Maclean, *Surviving Divorce*, *op. cit.*, note 4 above, p. 59.

154 See, for example, Krause, *op. cit.*, note 117 above.

155 Note 99 above, p. 194.

156 Maclean *op. cit.*, note 4 above, p. 517.

157 Davis, Cretney, *et al.*, *op. cit.*, note 103 above, p. 319.

158 Sara McLanahan, 'Intergenerational Consequences of Divorce: The United States Perspective,' in Weitzman and Maclean, *op. cit.*, note 76, p. 302.

159 Maclean, *Surviving Divorce*, *op. cit.*, note 4 above, p. 82, citing SBC, 1979, p. 12.

160 *Ibid.*, p. 83.

161 See, in particular, M.D.A. Freeman (1984), 'Legal ideologies, patriarchal precedents, and domestic violence', in M.D.A. Freeman (ed.), *The state, law and the family: critical perspectives*, London and New York: Tavistock Publications, Sweet and Maxwell.

162 See, for example, Fuchs, England and Farkas, Becker, Parkman.

163 For a summary of the conservative position, see Maclean, Houston, pp. 516–21. There is a separate issue as to whether or not public support is sometimes structured to encourage otherwise happily married couples to divorce for financial gain, but this does not appear to be a factor in the current debate. See Freeman, note no. 161, pp. 60–61, for a discussion of the effect of the 'cohabitation rule.'

164 *Op. cit.*, note 98 above.

165 See Weitzman, *op. cit.*, note 2, p. 388 (emphasis in original deleted).

166 See note 88, pp. 165 and 183 (emphasis in original deleted).

167 See Fineman, *op. cit.*, note 6, p. 176, and n. 232 and H.H. Kay (1987), 'An appraisal of California's no-fault divorce law', *California Law Review*, **75**; pp. 291–319, 318–19, n. 196.

168 Ekelaar and Maclean, *op. cit.*, note 49 above, pp. 104–37.

169 Singer, *op. cit.*, note no. 55, p. 1120. Singer undertook the article, in part, as an effort to set out a justification for Weitzman's income sharing suggestions, suggestions that also rest on the principle of recognizing the spouses' equal contributions to the marriage.

170 J. Rutherford (1990), 'Duty in divorce: shared income as a path to equality', *Fordham Law Review*, **58**; pp. 539–92.

171 Okin, *op. cit.*, note 98 above, p. 138; Rutherford, *op. cit.*, note 170 above. Mary Ann Glendon and Martha Fineman, without directly commenting on income sharing, have suggested that the first principle at divorce ought to be adequate provision for children, and that any division between the adults ought to follow the provision for children even if that imposes a greater hardship on the noncustodial parent than the custodial one: 'Family law reform in the 1980's', *Louisiana Law Review*, **44**, 1984, pp. 1553–73, 1560. For that reason, Fineman (*op. cit.*, note 6, p. 177) is critical of an exclusive reliance on equal division, reflecting marital *contributions*, and prefers an emphasis, like that of Okin and Rutherford's, on the custodial families' continuing *needs*.

Eekelaar and Maclean (*op. cit.*, note 49, pp. 113–31) have offered a complex blend of different principles. First, although they refer to their principle in terms of 'equalization of resources', they describe it as requiring that 'the absent parent will need to share his resources in such a way as to keep the children *and former spouse* as nearly as can be at a standard of living equivalent to that which they enjoyed at the time of separation'. Second, they would limit such a standard to an upper amount equal to 'the standard of living enjoyed by most children in their society'. Third, they would relax their equalization principle at the lower end of the income spectrum where it serves only to reimburse the state. Their proposal, however, stems not from a feminist account of the relationship between husband and wife, but from an effort to ground support in a combination of parental and societal obligations toward children.

To the extent, however, that these proposals rest on parental obligation toward children, rather than on the relationship between husband and wife, they raise the question of adjustments in light of new families. Eekelaar and Maclean, consistent with their characterizing the obligation as one toward children, adjust the amount of support owed to take into account the new family obligations (p. 133). Rutherford, consistent with her treatment of the obligation as one between husband and wife, does not.

172 I. Ellman (1989), 'The theory of alimony', *California Law Review*, **77**; pp. 1–81.

173 Ekelaar and Mclean, *op. cit.*, note 49 above, p. 142. More recently, Maclean noted:

> For women we did not argue for maintenance in order to perpetuate women's economic dependence on men, but for income transfers to compensate for the losses associated with motherhood, or with marriage, but with divorce. If marriage is a contract which can result in loss of earnings associated with child rearing, compensated during marriage by a share in the other partner's income during his working life and pension in retirement, it is this share which the divorced woman loses. This loss continues to affect her after children have grown up and left home and child support payments have ceased.

'Comment: Child support – wife support, or family support?', *Family Law*, **21**, 1991, p. 3. This rationale, which I have argued elsewhere, corresponds to the expectation interest in contract damages, depends, however, on fault. If a divorced woman leaves her husband for another man, or throws him out because she no longer wishes to live with him, why should she be entitled to the benefits of the marriage? It is only if he is at fault that this rationale works: see Brinig and Carbone, *op. cit.*, note 83 above. The claims based on losses associated with loss of earnings or motherhood, in contrast, are independent of fault.

174 Glendan and Fineman, *op. cit.*, note 171 above, p. 1560.

175 Singer, *op. cit.*, note 55 above, pp. 1113–18.
176 Whatever rationale is adopted, the tension between treating marriage as a shared enterprise and doing justice in individual cases acquires particular force when the higher-earning spouse and the primary caretaker are the same person. If the spouse of an unemployed alcoholic both supported the family and provided the only care the children received during the marriage, why should that spouse's income – the only income available for the support of the children after the divorce – be shared with the other spouse? This issue poses particular difficulties for feminists because of distrust of judicial discretion and a reluctance to recognize exceptions to the concept of marriage as an economic partnership. Jane Rutherford would nonetheless recognize a limited exception where a spouse had contributed neither income nor domestic services during the marriage, unless the lack of contribution resulted from incapacity.
177 Fineman, *op. cit.*, note 6 above, p. 11; Glendon, *op. cit.*, note 171 above, p. 1560. See also Eekelaar and Maclean, *op. cit.*, note 49 above, pp. 104–7. It is for this reason as well that feminists reject the assertion of fathers' rights groups that mothers' benefits from custody should be balanced against fathers' financial advantages. Divorce divisions are not two-way affairs; the children's interests are independent from the parents', not identical with the mother's. A mother's strong preference for, or benefit from, a particular custody arrangement should not justify the child's impoverishment.
178 Singer, *op. cit.*, note 55 above, p. 1117–18.
179 Bartlett and Stack, *op. cit.*, note 9, pp 28 and 32–3.
180 Becker, *op. cit.*, note no. 5 above, p. 142.
181 *Ibid.*, p. 167.
182 *Ibid.*, pp. 195–7. Becker notes an unusually high rate of reversal on appeal in these cases, but emphasizes the often prohibitively high cost of appeal.
183 Fineman, *op. cit.*, note 6 above, p. 181.
184 *Ibid.*, pp. 91–2.
185 *Ibid.*, pp. 183–4.
186 E.S. Scott (1992), 'Pluralism, parental preference, and child custody', *California Law Review*, **80**, pp. 615–72.
187 Bartlett and Stack, *op. cit.*, note 9 above, pp. 37–9.
188 *Ibid.*, pp. 20–1. See also M.D.A. Freeman (1984), 'Legal ideologies, patriarchal precedents, and domestic violence', in Freeman, M.D.A., (ed.), *State, Law and the Family*, London and New York: Tavistock Publications, Sweet and Maxwell. Demie Kurz (1995), *For Richer, For Poorer: Mothers Confront Divorce*, New York and London: Routledge. Documenting the high level of domestic violence in US divorce.
189 N.R. Cahn (1991), 'Civil images of battered women: the impact of domestic violence on child custody decisions', *Vanderbilt Law Review*, **44**, pp. 1041–97 at pp. 1072–4.
190 Fineman, *op. cit.*, note 6 above, pp. 6, 94, 180.
191 Bartlett and Stack, *op. cit.*, note 9, pp. 35–7. The authors, however, favour imposition of joint custody even when 'both parents do not at the outset agree to such an arrangement' and support greater research and experimentation to promote greater use of joint custody in relatively difficult cases. As evidence of the successful use of joint custody in acrimonious divorces, the authors cite T. McKinnon, and J. Wallerstein (1979), 'Joint custody and the preschool child', *Behavioral Science and Law*, **4**, pp. 169–83, at p. 177; J.B. Greif (1979), 'Fathers, children and joint custody', *American Journal of Orthopsychiatry*, **49**, pp. 311, 318; M. Roman and W. Haddad (1978), *The Disposable Parent*; P. Wolley, 'Shared custody', *Family Advocate*, summer, **1**; (6), pp. 7, 33; and Wallerstein and Kelly, *op. cit.*, note 73 above, pp. 130–1, p. 218.
192 Czapanskiy, *op. cit.*, note 11 above, p. 1468.

Index

Note: Page numbers appearing in **bold** refer to tables